Never Been a Time

Never Been a Time

The 1917 Race Riot That Sparked
the Civil Rights Movement

HARPER BARNES

WALKER & COMPANY

NEW YORK

Published by Walker Publishing Company, Inc., New York
Distributed to the trade by Macmillan

All papers used by Walker & Company are natural, recyclable products made from wood grown in well-managed forests. The manufacturing processes conform to the environmental regulations of the country of origin.

LIBRARY OF CONGRESS CATALOGING-IN-PUBLICATION DATA

Barnes, Harper, 1937–
Never been a time : the 1917 race riot that sparked the civil rights movement / Harper Barnes. —1st U.S. ed.
p.   cm.
Includes bibliographical references and index.
ISBN-13: 978-0-8027-1575-3 (alk. paper)
ISBN-10: 0-8027-1575-3 (alk. paper)
1. East Saint Louis (Ill.)—Race relations—History—20th century.   2. East Saint Louis (Ill.)—Social conditions—20th century.   3. Race riots—Illinois—East Saint Louis—History—20th century.   4. Violence—Illinois—East Saint Louis—History—20th century.   5. African Americans—Illinois—East Saint Louis—Social conditions—20th century.   6. African Americans—Crimes against—Illinois—East Saint Louis—History—20th century.   7. African Americans—Civil rights—Illinois—East Saint Louis—History—20th century.   I. Title.
F549.E2B37 2008
977.3'89—dc22
2008000368

Visit Walker & Company's Web site at www.walkerbooks.com

First U.S. edition 2008

1   3   5   7   9   10   8   6   4   2

Typeset by Westchester Book Group
Printed in the United States of America by Quebecor World Fairfield

For Roseann Weiss
In memory of Julia Davis

Germany [in World War I] has nothing on East St. Louis when it comes to "frightfulness." Indeed in one respect Germany does not even approximate her ill-famed sister. In all the accounts given of German atrocities, no one, we believe, has accused the Germans of taking pleasure in the sufferings of their victims. But these [white] rioters combined business and pleasure.

—W. E. B. Du Bois

There has never been a time when the riot was not alive in the oral tradition.

—Eugene Redmond, poet laureate of East St. Louis

Contents

A History of Violence

[T]he East St. Louis race riot in 1917 was supposed to be about . . . black workers replacing white workers in the packing houses. So, the white workers got mad and went on a rampage killing all them black people . . . just shot them down like they were out shooting pigs or stray dogs. Shot them in their houses, shot babies and women. Burned down houses with people in them and hung some black men from lampposts. Anyway, black people who survived used to talk about it. When I was coming up in East St. Louis, black people I knew never forgot what sick white people had done to them back in 1917.

—Miles Davis

The mob and entire white populace of East St. Louis had a Roman holiday. They feasted on the blood of the Negro.

—Marcus Garvey

Race riots, as black militant H. Rap Brown famously suggested in the incendiary 1960s, are "as American as cherry pie." Long before the black riots of the sixties, whites rioted against blacks in cities across the country. Decades before the Civil War, in such Northern bastions of abolition as Cincinnati, Boston, Pittsburgh, Philadelphia, and New York, and in smaller cities and towns throughout the North, blacks were attacked in the streets by gangs of whites and their neighborhoods were invaded and sacked. African Americans were severely beaten and even killed, and black homes and institutions—including schools, churches, and even orphanages—were destroyed by white mobs long before the end of slavery. Carter G. Woodson, the pioneering black scholar who became known as the Father of Black History, wrote, "The Negroes . . . were not generally welcomed in the North. Many of the northerners who sympathized with the oppressed blacks in the South never dreamt of having them as their neighbors."[1]

In the second decade of the twentieth century alone, half a million African Americans moved from the impoverished rural South to the booming industrial cities of the North, wooed by the promise of jobs and freedom. The migration intensified in the second half of the decade in an industrial boom fueled by the First World War. Blacks arrived in Northern cities by the trainloads, and many whites responded to the African American incursion with a horrific series of racial confrontations, riots, and massacres that broke out in cities across the nation, beginning in the summer of 1917 in East St. Louis.[2]

The East St. Louis race riot was not only the first but officially the deadliest of a series of devastating racial battles that swept through American cities in the World War I era. The death toll in East St. Louis was at least forty-eight, a figure not exceeded in the twentieth century until the 1992 Rodney King riot in Los Angeles, with fifty-five deaths. Officially, thirty-nine African American men, women, and children were killed in East St. Louis. But, as with other riots in the period, including those in Tulsa and Chicago, it is likely that the official East St. Louis figures on the deaths of black men, women, and children, many of them undocumented, are too low. Historians, journalists, and civil rights leaders who have studied the East St. Louis riot believe that more than one hundred African Americans, and perhaps as many as two hundred, were killed in the impoverished industrial city on the east bank of the Mississippi, with many of their bodies, including those of small children and infants, burned beyond human recognition in gasoline-ignited shacks or dumped in the deep, fast-flowing waters of America's largest river and its sewage-ridden tributaries. What happened in East St. Louis in the summer of 1917, wrote Gunnar Myrdal in *American Dilemma*, his landmark study of race in this country, was not so much a riot as a "terrorization or massacre," a "mass lynching."[3]

East St. Louis, Illinois, an industrial and meatpacking town of about seventy-five thousand people, about twelve thousand of them black, lay across the Mississippi River from what was in 1910 America's fourth-largest city, St. Louis, Missouri. In the years leading up to 1917, blacks had moved North to both cities by the thousands, looking for work. Many blacks could not find jobs and ended up homeless or crowded into shanties in the river bottoms at the southwest end of East St. Louis, and sensationalist stories in some local newspapers led many whites to believe blacks were on a rampage of crime. But the city was riddled with vice and corruption long before large numbers of blacks came to it in search of work. A Wild West atmosphere had long prevailed in East St. Louis, further fueled by a wartime boomtown mentality in a city with thousands of jobs dependent on military contracts.[4]

Although there is little evidence of the "reign of crime" blacks were accused of, there were a few particularly lurid crimes with racial overtones, at least as they were presented in the local press, and whites generally blamed blacks for the increasing dangers of walking the streets. Perhaps more importantly, blacks were competing with whites for jobs, encouraged by the powerful white industrialists who controlled the city from behind the scenes, polluting its air and streams while paying very low taxes. Employers used non-union strikebreakers, some of them black, to force white unions into disarray and collapse, and continued to lure blacks North with promises of jobs long past the time when the job market was saturated.

Blacks were blamed for the city's troubles, and were attacked by white mobs in the street throughout the spring and early summer of 1917, leading up to a full-scale riot on July 2. By the end of the long, sweltering midsummer day, hundreds of blacks had been brutally attacked, thousands fled the city, and more than three hundred homes and places of business had been destroyed by fire. At military and congressional hearings in the aftermath of the riot, dozens of eyewitnesses, black and white, described their experiences in sometimes very painful detail, and many of these descriptions are quoted here for the first time.

In an atmosphere of racial and economic fear, whites and blacks had been pitted against one another by the purposeful acts of wealthy and powerful whites. It was the work not just of industrialists but of politicians as well, ranging from the Democratic mayor of East St. Louis to the president of the United States, Woodrow Wilson, who used a "Southern Strategy" in his bitterly fought reelection campaign in the fall of 1916 that increased the division between black and white in the region that included East St. Louis. In the riot's immediate aftermath, the tragedy was investigated by, among others, NAACP founder W. E. B. Du Bois and pioneering black feminist and anti-lynch-mob activist Ida Wells-Barnett, both of whom interviewed survivors and wrote of the terror visited upon the twelve thousand black citizens of East St. Louis. Their accounts, which are also part of this book, became rallying points for the growth of the NAACP, the Urban League, and other black organizations, including Marcus Garvey's "back-to-Africa" United Negro Improvement Association.

The terrible events of July 2, 1917, were the precursor to a horrific riot later that summer in Houston and to the Red Summer of 1919, when two dozen American cities and towns—including Chicago and Washington, D.C.—exploded in riot. Two years later, a riot tore through Tulsa, and once again the official death toll—thirty-six people, two thirds of them black—was widely considered to represent only a fraction of the tragic reality of the racial massacre.

The riots of the World War I period, one of the most violent times in the history of the world, were fueled by white resentment over blacks moving into previously segregated neighborhoods and jobs; sensationalist reports of black crime; lax, corrupt, and biased law enforcement; exploitation of or capitulation to racism by business, labor, and political leaders; overcrowded, crime-festering slums; neglect of the central cities by absentee owners; and deep poverty among both races. Ultimately, of course, like all racial confrontations in America from its earliest history to the present, the riots were part of the deadly legacy of slavery.

CHAPTER I

Brotherly Love

Racial prejudice seems stronger in those states that have abolished slavery than in those where it still exists . . . In the North, the white man no longer clearly sees the barrier that separates him from the degraded race, and he keeps the Negro at a distance all the more carefully . . . lest one day they be confounded together.

—Alexis de Tocqueville, *Democracy in America,* 1835

In the late eighteenth and early nineteenth centuries, Northern states one by one officially outlawed slavery, generally in gradual stages. In 1800, about eighty-three thousand blacks lived in the North. Between then and the Civil War, more than two hundred thousand escaped slaves, freedmen, and blacks from the Caribbean moved to the North—often at great peril—seeking asylum, social and political freedom, jobs, and equality. Instead, they met harsh inequality, widespread segregation, and cruelly limited opportunities for employment. As their population grew, more and more so-called Black Laws were passed that sharply curtailed or eliminated their right to vote, to educate their children in public schools, and to use the courts to ensure their rights.[1]

In the first decades of the century, the largest concentration of free blacks in the Northern United States was in Philadelphia, the location of the worst racial attacks. Philadelphian Charles Godfrey Leyland remarked in his memoirs of the period, "Whoever shall write a history of Philadelphia from the Thirties to the era of the Fifties will record a popular period of turbulence and outrages so extensive as to now appear almost incredible."[2]

Philadelphia was founded as the City of Brotherly Love by the Quakers, who would become vehement opponents of slavery. The city was the head-quarters for such prominent abolitionists as Benjamin Rush, a signer of the Declaration of Independence; Grace and Robert Douglass, head of a family of blacks active against slavery; and, in the 1850s, legendary Underground Railroad conductor Sojourner Truth. As the closest major Northern city to the slave states of the Southeast, Philadelphia became the Promised Land—Canaan—to thousands of Southern blacks in the first decades of the nine-teenth century, an important stop on the Underground Railroad.

Between 1800 and 1830, the black population of Philadelphia more than doubled to over fifteen thousand. Although most Philadelphia blacks were laborers or servants, African Americans also became clergymen and teachers, doctors and lawyers, carpenters and musicians. They founded black churches and schools and charitable societies, and some of them became quite prosperous, even wealthy, inevitably arousing envy and anger in less-fortunate whites.

In his landmark 1899 study, *The Philadelphia Negro*, the young black sociologist W. E. B. Du Bois wrote that the rapid growth in the working-class population of the city caused by the industrial revolution and the eco-nomic recovery following the War of 1812, both of which provided new jobs that attracted many thousands to the city, would "prove disastrous to the Philadelphia Negro" beginning in the second decade of the nineteenth century. Du Bois wrote:

> Philadelphia was the natural gateway between the North and the South, and for a long time there passed through it a stream of free Negroes and fugitive slaves toward the North, and of recaptured Negroes and kidnapped colored persons toward the South. By 1820 the northward stream increased [and] new installments of Pennsyl-vania freedmen, and especially their children, began to flock to Philadelphia. At the same time the stream of foreign immigration to this country began to swell, and by 1830 aggregated half a mil-lion souls annually [creating] a fierce economic struggle . . . The new industries attracted the Irish, Germans and other immigrants; [Native-born] Americans, too, were flocking to the city, and soon to natural race antipathies was added a determined effort to displace

W. E. B. Du Bois

Negro labor—an effort which had the aroused prejudice of many of the better classes, and the poor quality of the new black immigrants, to give it aid and comfort. To all this was soon added a problem of crime and poverty. Numerous complaints of petty thefts, house-breaking, and assaults on peaceable citizens were traced to certain classes of Negroes.[3]

During that period, blacks never made up more than 9.5 percent of the city's population. But there were much higher percentages of blacks in some neighborhoods, and those tended to be the neighborhoods where recent immigrants and other poor people lived. Poor whites and blacks also were competing for the same menial jobs. And there was a widespread and partly accurate belief among white working men that blacks were so desperate for work and so beaten down by slavery they would take the most menial jobs for less money, thus driving wages down.

At the same time, the militance of Philadelphia's many abolitionists— some of whom went so far as to suggest that blacks should not only be free but equal in all ways to whites, which was unthinkable even to many opponents of slavery—aroused equally passionate opposition among many whites. As Du Bois put it, "The agitation of the Abolitionists was the match that lighted this fuel."

In 1819, three white women stoned a black woman to death on a Philadelphia street. There were further attacks on blacks in the 1820s, and anti-abolitionist and antiblack riots broke out in 1829, in 1833, and most terribly in 1834, when, in the heat of August, hundreds of white men and boys, inflamed by a fight between white policemen and blacks, marched into black neighborhoods wielding clubs, brickbats, and paving stones. They attacked people on the streets and wrecked houses and churches, killing one black working man and seriously injuring several others. The riot lasted for three days. The rioters, who called what they were doing "hunting the nigs," succeeded in driving many black families out of their homes into other parts of Philadelphia, into rural Pennsylvania, and across the Delaware River into New Jersey. It took three hundred special constables and a troop of armed militia to stop the rioting.[4]

A committee that investigated the riot reported that the rioters felt the blacks were flooding the labor market, driving down wages, and taking jobs away from whites. The rioters were also angry because some blacks, particularly in the worst slum neighborhoods where criminals held great power, refused to turn black lawbreakers over to the police. One of the complaints heard from rioters suggests that violence against blacks was so easily provoked that it could even spring from a seemingly inoffensive difference in religious practices. The report cited white objections to "the disorderly and noisy manner in which some of the colored congregations indulge, to the annoyance and disturbance of the neighborhood in which such meeting houses are located." The goal of the rioters, the committee determined, was to drive blacks out of the city.[5]

Racism and racial violence were ingrained in the makeup of the United States, starting with European settlers taking possession of the continent by racial slaughter, telling themselves that the bronze-skinned people who already lived there were not really human, and thus the land was essentially unoccupied. Even a difference in skin color was hardly necessary for tribal prejudice to emerge in a land enmeshed in an experiment that had never been tried before—bringing together from across the seas millions of people who had previously lived in nations or states or regions or cities or tribal enclaves that had been battling one another across ever-shifting borders for hundreds and even thousands of years. If a white man whose family had lived for generations in the British Isles burned with hatred for another white man whose family was also from the British Isles but from a different clan, how much more easily might his animosity be aroused by a black man who he thought wanted his job.

The Philadelphia rioters were in great part Irish immigrants. They were Irish Catholics, not the Protestants known as Scotch Irish, who had begun immigrating to America somewhat earlier, encountering in their turn the prejudice and the territorial resistance from native-born Americans that seems to be a part of the American immigrant experience going back to Revolutionary days. Even Benjamin Franklin, thought of as a great egalitarian, referred to the Scotch Irish as "white savages."[6]

Thousands of Irish Catholics crossed the Atlantic every year in the first decades of the nineteenth century. The number increased when the British removed all legal barriers to immigration in 1827, and jumped again around 1845, when the potato blight produced a famine. Irish immigrants crowded into the cities of the Northeast, often living close to poor blacks. The newcomers found themselves under attack, not from blacks but from other whites. American-born Protestants staged ugly anti-Irish and anti-Catholic riots in Philadelphia, Boston, New York, and other American cities. They blamed the Irish Catholics for taking away jobs from "native Americans" (their term for native-born whites) and causing an increase in crime, public drunkenness, and pauperism, and a general lowering of the standards of this nation founded by Puritans.

The Irish had come to this country expecting "a sort of Halfway stage to Heaven," according to Thomas Grattan, the Irish-born British consul in Boston in the period. Instead, they found a nightmarish existence in crowded and disease-ridden slums, slaving from dawn to dusk in the most menial sort of labor, when they could find work at all. An Irish immigrant who found a life of "shame and poverty" in the United States wrote home that he had recently heard a black man say, "My master is a great tyrant, he treats me as badly as if I was a common Irishman."[7]

Like the blacks they encountered in the slums, the Irish who were pouring into Philadelphia were poor and badly educated, came mostly from rural areas, and had little or no training or skills in the new industries that were coming to dominate the American economy. Irish immigrants discovered bitterly that they had to compete with blacks for low-paying jobs, and they were enraged that some employers seemed to prefer blacks and that some blacks appeared to be rising above them—in a few cases, well above them— in society. Blacks became the scapegoats for the failure of the Irish immigrants to achieve anything remotely resembling the American dream.

The three-day riot in 1834 in Philadelphia mentioned above was similar in a striking number of ways to later race riots in American cities, including the racial massacres of the World War I period in East St. Louis and other cities. Most of the rioters were young men and boys, many of them still in their teens. They were mainly from lower social classes. A newspaper referred to them as "the most brutish and lowest caste of society," although also among those arrested were two house painters, a cabinet maker, a carpenter, and several other artisans.

Rioters, as well as many whites who did not take part, justified the riots as a defensible vigilante response to an increase in black crime. However, many white participants in the riot were recognized thieves, hoodlums, and ex-convicts. The *Philadelphia Inquirer* remarked, "There was little doubt that a large portion of the offenders were actuated solely from motives of plunder, as the pockets of some of the most active were found on examination filled with silver spoons and other valuables stolen from the blacks."

There was a large group of onlookers, generally older and of a higher social class than the actual rioters, whose presence contributed to the mayhem. One observer of the Philadelphia riot said that it appeared that the "large body of spectators" who did nothing to stop the violence gave the rioters "more than common confidence in themselves." It seemed as if the spectators "countenanced their operations and in one or two instances coincided with their conduct by clapping"—their approval encouraging the rioters to beat blacks savagely with clubs and bricks and demolish their homes and churches.

Initially the rioters seemed to focus mainly on young black men and places where they assembled, but as the riot progressed, according to one eyewitness, "The mob exhibited more than fiendish brutality, beating and mutilating some of the old, confiding and unoffending blacks, with a savageness surpassing anything we could have believed men capable of."

And there was yet another crucial similarity to the attacks on blacks by mobs of whites that would follow in decades to come: Although sixty white rioters were arrested, only ten actually appeared in court and none of them was fined, jailed, or otherwise punished.[8]

In 1835, a mob of whites burned down an entire row of houses in a black neighborhood, and hundreds of black women and children fled Philadelphia, fearing a racial massacre was soon to come. Three years later, a riot erupted at the dedication of Pennsylvania Hall, a large abolitionist meeting place. The hall was burned to the ground. The next night, a mob burned down the Shelter for Colored Orphans. Antiblack riots continued into the next decade. In 1842, more than one thousand African Americans marched in Philadelphia to support the temperance and abolition movements, often allied in those days. They were met downtown by a mob of whites—mostly Irish—attacked, and beaten. The mob burned down a black meeting hall and church and looted homes until finally the militia was able to stop it by bringing in artillery.

In this and other riots in Philadelphia and elsewhere, the frequent attacks on churches, homes, and well-dressed blacks in particular seems to suggest that the rioters were in part motivated by resentment against the rise of a black middle class in a city with so many poor whites. But there seems to be no question that black crime was among the precipitating factors. The riots, Du Bois wrote, "received their chief moral support from the increasing crime of Negroes; A Cuban slave brained his master with a hatchet; two other murders by Negroes followed, and gambling, drunkenness and debauchery were widespread wherever Negroes settled."[9]

Du Bois, who had been commissioned by the University of Pennsylvania in 1896 to study what was generally referred to as "the Negro problem," lived in Philadelphia's Seventh Ward, the predominantly black area he studied. The young sociologist, who ventured forth every day from the one-room, second-floor apartment he shared with his wife into a rough but vital African American neighborhood, did not—could not—deny that crime in the city's black slums was a real problem. It was one that neither his polite if threadbare upbringing in the Massachusetts Berkshires nor his education at Fisk, Harvard, and the University of Berlin did much to prepare him for. Although he noted that arrest and prison records could be misleading because blacks traditionally had been arrested "for less cause and given longer sentences than whites," Du Bois still argued in *The Philadelphia Negro* that "the problem of Negro crime in Philadelphia from 1830 to 1850 arose from the fact that less than one-fourteenth of the population was responsible for nearly a third of the serious crimes committed."

He wrote that there were unquestionably special causes for the prevalence of crime among African Americans. The black man "had lately been freed from serfdom, he was the object of stinging oppression and ridicule, and paths of advancement open to many were closed to him. Consequently, the class of the shiftless, aimless, idle, discouraged and disappointed was proportionately larger." At the root of the Negro problem, Du Bois said, was racial discrimination. "How long can a city teach its black children that the road to success is to have a white face?" he asked.

"Such discrimination is morally wrong, politically dangerous, industrially wasteful and socially silly. It is the duty of the whites to stop it, and do so primarily for their own sakes . . . [T]he cost of crime and pauperism, the growth of slums, and the pernicious influence of idleness and lewdness, cost the public far more than would the hurt to the feelings of a carpenter to work beside a black man, or a shop girl to start beside a darker mate."[10]

Attacks on blacks in Pennsylvania and other states of the Northeast proceeded on the legal front as well. New Jersey and Connecticut had already disenfranchised blacks by 1837 when a state constitutional convention in Pennsylvania, where free blacks had been able to vote for nearly fifty years, inserted the word "white" in the qualifications for the right to vote. Du Bois wrote:

> A curious comment on human nature is this change of public opinion in Philadelphia between 1790 and 1837. No one thing explains it—it arose from a combination of circumstances. If, as in 1790, the new freedmen had been given peace and quiet and abundant work to develop sensible and aspiring leaders, the end would have been different; but a mass of poverty-stricken, ignorant fugitives and ill-trained freedmen had rushed to the city, swarmed in the vile slums which the rapidly growing city furnished, and met in social and economic competition equally ignorant but more vigorous foreigners. These foreigners outbid them at work, beat them on the streets, and were enabled to do this by the prejudice which Negro crime and the anti-slavery sentiment had aroused in the city."[11]

Most of the black newcomers were just emerging—or escaping—from slavery. They were so poor they often arrived with little more than the clothes on their backs. They were forcibly uneducated—slaves were beaten for trying to learn to read and write—and untrained for any employment except farm labor. Prejudice blocked them from most jobs and from advancement when they found jobs. And often they had been brutalized from childhood, learning in the cruelest and most painful ways to be dubious and fearful when white men began talking about right and wrong, law and justice. Like the Irish, they had come to the cities of the American North in pursuit of a dream, and had been forced into deep poverty in the young nation's growing slums. Some of them became criminals. But in nineteenth-century Philadelphia and other Northern cities, as in twentieth-century East St. Louis, Washington, Chicago, and Tulsa, when whites attacked blacks on downtown streets and rampaged through black neighborhoods, burning and looting and killing, the victims were almost entirely ordinary, law-abiding men and women and children, not criminals. If whites were driven to riot by the crimes of blacks, they attacked the wrong people, as lynch mobs and race rioters so often do.

The rapid growth of urban slums in America as the century progressed would have horrified Thomas Jefferson, who had envisioned America as a nation of independent farmers and feared the coming of the industrial age and the replication of the urban slums of Europe. "The mobs of great cities," he wrote, "add just so much to the support of pure government, as sores do to the strength of the human body." Well more than a century later, black sociologist E. Franklin Frazier would contemplate the effects on African Americans of the nation's urban slums—places like New York and Detroit and Chicago that had proved so alluring to his race for so many years—and call them "the cities of destruction."[12]

In the 1820s and 1830s, European immigrants in the urban slums, as well as small farmers from states like Ohio, Indiana, and Illinois, felt left out of the new industrial capitalist economy. They flocked to support Democrat Andrew Jackson, a slave owner and white supremacist from Tennessee whose election to the presidency in 1828 and again in 1832 added legitimacy and political clout to the already-powerful forces that were fighting to maintain slavery. At the same time, Democrats took political power in many cities. Supporters of Jackson railed at the hypocrisy of the wealthy abolitionists, mainly gathered in the Whig party, for campaigning to free the slaves while ignoring the poor white men and women who, in many cases, worked like slaves for the companies these very abolitionists owned. "The abolitionists of the north have mistaken the color of American Slaves," said Theophilus Fisk, a Boston labor leader. "All the real slaves in the United States have pale faces . . . I will venture to affirm that there are more slaves in [mill towns] Lowell and Nashua alone than can be found South of the Potomac."[13]

In the Jacksonian period, antiblack riots struck throughout the North, in large cities and small. Some of the worst were in New York City. In July of 1834, America's largest city suffered the worst of several brutal anti-abolitionist and antiblack riots of the era. The riot was apparently triggered by sensationalist newspaper reports of widespread miscegenation and inter-marriage between whites and blacks. A mob invaded black neighborhoods, beating the residents and destroying hundreds of homes. This time, the riot-ers were in the main nativists, not Irish immigrants. Indeed, several hundred Irish Catholics signed up as citizen volunteers to help control the rioters.

Riots were not confined to the Eastern cities. Cincinnati, across the Ohio River from the slave state of Kentucky, was notable for its abolitionists and by 1829 had a black population of about two thousand. In that year, a mob of whites rioted for three days, killing and seriously injuring free blacks and es-caped slaves and destroying their property. About twelve hundred Cincinnati blacks fled into Canada. There were further riots in Cincinnati in the 1830s and another terrible one in 1841, when immigrant Irish dock workers marched against black dock workers and fired on them with a cannon.[14]

Farther west, blacks had begun moving into Illinois decades before the Civil War, rowing and even swimming across the Mississippi and Ohio rivers from nearby slave states. In the 1820s, in the southern part of the state, tiny Brooklyn, Illinois—located just north of a small Mississippi River settlement that in the 1860s became East St. Louis—was settled by free blacks and es-caped slaves and became one of the oldest black-founded communities in the United States. But much of the white population of southern Illinois sup-ported slavery, and many in the predominantly rural region of mines and small hardscrabble farms were adamant and sometimes brutal in their resis-tance to abolition.

Alton, Illinois, on the east bank of the Mississippi a few miles north of Brooklyn, was the headquarters of antislavery crusader Elijah Lovejoy, a Presbyterian minister whose home was an important stop on the Underground Railroad for escaping slaves. In the 1830s, he published the newspaper the *Observer*, an increasingly passionate advocate of immediate emancipation of the country's slaves. Enraged separatists smashed his press and dumped it in the river. He ordered a new press and resumed publishing his calls for freedom. On July 21, 1836, white mobs from southern Illinois attacked the printing plant and murdered Lovejoy. The black citizens of Brooklyn honored him by informally referring to their hometown as "Lovejoy."[15]

Elijah Lovejoy became the first important martyr of abolition. And in New York, influential publisher Horace Greeley declared that Lovejoy's death had convinced him "that Slavery and Freedom could not coexist on the same soil," and he intensified his attacks on slavery. As if the two sides were armies marching in step toward one another, every time the forces of abolition became bolder and less equivocating in their call for an end to slavery, the anti-abolitionists grew more fervent in their resistance.[16]

The first half of the nineteenth century—a cataclysmic era of the rapid and uncontrolled growth of cities, of a shift to an industrial economy, of growing wealth and growing poverty—was an exceptionally violent time in America. In addition to riots inspired by the dual issues of race and slavery and those inspired by prejudice against Irish Catholics, there were anti-German riots, anti-Protestant riots, riots of tenants against landlords and of workers against bosses, anti-dissection riots, riots between political parties, riots over theatrical performances, riots over the licensing of whiskey, brothel riots, and, of course, riots over taxes, the very sort of riot enshrined in the myth of the young country's war of independence. The United States was born in riot and rebellion, and remained true to its birthright.

In 1838, a young Illinois legislator named Abraham Lincoln contemplated his fractious nation and bemoaned "the increasing disregard for law which pervades the country" and the "worse than savage mobs" that across the nation seemed to be replacing the rule of law. He said, "Accounts of outrages committed by mobs form the every-day news of the times. They have pervaded the country, from New England to Louisiana; they are neither peculiar to the eternal snows of the former, nor the burning suns of the latter; they are not the creature of climate, neither are they confined to the slave-holding, or the non-slave-holding States. Alike, they spring up among the pleasure hunting masters of southern slaves, and the order loving citizens of the land of steady habits. Whatever, then, their cause may be, it is common to the whole country."

Lincoln warned, "Whenever the vicious portion of population shall be permitted to gather in bands of hundreds and thousands, and burn churches, ravage and rob provision-stores, throw printing presses into rivers, shoot editors, and hang and burn obnoxious persons at pleasure, and with impunity; depend on it, this Government cannot last."[17]

In the 1850s, the violence in word and deed focused increasingly on the battle over slavery. Congress created a new and significantly more draconian Fugitive Slave Law, imposing heavy penalties on anyone who helped a runaway slave and giving black men in so-called free states who could not prove they were freedmen very little legal recourse against any white man who claimed to own them. The *Dred Scott* decision, which ruled that African Americans could not be citizens, further weakened the position of blacks in America. Slave catchers mounted intensive hunts in Northern states, seizing blacks who had lived free for many years. Abolitionists fought back, in some cases rescuing captives and setting them free again. The nation's racial gulf widened ever further, and war seemed inevitable.

By the time Lincoln was sworn in as president of the United States, in March of 1861, six states had already seceded from the Union over the question of slavery. A month later, the Civil War began. Major Democratic politicians in New York and Philadelphia, both of which had close commercial ties to the South, put forth serious if ultimately fruitless proposals that those cities also secede and at least be neutral, if not pro-Confederate.

In some parts of the North, the beginning of the war deepened anti-black attitudes. Democratic leaders in New York and other Northern cities had preached to their working-class followers that the federal government was marching white men off to die in a war to free the black men who would replace them in the factories of the North. As if to confirm the charge, blacks—who were excluded from virtually all labor unions—were used as strikebreakers in many Northern cities, leading to attacks by white workers in Detroit, Cleveland, Buffalo, Boston, Camden, New Jersey, and other cities, including New York.[18]

On January 1, 1863, Lincoln issued his Emancipation Proclamation, freeing slaves in rebel states "thenceforward and forever." Two months later, a federal draft was instituted. The anger of poor young white men subject to induction was further stirred by the knowledge that any man wealthy enough to fork over $300 could opt out of the draft. Antidraft riots struck Detroit and other Northern and midwestern cities. By far the worst was in New York.

In mid-July of 1863, in the depths of the war and not long after blacks with police protection were brought in as strikebreakers in a longshoreman's strike, a riot swept across New York that far exceeded in destruction and brutality anything that had happened in Philadelphia or other cities. The riot occurred at a seeming low point in the war for the North, in a city that had already contributed fifty thousand men to the Union cause and that (unlike Philadelphia) had not voted for Lincoln in the November election. By then, the Irish had become New York City's largest immigrant group. They numbered more than two hundred thousand, about one fourth of the population. But they were still competing with blacks for jobs and were considered by many whites to be merely "blacks turned inside out," or even inferior to blacks because of their supposed lack of industriousness and dissolute living.[19]

The New York Draft Riots began on July 13, 1863, with the torching of a draft office on Forty-sixth Street, and quickly spread to other parts of the city and into outlying areas. Mobs of poor whites numbering well into the thousands, many of them Irish, rioted for four days, attacking the mansions of the rich as well as the hovels of poor blacks, assaulting blacks on the streets, burning down a black church, killing more than one hundred men, women, and children, and forcing thousands of blacks to flee the city. Not for the last time in an American city, blacks were chased or hurled into the adjoining rivers and hanged from lamp poles above the city streets. And white public officials repeatedly refused to respond with adequate force as rioters sacked, looted, and burned a city and murdered its citizens. In the most notorious attack, five hundred armed rioters stormed and torched the Colored Orphan Asylum on Fifth Avenue. Despite cries of "murder the damned monkeys," the 233 children were rescued before the building, a symbol of white charity toward blacks, burned to the ground.[20]

The New York riot of 1863 shared crucial foreshadowing elements with other major American race riots, from Philadelphia in 1834 to East St. Louis in 1917: bitter competition between blacks and whites for scarce jobs; use of blacks as strikebreakers; deep mistrust of government, politicians, and law-enforcement officials; a high crime rate; sensationalist newspaper reports of black rape and other heinous crimes; bitterness over what many poor white people saw as unfair advantages given to blacks; and murderous resentment of any small sign that blacks had risen from the lowest rung of the social and economic ladder.

A little less than two years later, Robert E. Lee surrendered to Ulysses S. Grant at Appomattox to end the Civil War. By then more than six hundred thousand Americans, white and black, had been killed. Just under four million American slaves were free. But the fight for black freedom—and the Northward migration by blacks—had just begun, along with violent white resistance to black hopes and aspirations, resistance that often led to lynching, riot, and racial massacre.

CHAPTER 2

Reconstruction and Redemption: From Hope to Despair

From the uncertain early months of the Civil War until its scorched-earth conclusion, as Northern armies drove into Southern states, thousands of slaves fled North behind the protection of Union lines. Although more than 90 percent of the freed slaves ended up staying in the South after the war was over, at least a hundred thousand Southern blacks migrated to the North in the 1860s.[1]

Thousands more headed for the cities of the South, where whites resisted the arrival of the African American immigrants as fiercely as Northerners had decades earlier. One reason for white antagonism was simple fear, based on a persistent and terrifying rumor that blacks—who outnumbered whites in many areas, including the states of Mississippi and South Carolina—were plotting a vengeful uprising, a mass slaughter, and political and economic takeover of the South. In the anarchic early period of Reconstruction during the weak administration of the Democrat Andrew Johnson—a period of so-called white home rule—Southern states passed Black Codes limiting areas where blacks could live, establishing large fines or jail terms for blacks who attempted to quit their jobs, and denying blacks the right to testify against whites in court. Because the Thirteenth Amendment ending slavery had left open the issue of black suffrage, Southern states were able to pass laws barring blacks from voting.

Throughout the South, from major cities to the most remote pine barrens and bayous, white mobs physically assaulted blacks trying to exercise their civil rights. The attacks sometimes escalated into race riots. The worst were in Memphis and New Orleans.

The black population of Memphis more than quadrupled from the beginning of the Civil War to 1866. Some of the newcomers found jobs or made work for themselves and were doing relatively well, as were some African Americans who had been in Memphis before the war, but the streets swarmed with impoverished unemployed blacks. Some of them were looking for work. Others gave up and became beggars or thieves, stealing from blacks as well as whites, and some neighborhoods became infested with crime. In late April 1866, the *Memphis Argus* declared of the newcomers, "Would to God they were back in Africa or some other seaport town . . . anywhere but here." Whites began attacking blacks almost indiscriminately, and as usual the victims were often respectable, hardworking citizens who were as horrified by the crime wave as their white neighbors.[2]

On May 1, a horse-drawn hack driven by a white man collided with one driven by a black. Crowds of both races gathered. Police arrived and arrested only the black driver. A group of black Civil War veterans tried to intervene. Fights broke out between whites and blacks, who were badly outnumbered, and escalated into three days of mayhem as white rioters, many of them Irish policemen and firemen, invaded black neighborhoods in South Memphis, including a shantytown that housed the families of black soldiers stationed nearby. The federal Freedman's Bureau, established to aid former slaves, was impotent to stop the attacks, and the area's military commander refused to send in troops of either race, even to help the families of the black soldiers. The rioters burned and looted, viciously assaulting blacks, battering and shooting them. At least forty-six blacks were killed, five black women were raped, and hundreds of black homes, churches, and schools were destroyed.

Three months later, in the swelter of late July in New Orleans, the Radical Republican governor of Louisiana convened a constitutional convention to enfranchise blacks—and at the same time to prohibit former Confederate soldiers from voting. On the day of the convention, fighting between blacks and whites broke out on the streets outside the convention hall. Police—mostly former Rebel soldiers—arrived en masse and joined the white rioters, wielding billy clubs and firing guns. The melee turned into a massacre. Outnumbered blacks and their supporters were shot down when they tried to flee, despite white flags of surrender. By the time federal troops arrived and intervened, thirty-four blacks and three white Radical Republicans had been killed. One veteran of the Civil War said later that "the wholesale slaughter and the little regard paid to human life" surpassed anything he had seen in battle.

In his pioneering, myth-dispelling 1935 book, *Black Reconstruction*, W. E. B. Du Bois agonized over the mass racial violence he had studied so extensively and reached strikingly humanistic conclusions about its causes, causes that could as easily have been ascribed to other racial massacres throughout our history, from the Philadelphia and Cincinnati riots long before the Civil War to the New York Draft Riots during it, to the terrible urban slaughters of the period of World War I:

> Total depravity, human hate and *Schadenfreude*, do not explain fully the mob spirit in America. Before the wide eyes of the mob is ever the Shape of Fear. Back of the writhing, yelling, cruel-eyed demons who break, destroy, maim and lynch and burn at the stake, is a knot, large or small, of normal human beings, and these human beings at heart are desperately afraid of something. Of what? Of many things, but usually of losing their jobs, being declassed, degraded or actually disgraced; of losing their hopes, their savings, their plans for their children; of the actual pangs of hunger, of dirt, of crime. And of all of this, most ubiquitous in modern industrial society is that fear of unemployment.
>
> It is its nucleus of ordinary men that continually gives the mob its initial and awful impetus. Around this nucleus, to be sure, gather snowball-wise all manner of flotsam, filth and human garbage, and every lewdness of alcohol and current fashion. But all this is the horrible covering of this inner nucleus of fear.[3]

There was much to fear for both blacks and whites in the physically devastated Reconstruction South. Its agriculture and slave-based economic system lay in ruins while the rapidly industrializing and expanding North was booming. And nature added its toll. Heavy floods in 1866 and 1867 on the Mississippi and its tributaries and infestations of army worms caused massive losses of cotton, corn, and other grains, ruining the few blacks who had set up small independent farms and battering large planters. In the Deep South, sugar and rice fields lay ruined by war and weather. Many thousands of blacks were evicted from plantations and found themselves homeless and destitute. They crowded the growing black ghettos of the cities of the South, or roamed the countryside, desperately searching for food and shelter.[4]

"Armed bands of white men patrolled the county roads to drive back the Negroes wandering about," said social reformer Carl Schurz, a former Union general, in his lengthy 1866 testimony at congressional hearings on Reconstruction. "Dead bodies of murdered Negroes were found on and near the highways and byways. Gruesome reports came from the hospitals—reports of colored men and women whose ears had been cut off, whose skulls had been broken by blows, whose bodies had been slashed by knives or lacerated with scourges. A number of such cases, I had occasion to examine myself. A veritable reign of terror prevailed in many parts of the South."[5]

The massacres at Memphis and New Orleans and the violence against blacks throughout the South horrified many Americans, and Republicans seized the mood to put forward a series of new Reconstruction acts. Passed in 1866 and 1867 over the veto of Andrew Johnson, the new laws put the South under military control, and ensured black males the right to vote while disenfranchising many former Confederates—thus helping Republican Ulysses S. Grant carry much of the South in the election of 1868. The period of Radical Reconstruction had begun, and soon hundreds of blacks were serving in the state legislatures and other governing bodies of the South, and more than twenty reached the Congress of the United States.

As Southern whites ceaselessly pointed out at the time and would continue to point out for decades to come, blacks had their share of crooked or incompetent politicians during Reconstruction. But so did whites. Reconstruction was a time of almost unprecedented political corruption in both the North and the South. Blacks did not invent public plunder or legislative idiocy in states like Louisiana and Mississippi. Cities in both the South and the North were ruled by breathtakingly corrupt political machines like that of Boss Tweed in New York. And the president of the United States had managed to so surround himself with wealthy crooks that the term "Grantism" became synonymous with audacious thievery of millions in public funds by political cronies.

The Fourteenth Amendment, ratified in 1868, granted blacks equal protection under the law, and the Fifteenth Amendment, ratified in 1870, made it illegal to deny voting rights on the basis of race. Southern whites fought back against the new status of African Americans. Their tactics ranged from legal and political maneuvering and sheer fraud and trickery—such as requiring blacks to read the Declaration of Independence aloud, in German—to physical intimidation, lynching, and riot. As Du Bois observed, "A lawlessness which in 1865–1868 was still spasmodic and episodic now became organized . . . [U]sing a technique of mass and midnight murder, the South began widely organized aggression upon the Negroes."[6]

The White Knights of the Ku Klux Klan and the Knights of the White Camellia were the most powerful of dozens of vigilante groups with genteel-sounding names that terrorized the countryside. In the last thirty-five years of the nineteenth century, racist vigilante groups killed thousands of African Americans in the South and often justified the murders by accusing the victims of raping white women. An 1871 investigative report to a congressional committee considering anti-Klan legislation pinpoints in microcosm the regionwide terror, and the reality behind the fantasies of rape: "In the nine counties [of South Carolina] covered by the investigation for a period of approximately six months, the Ku Klux Klan lynched and murdered 35 men, whipped 262 men and women, otherwise outraged, shot, mutilated, burned out, etc., 101 persons. It committed two cases of sex offenses against Negro women. During this time, the Negroes killed four men, beat one man, committed sixteen other outrages, but no case of torture. No case is found of a white woman seduced or raped by a Negro."[7]

In the late 1860s and early 1870s, in addition to the vigilante campaigns of terror, deadly race riots erupted in Meridian, Mississippi, again in New Orleans, and in other Southern cities and towns. On Easter Sunday, 1872, in the parish (county) seat of black-governed Colfax, Louisiana, hundreds of blacks and a few white supporters barricaded themselves inside the parish courthouse for protection from an advancing white militia, heavily armed and made up mainly of former Confederate soldiers. The mob rushed the courthouse and burned it to the ground and at least seventy-one blacks were killed, many of them executed in the roads and fields after they had marched out of the burning courthouse under a white flag of surrender. The event came to be called the Colfax Massacre.[8]

Two years later, another horrific riot hit Vicksburg, Mississippi, after an election in August. By then, the right to vote and participate in the political process had been restored to virtually all former Confederates in a federal amnesty. Thugs from the so-called People's Party—also known as the White

Man's Party—patrolled the streets and physically intimidated blacks from voting, with the result that the city's Republican administration was voted out of office and white supremacists took power. In December, when the new administration physically evicted a black sheriff from his office and literally chased him out of town, a posse of rural blacks, some of them carrying shotguns and pistols, marched to Vicksburg, where they were met by a white mob armed with military and hunting rifles. The blacks were both outnumbered and outgunned, and at least seventy-five were killed in the resulting melee. For days armed white gangs terrorized the area, killing hundreds more.[9]

The unrelenting and often violent resistance from Southern whites—and a deepening economic depression that began with the financial panic of 1873—weakened the resolve of the North to enforce the Reconstruction statutes, and President Grant became less and less willing to send in federal troops to protect blacks against what many white Southerners referred to as "Redemption": the eradication of black and Northern political power. African Americans were attacked and killed at political gatherings across the Deep South. In the name of Redemption, whites waged a paramilitary campaign in Mississippi to intimidate blacks physically from voting in the elections of 1875. Aided by flagrant ballot stuffing on a grand scale, Democrats gained control of the state, winning overwhelming majorities in many places that had been strongly Republican in the previous election.

Violence did not end with the election. Dozens of black and Republican officeholders were given a stark choice: resign or be assassinated. In the midst of the campaign, Republican governor Adelbert Ames, a former Union general, wrote, "A revolution has taken place—by force of arms—and a race are disenfranchised—they are to be returned to a condition of serfdom—an era of second slavery."[10] For all practical purposes, Reconstruction ended with the disputed presidential election of 1876. To break a deadlock, Republicans in Congress finally agreed to a deal in which their candidate, Rutherford B. Hayes, was handed the presidency in return for the withdrawal of federal troops from the South. White home rule was reestablished; blacks were shut out of the electoral process in state after state by threats, trickery, fraud, and racist legislation; segregation was imposed by law in schools, public accommodations, public transportation, and many other aspects of daily life; blacks' legal, property, and employment rights were severely curtailed; inequitable, debt-accruing sharecropping and tenant-farming arrangements turned black agricultural workers into virtual serfs; and Jim Crow ruled the South.

As W. E. B. Du Bois would write, "The slave went free; stood a brief moment in the sun; then moved back again toward slavery."[11]

In the last years of the war and the early years of Reconstruction, as the North boomed economically, the American labor movement grew rapidly, and many hundreds of local unions were created. Umbrella assemblies of trade unions sprang up in every major American city from New York to San Francisco, and in the decade beginning in 1863, twenty-six new national trade unions were formed, bringing the total to thirty-two. But almost all of them excluded blacks. The few black unions that did exist were usually ignored when it came to strikes and other decisive action.

Employers in Northern cities continued to stoke racial antagonism during strikes by replacing white workers with low-paid blacks. Sometimes just the threat of bringing in black strikebreakers was enough to break union militancy, and such tactics fed into the bitterness many white workers felt toward blacks. For example, the *Boston Post* in 1866 reported that a business-sponsored emigration society was contemplating shipping two hundred thousand or more black workers to New England to lower the cost of labor. The report was false, but it had a chilling effect on white labor militancy.[12]

The National Labor Union, the first successful nationwide labor federation, was formed in 1866 and initially seemed to offer some hope for integrating blacks into the American labor movement. It would be "an act of folly" to reject members from "the African race," the federation stated, arguing that employers would use the rejection to "foment discord between the whites and blacks, and hurl the one against the other." But most local and regional unions in the federation insisted on excluding African Americans from membership. Typical was the response of the powerful Carpenters and Joiners National Union, which announced in 1869 that "the prejudices of our members against the colored people are of such a nature that it is not expedient at present to admit them as members, or organize them under the National Union." There was never any significant integration of blacks into the organization.[13]

Then, in 1873, economic disaster struck. The postwar period of industrial and financial growth reached overexpansion and came to a halt in a wave of defaults, business failures, and bankruptcies. The Panic of 1873 triggered what, until the 1930s, was referred to as the "Great Depression." By 1876, more than half the nation's railroads had defaulted on their bonds and were in receivership, and when the railroads slashed jobs and cut wages, eighty thousand railroad employees, black and white, walked off the job across the country. They were supported by hundreds of thousands of workers and unemployed people of both races in what became the Great Strike of 1877. For a brief period, desperation drove poor blacks and whites together. In Philadelphia, Pittsburgh, Chicago, St. Louis, East St. Louis, and other rail hubs, strikers trying to halt all railroad traffic battled police and militia. The strike lasted for more than a month before state and federal troops and private police brought it under control. Dozens of strikers of both races were killed. Unions collapsed across the country, and those that remained found themselves more concerned with public relief for their unemployed members than with adding blacks to their membership.[14]

In the wake of the Great Strike and the virtual disintegration of the existing labor movement, the Knights of Labor, a radical, militant national group organized by industry rather than craft, emerged as a national force and grew rapidly for a decade. It welcomed blacks (and women) as members. At the organization's height in the mid-1880s, about sixty thousand African Americans were among its seven hundred thousand members, but the organization went into a rapid decline after losing several crucial strikes and being accused of involvement in the bombing that killed eight policemen at the Haymarket Square riots in Chicago in 1886. Labor violence continued at a ferocious level into the following decade, with workers generally on the losing end of bloody battles. The Knights of Labor were shattered and moribund by the turn of the century.

The American Federation of Labor—an umbrella group of craft unions that was considerably more conservative than the socialistic Knights of Labor—gained a national following as the Knights of Labor declined, and at its convention in 1890, the federation declared that it looked "with disfavor upon trade unions having provisions which exclude from membership persons on account of race and color." But many independent craft unions, such as the large National Machinists Union, refused to join if they had to accept black members. The federation changed the rule, and unions could enter if they did not openly exclude African Americans in their constitutions. Many all-white unions simply took the racial exclusion clause out of their constitutions while maintaining the policy.

The American Federation of Labor grew rapidly in the late nineteenth and early twentieth centuries as an overwhelmingly white organization. At the same time, few independent black unions succeeded against the virtual monopoly held by white unions. For decades after the decline of the Knights of Labor, blacks had little representation and essentially no clout in the mainstream of the American labor movement.[15]

After the collapse of Reconstruction, many thousands of blacks—angry, frustrated, and fearful of what would come next—left the South. The black population of the North rose from about 450,000 in 1870 to 615,000 in 1880.[16] In the late 1870s, as the noose of white supremacy tightened on millions of Southern blacks, Benjamin "Pap" Singleton, a dynamic black Tennessean with an audacious vision and a gift for promotion, decided it was time for African Americans to leave the South and that the appropriate Canaan for a black exodus was Kansas, where John Brown had waged bloody guerilla warfare in the name of abolition. Singleton established a real estate company to arrange for blacks to be transported to Kansas and, with the cooperation of steamship companies and the railroads, dispatched circulars throughout the black South with the help of itinerant preachers, railway porters, and steamboat workers.

Singleton was not alone in promoting an exodus to the West. An uneducated black Union soldier named Henry Adams—who had returned home to Louisiana in 1869 to find the treatment of former slaves unbearable—organized a committee of more than one hundred blacks to travel throughout the South and "see the true condition of our race, to see whether it was possible we could stay under a people who held us in bondage or not." Confronted almost everywhere with terrible conditions, the committee reported in the late 1870s that blacks had to leave the South. Adams's colonization council soon had tens of thousands of members from Louisiana, Mississippi, Alabama, and Texas who were committed to a black exodus to the North and West.[17]

The exodus movement spread as far east as North Carolina, and in the late 1870s thousands of blacks crossed the South on foot to the Mississippi

River, where they crowded onto steamboats headed North for St. Louis. From there they could continue west by land or water. A contemporary report described the scene at St. Louis:

> Homeless, penniless and in rags, these poor people were throng-
> ing the wharves . . . hailing the passing steamers and imploring
> them for a passage to the land of freedom, where the rights of
> citizens are respected and honest toil rewarded by honest compen-
> sation. The newspapers were filled with accounts of their destitu-
> tion, and the very air was burdened with the cry of distress from
> a class of American citizens flying from persecution which they
> could no longer endure. Their piteous tales of outrage, suffering
> and wrong touched the hearts of the more fortunate members of
> their race in the North and West, and aid societies, designed to
> afford temporary relief and composed almost entirely of colored
> people, were organized in Washington, St. Louis, Topeka and
> various other places.

The black immigrants to Kansas, who spilled over into Nebraska and other farm states west of the Mississippi, became known as Exodusters. Southern officials—alarmed at the departure of so many workers, some of them skilled—tried with little success to stop the exodus by various means, from trying to put pressure on steamship companies to stop selling tickets to blacks to arresting blacks on false charges as they waited to board ships or trains. Still, between fif-teen and twenty-five thousand blacks moved to Kansas in the late 1870s.[18]

There were far more Exodusters than there was employment or land in Kansas for them, and many became refugees who crowded into some of the cities and towns. The immigrants were not always welcome, or even tolerated. At Leavenworth, on the Missouri River, police and city officials prevented a steamboat full of blacks from landing, and in Topeka a gang of whites tore down barracks being built to house black refugees. But there was nothing close to a riot. Aided by large contributions from church and charitable groups in other Northern states, Kansans founded organizations to provide food, shelter, and work for the refugees, and most of the Exodusters stayed, establishing at least one all-black town and large black enclaves in Topeka and Kansas City, Kansas. Black historian Carter Woodson observed in 1918,

"The people of Kansas did not encourage the blacks to come. They even sent messengers to the South to advise the Negroes not to migrate . . . When they did arrive, however, they welcomed and assisted them as human beings."[19]

Although some of the Exodusters failed in Kansas and went back to the South, most did not return, despite hard times and the winter wind knifing across the desolate prairie. A letter from a white woman in rural Kansas to a friend in Chicago vividly points out why. She wrote in horror, "A respectable colored man came here last spring, worked hard, earned enough to buy a lot, build a cottage and save $100 and then returned to bring his wife and family. The brutal Regulators seized him, cut off both his hands, and threw him into his wife's lap, saying, 'Now go to Kansas and work.'"[20]

Black leaders disagreed about the wisdom and efficacy of migration. The venerable black abolitionist Frederick Douglass urged blacks to remain in the South, contending that leaving was not a permanent solution to ill treatment by whites and that the government should protect and defend its citizens no matter what their skin color or where they lived. The eloquent Douglass had been born a slave in Maryland in 1818 and, before his 1838 escape to the North, had been brutalized by a "slave-breaker" trying to cure him of his rebelliousness. He argued:

> Bad as is the condition of the Negro to-day at the South, there was a time when it was flagrantly and incomparably worse. A few years ago he had nothing—he had not even himself. He belonged to somebody else, who could dispose of his person and his labor as he pleased. Now he has himself, his labor, and his right to dispose of one and the other as shall best suit his own happiness . . . At a time like this, so full of hope and courage, it is unfortunate that a cry of despair should be raised in behalf of the colored people of the South, unfortunate that men are going over the country . . . telling the people that the government has no power to enforce the Constitution and laws in that section, and that there is no hope for the poor Negro but to plant him in the new soil of Kansas or Nebraska.[21]

But lawyer and educator Richard T. Greener, dean of the law school at Howard University and the first African American to graduate from Harvard, was among many blacks who argued that leaving the South would not only improve the lot of those who left, but would pressure Southern whites into better treatment for those who remained. Greener, who was born free in 1844 and had grown up in Philadelphia and Boston, contended that many blacks were actually worse off in the South than they had been in slave days. "Before the war," he said, "the Negroes in the Southern cities and larger towns were the carpenters, bricklayers, stonemasons, and in some instances, manufacturers on a small scale. Send him West and open up to him the life of an agricultural laborer, a small farmer, a worker in the mines or on the great lines of railways, and you will soon find out what a steady, cheerful worker he is."[22]

From 1880 through 1889, the black population of the North (including the North Central states) rose from about 615,000 to more than 700,000.[23] Black migration often came in waves provoked by events—new crop failures, harsher Jim Crow laws, an increase in lynching. One wave of migrants left for the North after Grover Cleveland was elected president in 1884. A rumor had swept the Black Belt that when Cleveland and the Democrats took power, they would reinstitute slavery.

In a 1954 judgment that has met wide acceptance in the years since, African American historian Rayford W. Logan described the years from 1877 to 1901 as "the nadir" of the black experience in America.[24] The Panic of 1893 brought an end to the so-called Gilded Age, which had been in part fueled by a modest economic recovery in the 1880s, and the nation sank back into depression as America's boom-and-bust economy seemed to be forever locked into a vertiginous twenty-year cycle. Unemployment soared, labor violence erupted across America, and in the South, seemingly defying the tenets of free market economics, agricultural prices continued to fall despite crop failures. As usual, times that were bad for whites were even worse for blacks. In the final decade of the nineteenth century, Southern blacks lost virtually all of what little political power they had left. Populism, beginning in the 1880s, briefly and tentatively united some Southern blacks and whites in dreams of a radical reconstruction of the American economic system, but the People's Party—a new national organization that bore no relationship to the party of the same name that murdered blacks in Vicksburg in 1874—and other manifestations of populism were undermined by the white supremacist campaigns of the Bourbon Democrats, campaigns filled with vicious antiblack propaganda that inevitably included charges of rape.

The maverick Georgia populist Tom Watson, defeated in an 1892 bid for reelection to Congress by a white supremacist Bourbon Democrat, cried out to poor Southerners, black and white alike, "You are made to hate each other because upon that hatred is rested the keystone of the arch of financial despotism which enslaves you both . . . [and] perpetuates a monetary system which beggars you both."[25]

Beginning in 1890 with the infamous "Mississippi Plan," a noxious mixture of high poll taxes, rigged literacy tests, and various color-coded standards of ancestry and supposed character, the states of the South one by one made it legally impossible for the great majority of blacks to cast a ballot. But the assault on African Americans was not just political. The murder of Southern blacks rose dramatically in the 1890s. According to the cautious tabulation begun in 1882 by the Tuskegee Institute in Alabama, lynching of blacks exceeded one hundred a year for the first time in 1891 and remained in the hundreds for all but two of the following ten years. The worst states were Mississippi, Alabama, Georgia, and Louisiana, and the worst year was 1892, when 161 blacks were lynched, almost twice as many as in 1890 and three times as many as in the years of the early 1880s.[26]

Sociologists E. M. Beck and Stewart Tolnay, in a close statistical study of the period, have shown a correlation between the politics and economics of the 1890s and the rise in lynching. They write, "The broad historical sequence is uncontested: The peak of black lynchings in the early 1890s coincided with a softening demand for southern cotton, the rise of populist and agrarian protest, and the birth of radical racism. The bloody 1890s were followed by several years of rising cotton prices and an apparent decline in violence against southern blacks."[27]

Poverty and economic fear among poor whites—out of work and desperate, with time heavy on their hands and no food on their tables—bred seething anger, and racist politicians made certain that the anger was directed at the blacks on the lowest rung of the societal ladder rather than upward at the political and economic moguls perched on the top step. Anthropologist Ruth Benedict succinctly described this kind of displaced rage, as it was played out in Nazi Germany, in her illuminating study, *Race: Science and Politics*:

Desperate men easily seize upon some scapegoat to sacrifice to their unhappiness; it is a kind of magic by which they feel for the

moment that they have laid [down] the misery that has been tor-
menting them. In this they are actively encouraged by their rulers
and exploiters, who like to see them occupied with this violence,
and fear that if it were denied them they might demand something more difficult. So Hitler . . . exhorted the nation in 1938 to
believe that Germany's defeat in 1919 had been due to Jewry, and
encouraged racial riots.[28]

Lynching became so commonplace in the South in the 1890s that, in
some cases, there was no need for sociological or anthropological analysis to
detect economic factors at work. In March of 1892, three black grocers were
lynched on the outskirts of Memphis. Outraged, Ida B. Wells, the twenty-
nine-year-old editor of a black Memphis newspaper called the *Free Speech
and Headlight*, charged in an editorial what most local people, black and
white, already assumed (or knew) was true—that the grocers were lynched
because they were successfully competing against a white-owned store in the
same black neighborhood. Wells urged Memphis's African Americans to
"save our money and leave a town that will neither protect our lives and property, nor give us a fair trial in the courts when accused by white persons."
Wells was fearless and fierce in her racial pride. At the age of twenty-one, she

Ida B. Wells

had unsuccessfully sued the Chesapeake, Ohio and Southwestern Railroad in Tennessee for violating her civil rights by forcing her (with some difficulty; she bit the hand of a conductor) to move to a "colored" car.[29]

Barely two months after her inflammatory editorials on the murder of the grocers, Wells became infuriated by the lynching in Southern states of several black men for allegedly raping white women, and wrote a thunderous editorial calling the rape charges a "threadbare lie" that hid—or exposed—the abiding white fear that white women were attracted to black men. Wells was fortuitously—or wisely—visiting New York when a mob descended upon the paper's office and demolished it. Threatened with lynching if she returned to Memphis, she remained in the North and became a leader in the antilynching movement, her personal experiences adding to the power of her speeches as she swayed large crowds in America and on tours of England.[30]

Militant leaders like Ida B. Wells found themselves in direct opposition to the increasingly influential Booker T. Washington, a growing force for caution, gradualism, self-reliance, and accommodation to whites in the improvement of the African American condition. Unlike Ida B. Wells, Washington accepted the reality of a segregated rail system, and had once written a rail company praising it for having first-class cars for both blacks and whites.[31]

In 1895, at the age of thirty-eight, the educator made the most important speech of his speech-filled life before a large audience in a convention hall at the Cotton States and International Exposition in Atlanta, a minor world's fair where the accomplishments of blacks were relegated to the Negro Building. The speech, proffering what came to be known as the Atlanta Compromise, made Washington nationally famous and would influence white attitudes and policies toward blacks for decades to come.

Booker Taliaferro Washington was the founder and principal of Tuskegee Institute in Alabama, which focused on vocational education. Having spent his childhood as a slave in Virginia—he proudly would title his autobiography *Up from Slavery*—Washington had worked long hours as a stevedore and saved his money by sleeping under an elevated sidewalk to pay for college at all-black Hampton Institute. He stayed in the South as an educator. "Cast down your bucket where you are," the famous advice he gave for the first time in his 1895 Atlanta speech, was a typically humble-sounding, backcountry metaphor for a conservative position he had advocated for years: Blacks should stay in the South, work hard to better themselves, concentrate

Booker T. Washington

on vocational training rather than academic education, and not make trouble by pushing for rights the white man was not willing to give them.[32]

Comparing the black race to a ship lost and adrift at sea, he intoned, "Our greatest danger is that in the great leap from slavery to freedom we may overlook the fact that the masses of us are to live by the production of our hands, and fail to keep in mind that we shall prosper as we learn to dignify and glorify common labor . . . It is at the bottom of life we must begin, and not at the top."

In a year in which blacks throughout the South were continuing to lose what little remained of their civil and political rights, a year in which, according to the educational institution he headed, 113 members of his race had been lynched, Booker T. Washington in his Atlanta speech advised blacks not to "underestimate the importance of cultivating friendly relations with the Southern white man, who is their next-door neighbor." Washington dismissed blacks who tried to force integration, saying, "The opportunity to earn a dollar in a factory just now is worth infinitely more than the opportunity to spend a dollar in an opera house."[33]

In essence, Washington chose jobs over justice. Openly concerned about unemployment and deep poverty among blacks, alarmed about blacks losing jobs to immigrants—"those of foreign birth and strange tongues and habits"—and having no reason to believe, either philosophically or pragmatically, that organized labor would provide relief, Washington said blacks would accept segregation in most aspects of life as long as they were given a chance to earn a living. What one observer described as "a delirium of applause" rose from the packed auditorium as Washington held his right hand high above his head, fingers splayed widely apart and then clenched into a fist as he said, "In all things that are purely social we can be as separate as the fingers, yet one as the hand in all things essential to mutual progress."

Earlier that year, Frederick Douglass, the embodiment of black pride and a tenacious foe of segregation, had died. After the Atlanta speech, the much more conservative Washington became the most prominent black man in America, a nation where public visibility is often equated with leadership. For whites at least, the time was right for the man who became known as the Great Accommodator. Enthusiastic white reaction to the speech was typified by President Cleveland's comment that the speech offered "new hope" for blacks and by the *Atlanta Constitution*'s editorial judgment: "The speech stamps Booker T. Washington as a wise counselor and a safe leader." White business leaders across the country agreed enthusiastically.[34]

Many prominent and successful blacks praised the speech as well, in part perhaps because of the singular nature of the event—a black man speaking of such important matters to a large audience of whites deep in the South, and bringing that audience to its feet. Even young W. E. B. Du Bois, teaching at Wilberforce University in Ohio, in the very early stages of his transition from intellectual elitist to radical populist, wrote to congratulate Washington on "a word fitly spoken" and said his proposal could be "the basis for a real settlement between whites and blacks in the South." Du Bois would later change his mind, to say the least.[35]

But some more militant blacks reacted to the speech with contempt, realizing that Washington had come dangerously close to confirming the belief of many whites that Americans of African descent were inferior to those whose ancestors had come from Europe, suited only to the most menial kind of labor, content with segregation, and happy to live off the crumbs that spilled from the white man's table. "He said something that was death to the Afro American and elevating to the white people," wrote W. Calvin Chase, editor of the *Washington Bee*. "What fool wouldn't applaud the downfall of

his aspiring competitor?" Ida B. Wells accused Washington and his followers
of advising blacks "to be first-class people in a Jim Crow car" instead of "insisting that the Jim Crow car be abolished."[36]

In fact, it would be decades before the Jim Crow cars on Southern trains
and the segregation they symbolized were abolished. Lawsuits against the
segregated rail coaches, like the one initiated by Wells, failed to advance beyond state courts until 1896, when the United States Supreme Court heard
a suit filed by a black man against segregated seating in Louisiana and
reached a decision that would prove to be disastrous to African Americans,
embedding the legality of segregation in federal law for generations to come.
In *Plessy v. Ferguson*, the court ruled that separate accommodations could
also be equal accommodations, and thus were not unconstitutional. Justice
John M. Harlan, although a Southerner and a former slaveholder, begged to
differ. The Great Dissenter wrote that the proposition that "colored citizens
are so inferior and degraded that they cannot be allowed to sit in public
coaches occupied by white citizens" was a despicable and unconstitutional
one that was certain to "arouse race hate" and "stimulate aggression, more or
less brutal and irritating, upon the admitted rights of colored citizens."[37]

The separate but equal doctrine quickly was used to justify and enforce
segregation in almost all aspects of public life in the South and to some extent
in the North, where blacks were generally segregated by custom—sometimes
brutally enforced—rather than by law. Racism was on the rise across America
and blacks were portrayed negatively at all strata in the dominant culture. On
one level, minstrel shows and "coon songs" enjoyed a revival in Northern
cities and blacks were routinely portrayed as bumblers and crooks of low in-
telligence in the popular press. On a higher intellectual plane, at the august
Smithsonian Institution, at the Museum of Natural History in New York,
and at the best universities—including Harvard, as 1890 graduate W. E. B.
Du Bois was infuriated to discover—distinguished academics espoused a
variety of social Darwinism that placed blacks a bare notch above the ape.
These notions were popularized in the extensive ethnographic exhibits at the
world's fairs that were so popular in the period. At the gargantuan expositions
in Chicago in 1893 and St. Louis in 1904, as well as at the lesser ones, including the Cotton States and International Exposition in 1895 in Atlanta,
American Indians and tribal peoples from what would later be called the
third world—living human beings—appeared in a kind of human zoo that

was meant to represent the evolution of humans from the lowest (and darkest) half-naked primitives toward the pinnacle of human development, the well-appointed northern European white men and women who attended the fairs in the tens of millions.

In the fall of 1898, the worst aspects of a terrible decade—tragically effective racist propaganda that often focused on alleged black rapes of white women; the disenfranchisement, disempowerment, impoverishment, and murder of blacks; the triumph of white supremacist politicians; and a sharp increase in racial segregation—coalesced in Wilmington, North Carolina's largest city, to produce the first major American race riot in some twenty years.

Wilmington, a thriving port city of some 20,000 people, about 11,300 of them black, sat on the Cape Fear River near its outlet to the Atlantic Ocean. The city and the state of North Carolina as a whole had in the years before the riot escaped many of the worst aspects of ever-increasing repression of blacks that characterized the 1890s in the South. The agrarian-based Populist Party, whose brief flame had been snuffed out by racist Democratic politicians by the mid-to-late 1890s in most of the South, had joined with black Republicans in North Carolina to mount successful campaigns for Fusion candidates, some of them black, in statewide and local races in 1894 and 1896. The white leader of the Fusion movement was Daniel Russell, who as a judge had ruled that business owners did not have a right to bar African Americans from their shops. It was a decision that would turn out to be roughly three quarters of a century ahead of its time. In 1896, Russell was elected to a four-year term as governor. By 1898, four blacks sat on Wilmington's ten-man board of aldermen, and the mayor, Silas Wright, was a Republican and a member of the Fusion movement.[38]

African Americans held other city offices and made up more than one third of the city's police force. There was a substantial and educated black middle class. The situation was too much to bear for North Carolina's white supremacists, particularly men whose wealth rested upon the large, docile contingent of poor people, both black and white, who were willing to work for near-starvation pay or under the terms of financially imprisoning sharecropping and tenant-farm contracts.

Although neither the Republican mayor of Wilmington nor the Fusionist governor of North Carolina was up for reelection in 1898, some of the most prominent white citizens of the city and the state, fearful of the radical economic notions associated with populism, chose the months leading up to the statewide biennial elections of that year to launch a vicious antiblack and anti-Fusionist propaganda campaign aimed at swaying the emotions of poor whites who had previously voted for Fusionist candidates. Leading North Carolina newspapers gave regular front-page banner headlines to trumped-up charges of corruption and ineptitude against Russell, Wright, and other Fusionist officeholders, black and white, and to wildly exaggerated tales of rampant rape of white women by blacks. Among the men orchestrating the campaign was nationally prominent Democrat Josephus Daniels, publisher of the *Raleigh News and Observer*, who openly proclaimed that his goal was "permanent good government by the party of the White Man."[39]

Thrust into the campaign was a much-publicized speech by the wife of a Georgia congressman who alleged that the greatest danger facing any rural white women was "the black rapist" and saying that such rapes must be stopped if it meant "lynching a thousand negroes a week." In reply, Alexander Manly, publisher of the *Wilmington Daily Record*—one of the few black-owned daily newspapers in America—wrote that, although it was true that black men were having sex with white women, the liaisons could hardly be called rape. "Our experience among poor white people in the country teaches us that women of that race are not any more particular in the matter of clandestine meetings with colored men than [are] the white men with the colored women." Manly's incendiary editorial was reprinted in white newspapers across the state under the headline ATTACK UPON WHITE CHRISTIAN WOMANHOOD. Manly's words added fuel to an already incendiary antiblack campaign. Alfred Waddell, a former Confederate soldier with a gift for passionate stump speeches, seized the day and uttered words of anti-Fusionist defiance that echoed from Wilmington across the state. "We will never surrender to a ragged raffle of Negroes, even if we have to choke the Cape Fear River with carcasses." Large crowds of poor whites turned out to cheer Waddell and curse the black race.[40]

In Wilmington and other North Carolina cities and towns, Red Shirts—Democratic paramilitaries—on horseback rode the country roads and the city streets in mounted Klan-like platoons, disrupting Fusionist political rallies and even bursting into church services, wielding clubs and whips, warning blacks that worse would come on election day if they dared to show up at the polls. And on November 8, in the streets of Wilmington and other North Carolina cities, black voters had to make their way past threatening pha-lanxes of Red Shirts. Through a combination of intimidation of blacks and arousal of racial fury in poor whites, the Democrats won strong victories across North Carolina.

But in Wilmington, the center of the racist campaign, the white su-premacists were not finished, not while the Fusionist mayor and the four black aldermen had two more years in office. Two days after the election, Waddell and an armed mob of two thousand men stormed the wooden building where the *Daily Record* was published—Manly had already fled the city—and burned it down. Then, led by Red Shirts on horseback, the mob laid waste to black neighborhoods, destroyed black businesses, and beat and slaughtered blacks. An estimated fifty or sixty blacks were murdered. Waddell installed himself as mayor and on his orders at least twenty-one prominent blacks and some of their white supporters were forced at bayonet point onto trains leaving town. In the immediate aftermath of the riot, about two thou-sand blacks fled town, and white supremacy reigned in Wilmington. The fol-lowing year, the newly elected Democratic state legislature took the vote away from blacks and instituted a regime of Jim Crow laws that remained in force for decades as North Carolina joined what came to be called the Solid South, the segregated fiefdom of racist white Democrats.

As the years went by, the Wilmington race riot, when it was discussed at all by whites, was portrayed as an understandable reaction against the black lawlessness that allegedly had plagued the state since the days of Reconstruc-tion. But the essential truth of the Wilmington riot as an assault on black success remained alive in the oral tradition of North Carolina's African Americans. In 2000, after repeated questions were raised by civil rights lead-ers and black politicians, the North Carolina General Assembly established the thirteen-member Wilmington Race Riot Commission to try and find out what had really happened on the streets of the small city more than a century before. Six years later, the commission issued a 464-page report that explains in detail that the events of November 1898 were not a spontaneous riot but a "coup d'état," an "armed overthrow of the legitimately elected municipal government" that was organized in a conspiracy by "men prominent in the Democratic Party, former Confederate officers, former officeholders and newspaper editors locally and statewide rallied by Josephus Daniels of the *Raleigh News and Observer*." The riot and the white supremacist reign that followed, the commission reported, resulted in devastating damage to the black community, with a significant loss in skilled occupations and an increase in "lower status jobs," along with major losses to the black businesses that remained, a sharp increase in residential segregation, and a drastic cut in funding to black schools and teachers. Among the recommendations to "repair the moral, economic, civil and political damage wrought by the violence" was to "support judicial redress to compensate heirs of victims."

The report noted, "An African American collective narrative developed to recall the riot and placed limitations on black/white public relationships. White stories of the riot claimed that the violence was necessary to restore order. The white narrative was perpetuated by historians."[41]

By 1900, more than 880,000 blacks lived in the North. The black population of the North had risen by more than 180,000 men, women, and children in ten years, more than twice the increase of the previous decade. Every year, many thousands of black men and women had abandoned the South to escape lynching, horrendous poverty, wretchedly unequal public education, and the virtual disappearance of their political and civil rights. But almost eight million American blacks still lived in the South. What is surprising today is not that so many African Americans fled to the North in the 1890s, but that so few did.[42]

CHAPTER 3

A Harvest of Disaster

In October of 1901, President Theodore Roosevelt set a surprising racial precedent by inviting Booker T. Washington to the White House for dinner, infuriating the Democratic South and dashing its hopes for both men, the hero of San Juan Hill (and American imperialism), who had been in office for barely a month following the assassination of William McKinley, and the "good negro" who had counseled blacks to back away from social equality. The black-owned *Washington Bee* whooped with glee. "The Southern Democrats hoped and expected to blarney the President so as to continue unrestrained in their wicked reign of terror and proscription against the coloured race. They are shocked, boiled, smitten, and exasperated . . . They are fuming with dire imprecations against him, and all because he took a meal of victuals with a coloured gentleman who had been entertained by the nobility of England and the best people of America."[1]

The meeting had symbolic value that helped both men politically with their own constituencies, black and white, but it didn't mean much in terms of better lives for blacks, North or South, and it didn't stop Southern Democrats from passing even more rigid Jim Crow laws. In the long run, the Progressive movement of the first two decades of the twentieth century did little to help African Americans, even when Republicans, the traditional party of blacks, sat in the White House. Still, the very early 1900s were a time when faint glimmers of hope flickered, often quite briefly, in the terrible darkness for American blacks. The price of cotton and some other farm products began to stagger upward in 1900, bringing modest economic improvement to the rural South, and within two years lynching of blacks had dropped from

105 a year to 85. Never again in the decade—nor since—did they approach 100. Black migration slowed a bit in the first ten years of the twentieth century, although more than one million blacks lived in the North by the end of the decade.[2]

At the turn of the century, a century that began with the United States still a predominantly rural nation and ended with most Americans living in cities or suburbs, seventy-two cities nationwide had black populations of five thousand or more. The largest concentration of blacks—eighty-six thousand—was in Washington, D.C. Over the years, particularly under Republican administrations, the federal government had made an effort to hire blacks. And Washington, a river's width from white-supremacist Virginia, maintained excellent if segregated schools for blacks. The capital was developing a solid African American middle class and a growing—and notably snobbish—black elite. Washington symbolized the protection that blacks hoped to find from the federal government. A black man driven by racial violence from the South in the early 1900s was asked by a reporter why he had chosen to go to Washington. He replied that he "wanted to be as near to the flag" as he could get.

Still, even in Washington, increasing numbers of poor urban blacks were crowded into disease-ridden ghettos that reeked of garbage and sewage—dangerous, ill-lit slums with flimsy, flammable housing, and high death rates among both infants and adults. Previously, small black neighborhoods had been scattered across cities. The new ghettos, growing in population but not always in geographical size, bred despair, anger, and crime—most of it inflicted on other blacks. They also bred disease; more than one fourth of black infants born in the North in the early years of the twentieth century died before they reached the age of one, which was twice the death rate of white infants.[3]

Blacks continued to be rejected by almost all trade unions and many blacks with a trade were forced to "stagger downward," as W. E. B. Du Bois vividly put it, into lower-paying unskilled jobs simply because of their race. After a wide-ranging survey in 1902, Du Bois concluded that the nation's 1.2 million union members included less than forty thousand nonwhites. This was not necessarily a problem for Booker T. Washington, who said that blacks "were not naturally inclined towards unions," being in the main "friendly" country folk who tended to "work for persons not wages," seeking out "a good white man" as a boss, and remaining loyal to him. Also, Washington said, there was "a very wide-spread prejudice and distrust of labor unions among Negroes generally." Why? Because, Washington said, spinning a circle of logic, white unions refused to admit blacks.[4]

Northward migration of blacks to small cities and towns in the southern Midwest led to numerous racial attacks in the first decade of the twentieth century. In 1901, after a young white woman was murdered by an attempted rapist in Pierce City, Missouri, a mob of one thousand stormed the city jail, lynched a black prisoner who apparently had nothing to do with the killing, and rampaged through an African American neighborhood, killing two more black men and driving hundreds of African Americans out of town. And in 1903, in Belleville, Illinois, just east of East St. Louis, a black schoolteacher who had shot and wounded the white superintendent of schools after learning that he had failed an examination for a teaching certificate was dragged from jail by a mob of five thousand, hanged, and set on fire. Race riots were triggered by the killing of black policemen in 1903 in Evansville, Indiana, and in 1904 in Springfield, Ohio. In both cases, racial tensions had been building up for years as blacks moved to these relatively small but rapidly growing industrial cities and competed with whites for jobs. Black homes and businesses were destroyed, and blacks were attacked and killed in both cities. In Springfield, a black neighborhood was rebuilt and, in 1906, again destroyed by an angry mob of whites.[5]

But the worst riot of the period took place in 1906 in the commercial capital of the Deep South, and it was a pivotal event in the struggle between Booker T. Washington and more militant black leaders who felt the future of their race had been betrayed for a handful of dubious coinage by the Atlanta Compromise.

During Reconstruction, blacks had established themselves economically and politically in Atlanta and, despite the steady march of Jim Crow across the South in the last decades of the 1800s, by the turn of the century Atlanta had a black elite, a strong black middle class, and many substantial black businesses and institutions. Indeed, it seemed to be fulfilling Booker T. Washington's dream of a "New South" where black economic success would prove that capitalism could trump racism. "The Negro merchant who owns the largest store in town will not be lynched," he assured blacks.[6]

Atlanta held six black private colleges, including prestigious if financially struggling Atlanta University. Most of its faculty was white and had come from Yale, although the intellectually demanding school also boasted a Harvard-educated black professor—W. E. B. Du Bois, who had come to Atlanta University late in 1897 and had completed *The Philadelphia Negro* there. Over the years, the more Du Bois experienced daily life for a black man in the Jim Crow South, whether as a college student and rural schoolteacher in Tennessee or as a Georgia-based scholar whose research took him deep into the rural South, the more he came to realize the profound blows racism had dealt blacks. Increasingly, he felt the need to be not just a student of the race, but an advocate, indeed a fighter, for it. In reaction to a ghastly lynching on the outskirts of Atlanta—a black farmer who killed a white man during an argument was set afire and a mob of two thousand white men, women, and children fought over pieces of his scorched flesh as souvenirs—he said in 1899 that "one could not be a calm, cool and detached scientist while Negroes were lynched, murdered and starved."[7]

Du Bois placed himself at the center of a movement of self-described "New Negro" men and women who espoused black pride and a constant struggle to assert black rights. Blacks, Du Bois proclaimed, "must insist continually, in season and out of season, that voting is necessary to modern manhood, that color discrimination is barbarism, and that black boys need education as well as white boys." Increasingly, Du Bois spoke and wrote in public opposition to Tuskegee Institute founder and president Booker T. Washington. Washington's presence in Atlanta was powerful despite his not living there because his nonthreatening notions of black progress were agreeable to the white Atlanta power brokers with whom he had close contact.[8]

In his passionate *The Souls of Black Folk*, a 1903 collection of essays on race, W. E. B. Du Bois delivered a devastating attack on Washington and his policies, saying that the Atlanta Compromise "practically accepts the alleged inferiority of the Negro races" and had sown the seeds "for a harvest of disaster to our children, black and white." Washington's "doctrine," Du Bois wrote, had resulted in the "disenfranchisement of the Negro," the "legal creation" of a "status of civil inferiority for the Negro," and the "steady withdrawal of aid from institutions for the higher training of the Negro." The Atlanta Compromise, he concluded, was a prescription for "the suicide of a race."[9]

Du Bois and the Boston journalist William Monroe Trotter, both in their thirties, became the leaders of a group of blacks, including educators, clerics, writers and journalists, doctors and lawyers, most of them urban Northerners, who stood in opposition to Washington's "Tuskegee Machine." In 1905, Du Bois went North to join Trotter and other anti-Washington blacks in a conference on the Canadian side of Niagara Falls and the "Niagara movement" was born. Du Bois was elected to the top post of general secretary. The movement's Declaration of Principles—written in great part by Du Bois—stated, "The Negro race in America stolen, ravished and degraded, struggling up through difficulties and oppression, needs sympathy and receives criticism; needs help and is given hindrance, needs protection and is given mob-violence, needs justice and is given charity, needs leadership and is given cowardice and apology, needs bread and is given a stone. This nation will never stand justified before God until these things are changed."[10]

The declaration condemned "two opposite classes of men": employers for "importing ignorant Negro American laborers in emergencies, and then affording them neither protection nor permanent employment" and labor unions for "proscribing and oppressing thousands of their fellow toilers, simply because they are black." But the most radical element was its emphasis on unyielding black protest to effect change. The declaration asserted, "The voice of protest of ten million Americans must never cease to assail the ears of their fellows, so long as America is unjust."

In the years before the 1906 riot, Atlanta grew rapidly in population as blacks and whites left farms and small towns and crowded into the city. Between 1900 and 1910, the population of the commercial and manufacturing boomtown rose from 89,000 to 155,000, with blacks making up between 35 and 40 percent of the total. Poor blacks and whites competed for work, and blacks were often forced into the most menial jobs. Many men of both races were unable to find work. Inevitably the crime rate went up, and thieves, pimps, and prostitutes ruled the streets of some poor neighborhoods—both white and black—particularly after dark. Arrest records suggested that poor blacks were committing a disproportionate number of crimes, and the race as a whole was excoriated in sensationalist newspaper stories.[11]

There were frequent racial skirmishes and attacks on blacks in the streets. A riot nearly broke out in 1905 between blacks and whites at a theatrical production of Thomas Dixon's notorious, inflammatory novel *The Clansman*, which portrayed hooded white vigilantes as Reconstruction-era heroes rescuing a screaming white woman from black rapists. (A decade later, *The Clansman* would become the most popular silent film of all time, *The Birth of a Nation*, and would again arouse whites to antiblack rage in cities and towns across America, including East St. Louis.)

For many months leading up the 1906 gubernatorial election, Atlantans were bombarded with antiblack propaganda by two white candidates competing for poor white voters and the crucial support of the Georgia populist Tom Watson, who once had courted black votes but now had revealed himself as an open and virulent racist. Watson set the hysterical tone of the election, calling for complete disenfranchisement of blacks and screaming in his eponymous propaganda magazine, "What does civilization owe to the negro? Nothing! *Nothing!* NOTHING!"[12]

One of the gubernatorial candidates was Clark Howell, the editor of the *Atlanta Constitution*, and the other, Hoke Smith, was the former publisher of the *Atlanta Journal*. Those dailies and other less respectable white-owned newspapers, in a frenzied circulation war, regularly splashed across their front pages highly exaggerated stories of black crime, particularly the "assault" of white women by black men. The verb "assault" in headlines may have referred to something as minor as an alleged purse snatching or even accidental contact on a crowded downtown street. But the implication was inevitably sexual to white readers who were alert to such matters. And hysterical news stories about "ebony devils" and "ravished white women" created an atmosphere in which white women were quick to see all black men as potential rapists.[13] The racial fear that permeated Atlanta in 1906 was dramatically described by a white woman who, in the wake of the riot, told investigative reporter Ray Stannard Baker of "a really terrible experience one evening a few days ago" on a downtown street:

> I saw a rather good-looking young Negro come out of a hallway to
> the sidewalk. He was in a great hurry, and, in turning suddenly, as
> a person sometimes will do, he accidentally brushed my shoulder
> with his arm. He had not seen me before. When he turned and
> found it was a white woman he had touched, such a look of abject
> terror and fear came into his face as I hope never again to see on a

human countenance. He knew what it meant if I was frightened, called for help, and accused him of insulting or attacking me. He stood still a moment, then turned and ran down the street, dodging into the first alley he came to. It shows, doesn't it, how little it might take to bring punishment upon an innocent man.[14]

In mid-August of 1906, Du Bois and a large contingent of black men from Atlanta took part in the second meeting of the Niagara movement, fully aware of the militant symbolism of their gathering place: Harpers Ferry, West Virginia, site of John Brown's bloody 1859 raid on the federal armory in the buildup to the Civil War. The concluding statement of the conference, written by Du Bois, proclaimed, "We claim for ourselves every single right that belongs to a freeborn American, political and civil, and until we get these rights we will never cease to protest and to assail the ears of America. The battle we fight is not for ourselves alone but for all true Americans. It is a fight for ideals, lest this, our common fatherland, false to its founding, become in truth the land of the thief and the home of the slave." Back in Atlanta, the race-baiting *Georgian* denounced "Negro tirades" and "Negro platitudes and resolutions against the injustice of the South," calling on black leaders to return to Washingtonian accommodation, stop making so much noise about lynching, and focus on the subject that was "pulsing in the aroused and indignant veins of Southern manhood" —rape. Otherwise, the paper warned, it was inevitable that black schools, churches, and other institutions would be destroyed.[15]

On August 22, Hoke Smith won the only gubernatorial election that mattered, the Democratic primary, and announced that as governor he would take steps to disenfranchise all blacks. But the daily papers did not let up on the sensationalist coverage of black crime. On the afternoon of Saturday, September 22, Atlanta newspapers put out multiple extra editions chronicling a series of four alleged assaults by black men on white women. The *Atlanta Evening News* issued five separate editions, devoting the top half of the front page to a series of alarming new headlines:

TWO ASSAULTS!

THIRD ASSAULT!

FOURTH ASSAULT!

The shouts of news boys spread the alarm throughout downtown Atlanta. "The whole city," reported Ray Stannard Baker, "already deeply agitated, was thrown into a veritable state of panic."[16]

It turned out that none of the four cases involved rape; one was a report of a black peeping tom, another of a woman knocked down by a black man running from her back yard, and the other two seemed be cases of pure racial fright. But that didn't seem to matter. "The news in the extras was taken as truthful," Baker reported, "for the city was not in a mood then for cool investigation." It was payday and thousands of men were downtown with money in their pockets, many of them spending the afternoon in the saloons that were thick in the Five Points area, the bustling center of the city, where black Atlanta met white Atlanta beneath towering new buildings. By evening a mob of ten thousand whites, mostly young men, was milling around downtown, vowing vengeance on blacks.

As the sun went down, the mob surged down Decatur Street—which was lined with black saloons—attacking men and women in the streets. Spreading out through downtown, the rioters stopped streetcars by yanking loose their overhead trolleys and pulled black passengers out to be beaten and killed. They swarmed over black neighborhoods, beating and shooting residents and destroying homes and businesses. An African American bootblack was jerked out of the shop where he was shining the shoes of a white man and kicked and beaten to death. Barbers and clerks were pulled out of their shops and beaten and stabbed. Blacks were hung from lampposts and their bodies used for target practice. Police did little to stop the riot. "Had the Police Department opposed a determined front to the mob at the inception of the riot," a grand jury later determined, "all serious trouble could have been averted." The state militia was called in about midnight, but the mob did not relinquish control of the downtown streets to the soldiers until a drenching rain began to fall about two in the morning.

The next two days, with police and militia patrolling downtown streets, white mobs armed with shotguns, clubs, and crowbars invaded black neighborhoods on the outskirts of the city, including a mostly middle-class suburb called Brownsville with two black colleges. By then many blacks had armed themselves, and in some areas they fought back against the white mobs and managed to send them into retreat. When a policeman was shot to death in one black neighborhood, three companies of armed militia men were sent in and arrested 250 blacks.

When the three-day riot was over, at least two dozen blacks and two whites were dead. Witnesses, black and white, said the rioters had been mostly working-class young men and teenagers, although more prosperous-looking whites were seen cheering the whites on. And thousands of other citizens of Atlanta, who were "swept along by curiosity with no intention of crime," one reporter observed, "added by their mere presence to the ferocity of mob leaders."[17]

The riot, in Booker T. Washington's symbolic hometown, shattered the essence of the Atlanta Compromise—the notion that, as blacks succeeded in the economic realm, "friendly whites" would come to respect them and grant them the rights they deserved. In many cases, it was precisely the successful blacks, their property, and their institutions that came under attack.

W. E. B. Du Bois was in Alabama doing research for the United States Census Bureau when the riot struck. On the way home in a segregated rail car, worried sick about his wife and young daughter, he wrote an angry elegy he called the "Atlanta Litany." Without mentioning Washington by name, he indicted his policies. "Behold the maimed black man, who toiled and sweated to save a bit from the pittance paid him. They told him: *Work and Rise!* He worked." And now, Du Bois wrote, "this man lieth maimed and murdered, his wife naked to shame, his children to poverty and evil." Du Bois asked God to show him how his "mobbed and mocked and murdered people" could rise out of its suffering, and he heard no answer. But he admitted he felt "a clamoring and clawing within, to whose voice we would not listen, yet shudder lest we must, and it is red. Ah God! It is a red and awful shape." Increasingly, as time went by, Du Bois would advocate as a last resort the message of that "red and awful shape"—physical defense against the inhumane incursions of white America.[18]

In the meantime, Du Bois called for federal intervention to stop further racial violence in Atlanta. It never came. President Theodore Roosevelt made it clear that he felt racial problems—including lynching and riots—were best solved at the local, not the national, level. "Next to the negro himself," he announced not long after the riot, "the man who can do most to help the negro is his white neighbor who lives near him, and our steady effort should be to better the relations between the two."[19]

In the immediate aftermath of the riot, Atlanta's white leaders met with selected blacks—not including W. E. B. Du Bois, whose effect on whites, a colleague suggested, was generally to make them "angry or miserable"—to discuss how to prevent future racial violence. Periodic interracial meetings to head off potential trouble became known as "the Atlanta way." Some cheap saloons in the riot area, black and white, were closed down, and there was a crackdown on the illegal carrying of guns by both blacks and whites.

But the only real changes were retrograde. Segregation became even more rigid, as if putting further barriers between blacks and whites would dampen the fires of racial hatred, and scores of middle-class blacks fled the city. In trials growing out of the riot, the hand of the law landed much more heavily on blacks than on whites. Some fifty-four African Americans were convicted on weapons charges as opposed to about five whites. Numerous felony charges against whites accused of brutal acts were reduced to misde- meanors or dropped completely. White Atlanta worked hard to forget the un- pleasantness. Only two days after the riot, one newspaper declared, "Atlanta is herself again, business is restored, and the riot is forgotten." For months af- ter the riot was officially over, blacks were assaulted on the streets of Atlanta by small gangs of whites.[20]

The following year, the Georgia legislature, which had only one black member, passed the new governor's disenfranchisement bill, a bundle of re- strictions based on ancestry, economic status, and "character" designed to shut most blacks out of voting. "Nowhere in this bill," boasted one white leg- islator, "is the word 'nigger' written." In a subsequent referendum, the voters of the state by a 2 to 1 margin approved making the bill an amendment to the Georgia constitution. Neither the national Republican Party nor its Geor- gia branch gave any support to the blacks who opposed the new law. By 1910, the percentage of Georgia's blacks who were registered voters had plunged from 28 percent to 4.3 percent.[21]

Although the Atlanta riot initially energized the opposition to Booker T. Washington, political infighting between Trotter and Du Bois and their sup- porters split the Niagara movement, and the organization was languishing when the struggle for black rights was galvanized in 1908 by another riot, this one in the North.[22]

In Springfield, Illinois, the white wife of a streetcar conductor said that a black man had raped her. After the man was arrested, thousands of whites assembled downtown in front of the city jail. When they discovered that the accused rapist and another black man who had been accused of murdering a white railroad engineer had been taken to another town for safety, the mob burned and pillaged black neighborhoods, destroyed parts of downtown, including white-owned businesses, and lynched two law-abiding, middle-class black men, including a black barber who was hanged from a tree in front of a saloon. It took state militia men, who eventually numbered in the thousands, two days to stop the riot.[23]

Springfield, the home and burial place of Abraham Lincoln, seemed like a highly unlikely place for a race riot. It had a very small black population of about twenty-five hundred out of a total of forty-seven thousand, and the black population had not being growing, as it had been in most other cities hit by race riots. What Springfield did have was a corrupt city government that permitted vice districts to flourish in and around downtown, serving the large population of well-heeled men who travel in and out of any state capital, men who are single, at least for the time being, and looking for a good time. Much of the shady activity was concentrated in and around Springfield's downtown, including a heavily black area of cheap saloons, whorehouses, and gambling joints known as the Badlands. According to stories in the newspapers and pronouncements from the pulpit, crime and public indolence were on the rise in downtown Springfield, and blacks were blamed.

After the riot, the local papers reported that white petty criminals and unemployed saloon loafers had formed the core of the rioters. That was undoubtedly true in part, as it often is in race riots. However, many of those arrested for rioting were single young white men with low-paying jobs, which is also often the case. Initially at least, the rioters were encouraged in their attacks by middle-class white spectators. Black criminals and their haunts may have been an original target of the rioters, but as the riot went into its second day, the attacks shifted to a middle-class black neighborhood about two miles from downtown. A black woman who had been a little girl during the riot recalled many years later, "See, the people that they harmed and hurt were not really the no-gooders. They were busy hurting the prominent . . . We owned property; many whites didn't. There was a great deal of animosity toward any well-established Negro who owned his house and had a good job." Historian

Roberta Senechal, who made a thorough reevaluation of the Springfield riot in the 1990s, concluded, "Although what triggered the riot may have been anger over black crime, very clearly whites were expressing resentment over any black presence in the city at all. They also clearly resented the small number of successful blacks in the city."[24]

Later, the woman whose rape accusation had ignited the riot admitted she had lied. It appeared that she had invented the story to hide an affair— with a white man. The accused rapist was set free, as were dozens of whites arrested for rioting. All-white juries acquitted all but one of the men whose cases came to trial. That man spent thirty days in jail.

The Springfield, Illinois, riot shocked the nation, perhaps in great part because the events took place not just in the North but in a city so closely associated with the Great Emancipator, a connection that was not lost on the rioters. Reportedly, members of the mob shouted "Lincoln freed you, now we'll show you where you belong!"

In reaction to the riot, an interracial organization called the National Negro Conference was formed to fight for African American rights. This time the impetus came from white liberals, who would dominate the organization in its early years, but W. E. B. Du Bois, Monroe Trotter, and Ida B. Wells-Barnett—in 1895, the fiery crusader had married black lawyer-journalist Ferdinand L. Barnett—were also among the founders of the conference.

After a long and volatile series of meetings in New York in May and June of 1909, the National Negro Conference, now one thousand strong, voted to reprimand new president William Howard Taft, who had said he would only appoint blacks who were approved of by the South to federal positions. The conference called for strict enforcement of civil rights laws, enfranchisement of African Americans in all parts of the country, and equal educational opportunities for blacks. The following year, the National Negro Conference became the National Association for the Advancement of Colored People and W. E. B. Du Bois left Atlanta University for New York to become the organization's director of publicity and research, the top salaried position. The first task he set for himself was to start a national monthly magazine that would focus on the black struggle in America. He wrote later, "Stepping, therefore, in 1910 out of my ivory tower of statistics and investigation, I sought with bare hands to lift the earth and put it in the path in which I conceived it ought to go."

The magazine, called the *Crisis*, was an almost immediate success. And within a few years the NAACP—and W. E. B. Du Bois, its principal spokesman—became dominant forces in American black thought and political action. By 1914, the NAACP had fifty branch offices and more than six thousand members.[25]

CHAPTER 4

East St. Louis and the Great Exodus

Every major city needs a workbench, a trash heap, a washbasin; some kind of repository for the unattractive yet essential elements of urban life—slaughterhouses, smokestacks, rail yards, and even those who make them work. Industrial suburbs house those elements. Philadelphia needs Camden, Chicago needs Gary, Cincinnati needs Covington, and St. Louis needs East St. Louis.
—Andrew J. Theising, *Made in USA: East St. Louis*

S t. Louis, Missouri, founded by French fur traders on the west bank of the Mississippi River in the late eighteenth century, became in the early nineteenth century the main beneficiary of the immense wealth generated by the virtual decimation of the beaver population of the western territories. Across the Mississippi in Illinois, a tiny mercantile settlement named Illinoistown struggled along on leavings from the fur bonanza. Between the two towns—near the middle of the Mississippi and carved by swift brown currents—lay a no-man's-land of shifting sands and the flood-bleached carcasses of dead trees that made a perfect locale for a popular male pastime of the era, the fighting of duels. The island where men shot and killed other men came to be called Bloody Island.

The St. Louis fur trade depended on the city being a viable port with direct access by water to the Ohio River, New Orleans, the Gulf of Mexico, and the world. Then something ominous began to happen. The channel along the west bank of the Mississippi, which carried the river past the long rows of head-high fur bundles on the St. Louis levee, was slowly silting up.

More and more of the water in the river, it appeared, was flowing along the east bank, deepening the channel on the Illinois side. When the largest boats began getting stuck in the muck at what was billed as a deepwater port at St. Louis, powerful Missouri businessmen and politicians decided something had to be done. They looked to the east, to Bloody Island.

Any doubts as to how to solve the problem, and to whose benefit, were overridden by the political reality. Democrat Thomas Hart Benton of St. Louis, who ironically had helped give the wayward island its name by shooting another lawyer dead on its river-washed sand, was the most powerful man in the United States Senate, in great part because he was an old friend and former military aide de camp of President Andrew Jackson. And so, in 1837, Lieutenant Robert E. Lee was dispatched with a group of muckers from the Army Corps of Engineers to the east bank of the Mississippi, and they built a dike between the Illinois shore and Bloody Island. Over the next few years, millions of tons of water, frustrated in its easterly course, flowed west of Bloody Island and scoured out the channel on the St. Louis side of the river so the city was once again a deepwater port. To the east, sediment built up around the dike and soon attached Bloody Island to the mainland of Illinois. The island with its legacy of death became the riverfront, and, eventually, the railroad yards and westernmost slums of the town that in midcentury became East St. Louis.

It would not be the last time that the interests of the larger city to the west prevailed over those of its smaller and less-affluent namesake across the water, but the leavings for East St. Louis were not inconsiderable as the century advanced. Because of its location a short ferry ride east of America's fourth-largest city and westernmost metropolis, the gateway to the West, East St. Louis became one of the nation's major railroad centers, the western terminus for twenty-two eastern rail lines. And the rail yards attracted industry.[1]

Until the ruggedly graceful, latticed-iron Eads Bridge was built across the Mississippi at St. Louis in 1874, crossing the southern tip of the land that had been Bloody Island, everything that went west from East St. Louis had to be unloaded off wagons or railroad cars, ferried across the wide, deep, swift, perilous river, and loaded up again on horse-drawn carts that would haul the goods up the St. Louis levee to wagons and freight trains pointed west. And even after the bridge was completed, a monopoly held by minor-league robber barons in St. Louis, who had paid dearly for it in a fight with major-league robber baron Jay Gould, charged exorbitant rates to cross what they thought of as "their bridge," even though it, too, was in part built by the United States Army Corps of Engineers. Not until the fall of 1916 was something called the Free Bridge finally completed a mile or so downriver from the Eads Bridge. At that point, the Free Bridge accommodated only foot and automobile traffic, no trains or streetcars. But at least it was free.[2]

In the Civil War era, both St. Louis in eastern Missouri and the cities and towns of southern Illinois had been torn over the issue of slavery, as a population that in great part sympathized with the South found itself in states officially aligned with the Union. The area was touched by the violent demonstrations that broke out over the Civil War draft, but the focus of the draft riots was in the cities of the Northeast, particularly New York.

During the migrations of the late nineteenth and early twentieth centuries, a few thousand Southern blacks moved north to East St. Louis, got menial jobs in the growing number of plants in the area, and found homes downtown and south of Broadway in what became known as the South End. Perhaps the first black man of note to travel north to East St. Louis was a poor young Alabama musician named William Christopher Handy, who visited briefly in 1892. He spent a few weeks in East St. Louis, and got a job working for a company that manufactured railroad equipment. Years later, in a letter to a friend, he recalled, "I . . . pawned my watch for food and lodging to my employer, who stood in with corrupt East St. Louis Police. This [black] man took my two weeks' wages, and kept my watch for the board and lodging, and wouldn't let me have my laundry and clothes. I went to the police for redress, and they threatened to take me in for vagrancy if I pressed the charge. If you don't think that in those days there was corruption in East St. Louis, you have but to do a little research."

One night Handy was sleeping beneath a pier of the Eads Bridge on the Missouri side of the river when he was awakened by black hoboes plucking homemade guitars and singing a lament about East St. Louis. "It had numerous one-line verses," he later recalled, "and they would sing it all night." The song went on and on, but it kept returning to the same two lines:

I walked all the way from old East St. Louis,
And I didn't have but one po' measly dime.[3]

It was one of the first times he heard the blues. Handy wrote that "the primitive Southern Negro" would "bear down on the third and seventh notes of the scale, slurring between major and minor." The eerie modal sound, like nothing that came out of Europe, stayed with him. Handy would use flatted thirds and sevenths in his own blues-based compositions, and those two kinds of notes became known as "blue notes." It is worth mentioning that Handy and the singing black hoboes may have had the blues in St. Louis, but they got them across the Mississippi in East St. Louis.[4]

By the early twentieth century, St. Louis had become a prosperous industrial city sometimes called "Old Smoky." Its furnaces, fueled by sulfurous southern Illinois soft coal, polluted the air so badly that you sometimes couldn't see half a block down the street. Rich men built larger and larger mansions further and further west, taking advantage of the prevailing west winds to keep their eyes and lungs clear of the very pollution that provided their fortunes. A large middle class moved into the sturdy brick houses the rich had vacated, still comfortable, if noticeably etched by acid rain.

East St. Louis, downwind of the pungent sky-darkening pollution of the larger city to the west, also developed a middle class, but a small one that tended to live in modest brick and frame houses built with its members in mind, and the wealth flowed across the river to St. Louis, or north and east to Chicago and New York. East St. Louis was a poor city, which was made daily poorer by the crooked politicians and thieves who ran it through most of its history, and by its absentee landlords, most of whom didn't even pay taxes to support East St. Louis.

In the 1870s, East Coast money built the St. Louis National Stock Yards, but not in St. Louis, nor even in East St. Louis. The stockyards lay just north of the East St. Louis city limits in unincorporated St. Clair County. The Vanderbilts and other stockyard investors built a fancy hotel with a four-star restaurant that, naturally, specialized in beef. Soon meatpackers like Armour and Swift began moving in, right next to livestock pens that could accommodate 15,000 cattle, 10,000 sheep, and 20,000 hogs ready for slaughter. That capacity would double by 1917. None of these enterprises, known collectively as the Meat Trust, paid taxes in East St. Louis, although they polluted the city's air and water and depended on the city's fire department for help if a cattle shed suddenly burst into flame. The northeast side of East St. Louis, adjacent to the stockyards, stank of burnt cowhide and rotting pig guts. In 1907, Upton Sinclair's muckraking novel *The Jungle* exposed filthy conditions in the meatpacking industry and led to the passage of federal meat inspection laws. About the same time, East St. Louis began annexing unincorporated land. The Meat Trust responded to the threats by wrapping itself in a legal cloak, creating the village of National City, Illinois, with about 250 human residents, a mayor picked by the Trust, and a tax assessor who was also on the payroll of one of the meatpackers.

By then, William Neidringhaus, a St. Louis robber baron, had expanded his steel works into Illinois. He bought land north of East St. Louis and created Granite City. Other wealthy industrialists built plants in Granite City and on unincorporated land nearby, and eventually companies like Monsanto Chemical Company of St. Louis and the Aluminum Ore Company, an ancestor of Alcoa whose principal investors included Andrew Mellon of Pittsburgh, would also have their own little towns, relatively free of taxes and pouring out sulfur-laden smoke that seemed to find its way freely across municipal limits. At the time of the First World War, the largest single employer of East St. Louis men and women was the Aluminum Ore Company, which refined ore from Arkansas as part of the national aluminum trust. The company sprawled across the prairie in unincorporated

The Aluminum Ore Company

St. Clair County bordering East St. Louis, and its political clout was sufficient to beat back any attempts by St. Clair County to increase its minimal taxes. The Rockefellers' Standard Oil put a notably polluting refining plant in Wood River, in Madison County north of East St. Louis, and soon other refiners came and joined in.[5] As late as the end of the twentieth century, "Wood River" remained a synonym in the St. Louis area for lingering chemical pollution that could maim and kill and was particularly dangerous to small children.

As East St. Louis became known as the "Pittsburgh of the West" and, perhaps less flatteringly, as the "Hoboken of St. Louis," plants spread across the unregulated landscape, most of them paying wages that guaranteed little more than a lifetime of poverty. The first major strike in the East St. Louis area in the twentieth century came in the summer of 1904 at the packing houses of National City. At the same time, across the river, St. Louis was hosting its World's Fair, with millions of visitors from around the world coming to see the astonishing technological artifices of what came to be called the American Century. The St. Louis World's Fair was an unprecedented display of American might and ingenuity that trumpeted the Darwinian supremacy of the white race. A few miles and a wide river to the east of the fairgrounds where millions watched the Zulus and the pygmies dance near model industrial plants, Swift and Armour called out the Pinkertons and brought in strikebreakers to crush the uprising of men who butchered cows and pigs and waded in blood for a living.

Although some of the strikebreakers were black, the majority were recent immigrants from southern and eastern Europe. They stepped into jobs unwillingly vacated by men who called themselves "Americans" or "native Americans," the sons and grandsons of Irishmen and Scotsmen and Germans. The union men referred to the European strikebreakers as "white Sambos" or, if their skin was sufficiently swarthy, simply "niggers." As the century advanced, the southern and eastern European immigrants began to be accepted into the workplaces, the unions, the neighborhoods, and even the families of the northern European immigrants who had preceded them. In a sociological term of more recent currency, the Italians and Greeks and Poles and Turks "achieved whiteness," while African Americans remained the target of white America's racial prejudice. Most of the African Americans who had served as strikebreakers—and earned the persistent hatred of white union members for doing it—were gone from the stockyards within a few years, only to be summoned back the next time there was a strike.[6]

Nationwide, bringing in black replacement workers was a common tactic of management in the bitter labor battles of the era. In Chicago, black strikebreakers were used to defeat stockyard strikes in 1894 and in 1904. Blacks were physically assaulted in both strikes, and at least one black worker was killed in 1904. But it was a teamsters' strike in 1905 that seared the link between blacks and strikebreakers into the consciousness of Chicago whites, and led to blacks being referred to contemptuously as "a scab race." The strike lasted more than three months and labor violence spilled over into the city as a whole. In the early weeks, blacks were recruited and transported to Chicago by the trainload. And as they tried to go to work at plants or deliver milk, coal, ice, and other commodities, they were attacked, beaten, shot, and stabbed. The city council, fearing a widespread riot, hotly debated the question of "whether the importation of hundreds of Negro workers is not a menace to the community and should not be restricted," and the employers' association agreed to stop bringing in black strikebreakers but refused to discharge those already working.

"You have the Negroes in here to fight us," the president of the teamsters union told the employers' association, "and we answer that we have the right to attack them wherever found." Not only strikebreakers but ordinary blacks were attacked in the streets, particularly in a white working-class neighborhood bordering what was becoming the Black Belt on Chicago's South Side. Even schoolchildren joined in the attacks, gathering by the hundreds to throw rocks at scabs.[7]

Blacks fought back, some of them with guns. After two black strikebreakers leaving work fired into a jeering crowd and killed an eleven-year-old white boy, enraged whites stormed black neighborhoods, and met armed black resistance. Black men were dragged off of streetcars and beaten, and a white bartender killed a black man in a saloon brawl. For a week, blacks and whites fought in the streets of Chicago. By the end of the strike, almost twenty people, black and white, had been killed, and more than four hundred seriously injured.

The period was also marked by violence against blacks in the smaller cities of downstate Illinois, where antiblack bigotry was flavored by a sometimes deceptively bucolic racial climate. The farming and mining country of southern Illinois was geographically and culturally closer to the South than it was to the burgeoning industrial giant of Chicago. What that could mean for unwary blacks was demonstrated graphically in 1908 by the riot in Spring-field discussed in the previous chapter and in 1909 by a lurid racial murder in Cairo, a cotton port at the southern tip of the Little Egypt region of Illinois, where the Mississippi meets the Ohio. Cairo and environs differed little in racial attitudes from Jackson or Natchez or Baton Rouge. An accusation that a black man had raped and murdered a white woman triggered a day of vio-lence. The accused rapist was wrestled from custody, dragged down the main street of Cairo by a rope around his neck and hanged from a steel lamppost. According to Ida Wells-Barnett, who came down from her home in Chicago in the immediate aftermath of the lynching, five hundred bullets were fired into the body. Some of the bullets severed the rope and the body fell to the ground. Wells-Barnett wrote, "The body was taken near to the place where the corpse of the white girl had been found. Here they cut off his head, stuck it on a fence post, built a fire around the body and burned it to a crisp." Later that evening, the mob, still thirsty for vigilante justice, broke into the city jail and lynched a white man who had been accused of murdering his wife.[8]

Photographs of the carnival atmosphere that surrounded the lynching of the black man in Cairo were widely circulated on a popular set of picture postcards.

By 1910, St. Louis had grown to a population of 687,000 people, about 44,000 of them black. Its growth was slowing somewhat. Chicago, with 2,185,000 people, had long ago overtaken the old riverboat city and become the commercial capital of the Midwest. But St. Louis remained the fourth-largest city in America. Across the Mississippi, East St. Louis grew too, and by the 1910 census it had about fifty-eight thousand residents, most of them blue-collar workers and their families. Blacks made up about 10 percent of the population. Within five years, the black population of East St. Louis had increased to about seventy-nine hundred people—about 11 percent of the total. Then America's first great black migration began in earnest.[9]

On August 4, 1914, Germany marched into Belgium to begin the Great War, and while American industrial plants ratcheted up their output to supply the European armies, immigration slowed sharply, and hundreds of thousands of European immigrants went back home to fight for their countries of birth, leaving jobs open in plants across the country.

At the same time, the boll weevil, which had crossed the Rio Grande near Brownsville, Texas, in 1892 and steadily marched to the north and the east, was devastating cotton crops in much of Mississippi and parts of Alabama. Also, mechanization was eliminating much agricultural handwork, and many thousands of Southern blacks, sharecroppers, and hired hands alike found themselves out of work.

Then came the severe floods of 1916, and the migration from the cotton fields of the Mississippi Delta became an exodus. "They were selling out everything they had or in a manner giving it away; selling their homes, mules, horses, cows, and everything about them but their trunks," said one black Southern observer.[10] There were jobs to be had in cities of the North, Southern blacks were told, and not just by the labor agents for employers who took trainloads of blacks north every week from Southern cities. Thousands of blacks who had already made the trek to Northern cities sent cards and letters to their relatives and friends down home telling them that life was better in the North. And the black newspaper the *Chicago Defender*, widely circulated in the South, regularly ran stories and advertisements promoting the opportunities for black workers in Chicago, Detroit, and other Northern cities, including St. Louis and East St. Louis.

The *Chicago Defender* was founded in 1905 by Robert Sengstacke Abbott, a deceptively mild-mannered, Georgia-born preacher's stepson who, as a young man visiting the Chicago World's Fair, had been inspired by the fiery speeches of Frederick Douglass and Ida B. Wells. Abbott's slogan was "American race prejudice must be destroyed." He vowed that "education of the race is our job," and he was not afraid to take strong and even comparatively radical editorial positions. He called for all trade unions to open their membership to blacks, for blacks to be represented in the presidential cabinet and in all police forces across America, and for all public schools to be open to African Americans. Like any number of black leaders before him—and long after him—he also called for federal antilynching legislation.[11]

As the *Defender* evolved and its circulation grew, the paper became a feisty mixture of heart-warmers about the accomplishments of blacks in the North and shockers about the mistreatment of blacks across the country, particularly in the South. Stories on black heroes like boxer Jack Johnson and coverage of the black struggle for justice were mixed with such mainstays of commercial journalism as obituaries, want ads, comics, and cartoons. The paper really took off, not just in Chicago but nationally, in 1910 when Abbott brought aboard a flamboyant, alcoholic managing editor named J. Hockley Smiley who ran sensationalist stories with headlines in red ink, headlines like:

100 NEGROES MURDERED WEEKLY IN
UNITED STATES BY WHITE AMERICANS

There were many real atrocities to report, and Smiley splashed them across the front page after the white press ignored or downplayed them. On slow weeks, a former *Defender* reporter once recalled, Smiley relied on his imagination, which produced "lynchings, rapes, assaults, mayhems and sundry 'crimes' against innocent Negroes in the hinterlands of the South, often in towns not to be found on any map extant."[12]

Abbott set up a distribution network in the South through Pullman car porters, dining car waiters, and touring black entertainers and ballplayers. And later, working through black ministers in the South, he established "agent-correspondents," who both distributed the paper and reported local news in dozens and eventually hundreds of Southern cities and towns. The circulation rose dramatically. In 1915, the *Defender*, which had begun the size of a handbill, switched from a tabloid format and became an eight-column broadsheet. The *Defender* had become America's most successful black newspaper. By 1920 the paper's nationwide circulation had risen to more than two hundred thousand, and the paper claimed a readership of more than one million, probably not an inflated figure. The *Defender* was passed from hand to hand until it was worn and torn, and read aloud in barbershops and churches and other meeting places. Two thirds of the circulation was outside of the city limits of Chicago, and although the bulk of those readers were in the South, still home of almost nine out of ten black Americans, the paper's reach was truly nationwide. The *Defender* sold twenty-three thousand copies every week in New York City alone.

Abbott was a great admirer of Booker T. Washington—the entire front page of the November 14, 1915, edition was devoted to a giant headline announcing Washington's death—but he disagreed with Washington's advice to Southern blacks to "cast down their buckets" where they stood. Abbott advised, with tempered optimism, the opposite, "Come North, where there is more humanity, some justice and fairness."[13]

The *Defender* became a powerful engine in the Great Migration that began in the years of the First World War. Carl Sandburg, in his *Chicago Daily News* column, wrote in 1919 that "the *Defender* more than any one agency was the big cause of the 'northern fever' and the big exodus from the south." Abbott relentlessly urged Southern blacks to move to the "Promised Land"— Chicago, St. Louis, and other cities of the North where underpaid, hungry Southern blacks "could get the wrinkles out of their bellies and live like men." The *Defender*, and the black press in general, were very important in the black community and held considerable power to sway readers, particularly in the South, where, with the exception of the church, all the major institutions of life—the courts, the political system, the daily newspapers—were controlled by whites and almost inevitably were hostile or at best indifferent to blacks. After the *Defender* ran an ambitious series of stories detailing how much better blacks were treated in the North than in the South, the Chicago Urban League, which helped African Americans find jobs and places to live, received an extraordinary 940 letters from blacks who wanted to move North.[14]

The power of the *Defender* in the black community did not go unnoticed by whites. In a cruel reminder of the Redemption period in the South, the Ku Klux Klan had been revived in 1915 and was riding through the South and the lower Midwest, flogging, branding, and lynching blacks and terrorizing whites who were insufficiently racist. These crimes were ignored or given minor play in most white newspapers, while the *Defender* reported them in detail. Alarmed, white public officials across the South declared the *Defender* a menace to public order and confiscated copies as soon as they appeared in town. In response, the paper encouraged readers to subscribe and receive the paper by mail. In some areas of the Deep South, the *Defender* set up an underground distribution network, shipping the paper into town hidden in other merchandise.

Distributors were assaulted by members of the Klan and other racist groups and their papers were destroyed. In one incident that was far from unique, Klansmen told a black woman in Yazoo City, Mississippi, they would kill her if she didn't stop distributing the paper. She was forced to leave town.

Such threats and assaults were duly reported in the *Defender*, and in the long run only added to the reasons for blacks to leave the South.[15]

As crowds of migrants headed North, daily newspapers in the South tried to counter the influence of the *Defender* by running reports from Northern cities about mobs of ill-clad blacks, shoeless and hungry, shivering on the icy sidewalks and begging for money for train fare back to the Land of Cotton. The *Defender* responded that it was cold in the South too—particularly for people too poor to afford winter heat—and ran a series of stories about blacks literally dying of the cold in Southern winters, stories with headlines like the one on a report out of Atlanta in February:

NEGRO WOMAN FROZE TO DEATH MONDAY

The *Defender* concluded that report by saying, "If you can freeze to death in the North and be free, why freeze to death in the South and be a slave, where your mother, sister and daughter are raped and burned at the stake, where your father, brother and son are treated with contempt and hung to a pole, riddled with bullets at the least mention that he does not like the way he has been treated? Come North, then, all of you folks . . . For the hard working man there is plenty of work—if you really want it! The Defender says come!"[16]

They came.

Also promoting northward emigration was the Illinois Central Railroad, which had bought railroad lines through the Mississippi Delta in the 1890s and offered special weekend excursion rates and group discounts for tickets from the Delta to Chicago, Indianapolis, St. Louis, East St. Louis, and other midwestern cities, providing the infrastructure for much of the extensive black exodus to the North Central states of the early decades of the twentieth century.[17]

Between 1910 and 1920, at least half a million blacks moved North, the great majority of them—four hundred thousand or more—in the second half of the decade. Previously, the majority of the black emigrants had gone to New York, Philadelphia, and other eastern cities and towns. This time, more and more blacks from the Deep South were riding the railroad lines due north to the rapidly growing industrial cites of the Great Lakes, Cleveland, Detroit, and especially Chicago, as well as to St. Louis, East St. Louis, Indianapolis, and the smaller industrial cities of Ohio, Indiana, and Illinois. The immigrants to the Midwest came in the main from the beleaguered cotton states of Mississippi, Alabama, Georgia, and South Carolina, and it is not coincidental that those were the states with the harshest Jim Crow laws and the worst record on lynching and other forms of brutality against blacks.[18]

According to the conservative figures of the U.S. Census Bureau, while the black populations of New York and Philadelphia increased by roughly 60 to 65 percent from 1910 to 1920, the black population of Chicago went up 148 percent, from about 44,000 to more than 109,000. Detroit, which had a black population of only about 5,700 in 1910, saw the number soar more than sevenfold to almost 41,000 by 1920 as the city's automakers grew rapidly and began hiring blacks. And Cleveland's black population rose from about 8,000 to about 34,000.[19]

Many thousands of the immigrants to the North were lured by offers of jobs on the railroads. For decades in the South, the roughest work on railways—the laying and replacing of tracks and maintenance of rail yards—had been done mainly by blacks, with many miles of tracks in the pre–Civil War South laid by teams of Irish immigrants and slaves owned by the railroads. After emancipation, track crews on Southern railroads were predominantly black. After World War I began, in order to fill openings created by increased shipping and the departure of large numbers of immigrants, Northern railroads openly recruited crews of trackmen in the South. Labor agents from Northern cities, including the major rail hub of East St. Louis, made weekly hiring trips to Southern cities. Public officials became alarmed at the weekly departures of carloads of young black men headed for railroad work up North, with their friends and families crowding train stations to see them off, and passed laws restricting the activities of labor-recruiting agents, or rediscovered old laws dating back to the fight against Reconstruction.

In early August of 1916, two entire trainloads of men—about one thousand black laborers—set off from Union Station in Savannah, Georgia, for track-maintenance jobs in Pennsylvania. In response, the city council of Savannah created a license fee of $1,000 for agents who sent workers out of state. Later that year, the city arrested hundreds of blacks at the station on trumped-up charges, inspiring W. E. B. Du Bois to remark in the *Crisis,* "All the slave catching machinery of the South is being put into motion to stop migration."[20]

As they saw their work force heading North, some Southern employers raised wages and made other concessions to induce blacks to stay. An observer for the U.S. Department of Labor reported, "Negroes remaining in the South are being given a consideration never before accorded them . . . Owing to the scarcity of labor, a Georgia farmer near Albany this year laid aside his whip and gun, with which it is reported he is accustomed to drive his hands, and begged for laborers."[21]

Beginning early in 1916, steel mills and other large Northern employers added to the exodus by offering free transportation to blacks who wanted to work in the North. The result, an observer recalled, was "like the gold fever in '49." The muckraking Chicago journalist Ray Stannard Baker, among the first white reporters to cover the African American community extensively, reported that, in the spring of 1916, "trains were backed into southern cities and hundreds of Negroes were gathered up in a day, loaded into the cars and whirled away to the North . . . Negro teamsters left their horses standing in the streets or deserted their jobs and went to the trains without notifying their employers or even going home."[22]

No matter where they ended up, the great majority of the black migrants found themselves, at best, with low-paying, menial jobs. For example, Carnegie, the Pittsburgh steel giant, employed about fifteen hundred blacks before 1916. By the summer of 1917, the number had swollen to more than four thousand, but only ninety-five of them were doing skilled labor.[23]

Few black workers in any Northern city, skilled or unskilled, belonged to unions. The American Federation of Labor remained the dominant force in the American labor movement, and founder Samuel Gompers had given up his earlier attempts at unionizing blacks as futile and going against the grain of racial attitudes in the white rank and file. Although the radical Industrial Workers of the World, which welcomed blacks and unskilled workers, won some bitterly fought labor battles in the first two decades of the century, the overwhelming majority of American labor remained lily white, and serious and effective organizing of black workers by mainstream American labor would not come until the top-to-bottom industrial unionism movement of the 1930s. In some industries, like the railroads, blacks shut out of white unions formed their own labor organizations, but most black workers who emigrated to the North were without union representation.

Many of them were without jobs as well. Some industrialists used labor agents and newspaper advertisements to lure blacks North with inflated promises, creating a highly visible ready reserve of workers desperate for jobs in case of a strike. As a result, when they arrived in the North, many blacks discovered there were no jobs at all, or that the jobs that were available paid well short of the living wage they had been promised. Some were able to find other jobs, usually at much lower pay than they had expected; a few went back to the South; some ended up on the streets, increasing social friction. But blacks continued arriving weekly in the cities of the North. Even blacks who had jobs paying relatively decent wages down South were heading North in numbers that were alarming to Southern whites. The *Telegraph* in Macon, Georgia, reported:

> Everybody seems to be asleep about what is going on right under our noses—that is, everybody but those farmers who waked up on mornings recently to find every Negro over 21 on their places gone—to Cleveland, to Pittsburgh, to Chicago, to Indianapolis. Better jobs, better treatment, higher pay—the bait held out is being swallowed by thousands of them about us. And while our very solvency is being sucked from underneath us, we go about our affairs as usual—our police raid pool rooms for "loafing Negroes," bring in 12, keep them in the barracks all night, and next morning find that 10 of them have steady jobs . . . Our country officers hear of a disturbance at a Negro resort and bring in fifty-odd men, women, boys, and girls to spend the night in jail, to make a bond at 10 percent, to hire lawyers, to mortgage half of two months wages to get back their jobs Monday morning, although but a half dozen could have been guilty of the disorderly conduct . . . It was a week following [such arrests] that several Macon employers found good Negroes, men trained in their work, secure and respected in their jobs, valuable assets to their white employers, had suddenly left and gone to Cleveland, "where they didn't arrest 50 niggers for what three of 'em done."[24]

The U.S. Department of Labor asked dozens of blacks why they had left the South. The reasons they gave included "ravages of boll-weevil, floods, change of crop system, low wages, poor housing on plantations, inadequate school facilities, inadequate crop settlements, rough treatment, cruelty of the law officers, unfairness in courts, lynching, the desire for travel, labor agents, the Negro press, letters from friends in the North, and finally advice of white friends in the South, where crops had failed."[25]

As the northward migration was gathering strength, the flames of racial prejudice, North and South, were fed by the unprecedented emotional power of a brilliantly constructed new movie celebrating the Ku Klux Klan and portraying Reconstruction Era blacks as ape men lusting after virginal white women. The cinematic innovations of one of the most talented filmmakers of the twentieth century—innovations such as multiple cameras, fast cutting, parallel editing, accelerating pacing, and point-of-view cinematography— made David Wark Griffith's *The Birth of a Nation*, initially released early in 1915, an emotional powerhouse. Over the next two years it played across the country, inspiring pickets and protests by the NAACP and, in some cities, attacks on blacks in the streets and brawls between blacks and whites. *The Birth of a Nation* was the most viscerally exciting movie of its time, and the most popular. It is no coincidence that the Klan reemerged as a powerful force, and lynching showed a marked increase as *The Birth of a Nation* was packing in crowds all over the country.

When it was shown in St. Louis, pickets from the NAACP competed for attention with men and women from something called the United Welfare Association, a group of white neighborhood associations well funded by real estate moguls. The United Welfare Association was gathering signatures on an initiative petition to enact "an ordinance to prevent ill-feeling, conflict and collision between the white and colored races" by requiring "separate blocks for residence," as well as segregation in churches and dance halls. Similar block-by-block segregation laws had been passed in other American cities in Southern and border states, including Louisville, Baltimore, Atlanta, and Richmond. These laws would be declared unconstitutional by the U.S. Supreme Court in 1917, but not before the citizens of St. Louis had given a clear indication of the racial mood of the area by voting approval of enforced segregation by a margin of 3 to 1.[26]

A special showing of *The Birth of a Nation* was arranged at the White House for President Woodrow Wilson, a Virginian and friend of the author of *The Clansman*, the novel on which the movie was based. Legend has it that Wilson was the one who gave the famous description of the movie, "Like writing history with lightning," and added, "My only regret is that it is all so terribly true."[27]

CHAPTER 5

A Nest of Crime and Corruption

Most of the blacks who arrived in East St. Louis between 1915 and 1917 were men from the slums of Southern cities like Memphis or Jackson or from the impoverished cotton farms of the Mississippi Delta. Some of them had rough manners. Few of them were used to the confusing racial signals of the North in general and the lower Midwest in particular, where they were supposed to be equal to whites, but were not treated that way. They arrived by the coachload and even the trainload. William Roach, who ran the Illinois State Free Employment Bureau in East St. Louis during that period, recalled that he talked to blacks as soon they arrived in town and "they told me they got cheap tickets, and that they were told by the white folks in the South, or some white man told them—sometimes the railroad agents would say it—that there was plenty of work in East St. Louis, good wages, and when they got to East St. Louis we didn't have anything for them at the time.

"When a great number of them came in," he said, "I notified all the railroad superintendents that we had a great many laborers on hand, colored track laborers, and I got jobs for pretty near all of them out of town. That was in 1915, and [even] a part of 1914, and I shipped a great many of them off . . . I shipped some of them to East Chicago, to Ohio, Indiana, Baltimore, Buffalo . . . all the way to Kansas City . . . I done all I could to take care of them. I notified the police department to send in every idle man they could get hold of, and that helped out too." Many thousands of men passed through his office in downtown East St. Louis between 1915 and 1917. At times, Roach would ship out three coaches, each holding eighty men, twice a week, which came to two thousand men a month.

Many of the men, he said, had spent their last cent on an excursion ticket to East St. Louis, hoping for work. "Some white fellows told them there was good wages in East St. Louis, in the north, and they headed this way," he recalled. In late 1915, as fall turned into winter, hundreds arrived every week, many with no luggage, wearing worn cotton overalls and thin work shirts. The men were from the Deep South, and were completely unprepared for snow and sleet and the freezing winds that blew from the west across the icy Mississippi.

So many of the men were able to buy tickets at such cheap rates that Roach became suspicious, and asked the United States attorney to find out who was subsidizing black migration. He never got an answer. But, he said, it seemed relevant that most of the men he talked to said they had been promised jobs on the railroad, and it was the railroads that were giving them the extraordinarily cheap rates.[1]

As job markets in other cities became saturated, the black men without jobs often stayed in East St. Louis, sleeping in vacant lots or alleys and begging on the streets. Some got hold of cheap guns and pulled holdups. Some of the victims were white. Although the official crime statistics for that period disappeared at least half a century ago into the dark maw of East St. Louis's corrupt city government, there is little question that the murder, rape, and robbery rate increased in the early years of the Great War, and no question that some of the worst crimes—or at least some of the most highly publicized crimes—were committed by blacks. But the abundance of street crime in East St. Louis could hardly be blamed solely on blacks in a city that essentially had been surrendered by its leaders—its politicians and businessmen and police—to thugs and gangsters, gamblers and prostitutes, and to saloon keepers and their clientele.

East St. Louis was nationally known as one of the most corrupt and crime-ridden cities in America. There was a widespread legend that a detective from New York who was visiting East St. Louis walked down Broadway one day and recognized three men—none of them apparently with either of the other two—and each of them was wanted for a felony in New York. All were white.[2]

In the wide-open red-light district known as the Valley, within sight of city hall and the main police station, hundreds of prostitutes, white and black, openly walked the streets or tapped on windows to lure potential customers inside—where, often, they were beaten and robbed rather than sexually entertained. The prostitutes worked twelve-hour shifts and were divided by the local vernacular into "women of the day" and "women of the night." They were often arrested, as were the pimps and muggers and gunmen who worked the Valley and adjoining areas of downtown East St. Louis. But those who hired the right lawyers and paid the requisite bribes to the police and the low-level city courts run by justices of the peace were soon released and working again after paying fines. Indeed, the East St. Louis political system depended upon bribes and fines to supplement the earnings of badly paid police and unsalaried justices of the peace, whose income came from court fees.

Most of the prostitutes and pimps and thugs in East St. Louis were white, even if much of the citizenry was led to believe otherwise. The *East St. Louis Daily Journal* emphasized and sensationalized black crime, particularly black on white crime. As a result, many East St. Louis whites came to feel as if they were under invasion, particularly on weekends when hundreds of blacks, coming and going, packed the downtown railroad station and roamed the nearby streets looking for food, drink, and amusement.

Despite the long-standing reputation of the state of Illinois as a haven for persecuted blacks, and despite a considerable body of nineteenth-century legislation forbidding discrimination in the state, much of public life in southern Illinois was segregated. In factories, blacks had separate washrooms and lunch rooms and were given the most menial jobs. Schools had legally been desegregated in the state of Illinois since 1874, but white children in East St. Louis and environs were assigned to all-white schools, and black kids to all-black schools. Although the Illinois legislature in 1885 had passed one of the nation's first laws forbidding discrimination in public accommodation, bars, restaurants, hotels, and boardinghouses were strictly segregated in the southern half of the state, as were all but the lowest whorehouses.[3]

Still, in the years before the Great War, many blacks and whites had lived very close to one another in East St. Louis—and sometimes worked side by side—without a great deal of trouble. Years later, at the height of the Depression but before the Second World War once again ripped the social fabric apart—with the memories of the riot somewhat dimmed, although certainly not forgotten—East St. Louis was again a city where a mixed population lived together in relative tolerance. Musician Miles Davis, the son of a dentist, grew up in the 1930s in East St. Louis near Fifteenth Street and Bond Avenue, where blacks and whites lived and worked very close to one another and racial incidents were rare.

The Davis family lived above a drugstore in their early years, as the father was establishing his practice, and next door was a tavern owned by a black man who played saxophone. Nearby was a soul food restaurant, but next to it was a white-owned dry goods store. "It was run by a German lady," Davis recalled. "All along 15th paralleling the river toward Bond street were all kinds of stores . . . owned by blacks, or Jews, or Germans, or Greeks, or Armenians, who had most of the cleaning places. Over on 16th and Broadway this Greek family owned a fish market and made the best jack salmon sandwiches in East St. Louis. I was friends with the son of the guy who owned it." But even as a boy growing up in a neighborhood where black and white kids played together, Davis, with the paradoxical "double-consciousness" that W. E. B. Du Bois identified as a necessary and crucial aspect of African American thinking, also understood that most East St. Louis whites were, as he put it, "racist to the bone."[4]

The sensationalist *East St. Louis Daily Journal,* an evening paper that was closely tied to the Democratic Party on racial and other issues, was East St. Louis's principal newspaper. But the five mainstream daily newspapers in St. Louis—the *Post-Dispatch*, the *Globe-Democrat*, the *Republic*, the *Star*, and the *Times*—covered East St. Louis, and were read by East St. Louisans. All five St. Louis papers had reporters assigned to East St. Louis and most had East St. Louis offices. The two most important, and most widely circulated, of the St. Louis papers were the morning *St. Louis Globe-Democrat*, which was known for solid, straightforward, sometimes tough-minded local coverage, and the evening *St. Louis Post-Dispatch*, which, under the leadership of Joseph Pulitzer II, was becoming one of the best newspapers in America. It excelled in national and international as well as crusading local coverage. Editorially, the *Globe-Democrat* leaned toward the Republicans and the *Post-Dispatch* tended to favor the Democrats (although it was relatively liberal on racial issues), but both the *Post-Dispatch* and the *Globe-Democrat* were modern newspapers in that they at least gave the appearance of being independent of party politics in their news coverage.

The *St. Louis Republic* was a struggling morning paper that was owned by a Democratic politician—David Francis, Woodrow Wilson's ambassador to Russia during the upheavals of 1917—and was old-fashioned in that it often seemed to parrot the party line, racially and otherwise. The *St. Louis Star* and the *St. Louis Times* were lavishly illustrated populist afternoon papers that stressed sports, entertainment, and local human interest stories.

For African Americans in both St. Louis and East St. Louis, the most important source of news about black affairs was the respected black-owned weekly, the *St. Louis Argus*.

In the summer of 1916, a brilliant young reporter named Paul Y. Anderson wrote a series in the *Post-Dispatch* excoriating the administration of Mayor Fred Mollman and police chief Ransom Payne for permitting illegal gambling and prostitution all over the city, including a couple of notorious vice dens virtually across the street from the city hall–police station complex on Main Street in the heart of downtown. Anderson reported that, in 1915, after Mollman had been elected on a "reform" ticket, he placated his more moralistic supporters by issuing an order closing the red-light district, an order that, after a brief flurry of token closings, was widely ignored by police and city officials, including Mayor Mollman himself. After utterly failing to get legendary cigar-chomping *Post-Dispatch* managing editor O. K. Bovard to fire Anderson for sullying the name of his fair city, Mollman, who was in his mid-forties, spotted Anderson, who was twenty years younger, near city hall one day and took a wild swing at him. He banned Anderson from the press

Paul Y. Anderson

Mayor Fred Mollman

offices in city hall and the police station, which didn't stop the tenacious young reporter from coming in and badgering recalcitrant city officials until cops shoved him out the door.[5]

Late in the summer of 1916, after Anderson's articles put pressure on the mayor to clean up open gambling, a member of the police vice squad named H. F. Trafton took it upon himself to close a downtown bookie joint. It happened to be owned in part by Frank Florence, the assistant chief of detectives. Florence walked in on the raid, pulled his service revolver, and told Trafton to put his hands in the air. Trafton complied, giving the assistant chief of detectives a clear shot at his vitals. Florence shot him dead. There were several witnesses who swore in court that they had seen the whole thing and that Florence was guilty of gunning down a man with his hands in the air, but after a year of legal maneuvering and backroom threats and dealing, Florence was acquitted of the charge of murder, confirming the general feeling that the police were among the last people in East St. Louis you would trust to enforce the law.[6]

In July of 1916, three dozen men were fired from National City's three largest meatpackers—Swift, Armour, and Morris—for trying to organize a union, and more than four thousand workers went out on strike. Management announced it would not negotiate with the strikers, and would only consider hiring them back if they left the union. "There will be no union at this plant," said the head of one large meatpacker. The meat companies brought in strikebreakers, including between eight hundred and fifteen hundred blacks. The hard stance of management quickly broke the back of the strike. Men began deserting the fledgling union in large numbers and going back to work. The strikers, except for union organizers, were rehired, at least for the moment.[7]

In August, management began a new wave of firings and replaced experienced men, some of them with many years of seniority, with cheaper untrained workers, some of them black. Earl Jimmerson, an official of the butchers and meat-cutters union, became alarmed at the potential social cost of continually bringing in black replacement workers. Jimmerson, who had political clout as a member of the St. Clair County Board of Supervisors, told Mayor Fred Mollman that trouble lay ahead unless something was done about "employing Negroes in place of white men . . . and throwing these [Negroes] right amongst these foreigners . . . You know what a foreigner is; he will fight at the drop of a hat and if you go to take his job he'll kill you if he gets the opportunity to do it." The mayor told Jimmerson to calm down, things weren't as bad as all that.[8]

Blacks were also used to break a strike against the streetcar monopoly in that period.

On Saturday, October 7, 1916, about six hundred workers walked off the job at the Aluminum Ore Company in protest against arbitrary pay cuts. On Monday, hundreds of strikers blocked rails and roads leading into the plant. The Aluminum Ore Company easily obtained a federal injunction so the plant could operate—there was a war in Europe, and aluminum was a vital raw material. The Aluminum Ore Company Employee's Protective Association, a local organization that was not affiliated with the American Federation of Labor—it was little more than a company union, other labor leaders charged—thrashed out an agreement with plant officials to return to work by the end of the week. As soon as the men came back, the company began getting rid of them a few at a time, laying off union men and hiring newcomers, some of them black, to replace them. By late fall two hundred men of a once union-friendly work force of about nineteen hundred had been replaced, and the firings continued into the winter. Workers became discouraged, or afraid, and left the union. Membership dwindled from a peak of about one thousand to a couple of hundred by the end of 1916.[9]

According to Aluminum Ore Company statistics, the number of black employees rose from a dozen in 1915 to 280 in November of 1916 and to 410 in December. Management was clearly aware of the effect black strikebreakers crossing picket lines had on white workers, and hoped that some of the anger focused on management would be redirected toward the blacks. That was part of the plan, as was evident when R. T. Rucker, assistant superintendent of the Aluminum Ore plant in St. Louis, spoke frankly of the racial attitudes of East St. Louis whites when he said that "Labor unrest . . . engendered bitterness against the negroes who came in here."

"The natural antipathy of a white man to a colored man . . . inherent in each of us," Rucker said, "was accentuated and exaggerated" by the arrival in East St. Louis of so many blacks.

Also, he said, in cities farther north, "an individual Negro on a streetcar caused no comment," but East St. Louis was more Southern in its attitudes, particularly when blacks on streetcars "voiced their privileges" and "made themselves nuisances." Rucker explained that he was talking, in the main, about black men taking empty seats next to white women, and even saying "good morning" to them.[10]

Most of the blacks hired by the aluminum company in 1916 had lived in East St. Louis for at least a few months, some for years. The aluminum workers union was able to break through racial suspicion on both sides and persuade a few of the new black employees to join the union. Then, according to the union, management changed its tactics. At the end of 1916 and the beginning of 1917, the company began giving preference to blacks who had just arrived from the South and were without jobs. The newly arrived blacks had been lured to East St. Louis with false promises, union leaders charged, were desperate for work, and would be disinclined to join any white-run labor organization, or afraid to.[11]

In early October of 1916, a month before the voters would choose between the incumbent Democrat Woodrow Wilson and Republican Charles Evans

Hughes for president of the United States, Democrats in St. Clair County charged that the Republicans were importing thousands of itinerant blacks into East St. Louis to vote the party line in what was described as "Negro colonization." The Republicans replied that the charges were spurious and purely political, but Democratic poll watchers appeared at all fifty-four polling places in the city and challenged the residency of all blacks trying to register to vote, even those who had lived in East St. Louis for many years. Something similar, it turned out, was going on across the lower Midwest in areas of recent black migration.[12]

The *St. Louis Argus* argued that the widespread challenges to black voters were yet another sign of the enmity toward blacks held by the Democratic Party and President Woodrow Wilson, who had received a significant minority of the black vote in the 1912 election. "Negroes who were seduced into supporting Wilson for President in 1912 are amazed at their own stupidity," the black weekly declared, "and all but those who are Democrats for revenue only have long since repented and returned to the Republican fold and are working hard to undo the harm they did four years ago."[13]

Wilson's numerous black supporters in 1912 had included W. E. B. Du Bois and the NAACP. Du Bois had met with Wilson and had been won over by his promise to be the "president of all the people." But after Wilson took office, he replaced a number of relatively high-ranking black officials left over from his Republican predecessors with white appointees, and he permitted his cabinet members—who included Josephus Daniels, the openly racist North Carolina newspaper editor—to segregate federal departments, creating separate black and white toilets and cafeterias. In many cases, blacks who supervised whites were demoted and replaced with white bosses. Wilson presided over the resegregation of federal Washington, which under his Republican predecessors had been a racially mixed haven for educated blacks.[14]

The *Argus* advised blacks to vote the straight Republican ticket. And justly wary of drawn-out challenges at the polls it also urged its readers, "Take no chances, vote early." W. E. B. Du Bois, disgusted with both Wilson and the Republicans, recommended that African Americans either vote for the Socialist candidate or stay home.[15]

Wilson's particular version of what later came to be called the Southern Strategy depended in part on minimizing the black electorate and arousing white voters in swing states like Illinois with the notion that blacks were trying to steal the election. The president personally stoked the fire by warning against vote frauds "perpetrated by conscienceless agents of the sinister forces." Racial antagonism already burned intensely in the border states and the lower Midwest and sometimes flared into deadly conflagration. For example, three weeks before the November election, in Paducah, Kentucky, little more than the width of the Ohio River from southern Illinois, a white mob of six thousand men and women lynched two black men—an accused rapist and a companion—and burned their bodies.[16]

As the election approached, the *East St. Louis Daily Journal*, which was backing Wilson, blasted its readers with a series of lurid stories about crimes committed by "black colonizers" who were in East St. Louis without jobs, supporting themselves by breaking into railroad cars in the flood plain that once had been Bloody Island. A white watchman for the Mobile and Ohio was shot dead, apparently by a black man looting cars, and police chief Ransom Payne blamed a recent rash of crime on "Negroes [who] come into East St. Louis, are not known, shoot or rob someone, and get out before we know who they are."[17] Ironically, in the midst of this supposed black crime wave, the suburban *Belleville News-Democrat* reported that blacks "must be behaving very well this fall." Population at the county jail in Belleville, black and white, was actually lower than it had been in recent years. The editor speculated that blacks didn't need to rob people because "it's election year and the negroes in East St. Louis are being pretty well taken care of." He added, "Jailers expect the rush to begin after Nov. 7."[18]

In mid-October, a strong rumor swept through East St. Louis that a large group of blacks was planning on voting in Chicago at dawn, catching a train south and stopping at some town along the way to vote again, and arriving in East St. Louis before the polls closed to vote a third time. Another battalion of blacks was allegedly going to make the same journey in reverse. In charge of the scam, according to Democratic state prosecutors in northern Illinois, was East St. Louis's own Dr. Leroy H. Bundy, a prosperous black dentist and entrepreneur who was the leading civil rights advocate in St. Clair County, a leader in the local chapter of the Afro-American Protective League.[19] (Although a branch of the NAACP had been founded in St. Louis in 1914, East St. Louis would not have one until 1924.)

A former member of the St. Clair County Board of Supervisors, Bundy was the proud—even at times prideful—son of a prominent black family in

Cleveland. In his mid-thirties, hard working, and ambitious, he invested money from his dental practice in a small car dealership, a gas station, and an auto repair shop. He was outspoken and sometimes argumentative in his support of full equal rights for blacks. He was the sort of "New Negro" resented by many whites. The *Chicago Defender* described him as a "natural" leader whom "the ordinary fellow looks to for guidance."[20]

Bundy was arrested in Chicago and held for questioning on allegations that he had masterminded at least three hundred illegal registrations in four predominantly black wards of that city's south and west sides. He was soon released for lack of evidence, and the charges eventually died away, but the *East St. Louis Daily Journal* played the report of Bundy's arrest as the turn story at the top of the right-hand column of the front page, the most prominent location in the paper. Below the Bundy report, in a secondary position, was a story headlined, HEAD OF MURDERED BOY FOUND IN DUMP. In the most horrific crime in years, a three-year-old boy had been kidnapped and beheaded by East St. Louis gangsters. The body and head were found in separate locations. The victim was white. So were the kidnappers.[21]

Two weeks before the November election, Wilson's Justice Department announced that it was launching investigations into voting fraud in Illinois, Ohio, and Indiana. The announcement was vague, but there was little doubt in the minds of Republicans that the principal targets were thousands of newly registered black voters in those three swing states. Four days later, the chairman of the Republican National Committee struck back, charging that the Democrats were trying to frighten black voters by false charges of colonization and by challenging the right to vote of thousands of legitimate black voters in cities like East St. Louis. He announced, "A bold attempt to disenfranchise Negro voters in the North as well as in the South is the latest scheme of the Wilson campaign managers." He further noted that the conspiracy, although clearly illegal, was proceeding without interference from Democratic federal prosecutors, who were interested only in Republican crimes.[22]

Woodrow Wilson won a narrow victory on November 7, carrying the South and the West while losing almost all of the Northeast and the North Central states. His victory was greeted in Washington with rebel yells. Wilson took St. Clair County by a few hundred votes, although his defeated Republican opponent, Charles Evans Hughes, carried the state of Illinois. The

Democratic machine kept all its seats on the East Side Levee and Sanitation Board, with its hundreds of thousands of dollars in county, state, and federal flood-control funds sitting in interest-free accounts in politically favored banks. Democratic mayor Fred Mollman was safe—he would not be up for reelection until the spring of 1917. And the powerful local congressman William Rodenberg, closely aligned with the East St. Louis political machine, won reelection. Rodenberg was a Republican, but that really didn't matter. At the end of the day, the politicians from both parties in East St. Louis would get together and carve up the pie once again.

A couple of weeks before the election, to insure the machine candidates got the church vote, Mollman and police chief Payne had closed a few shady establishments. Immediately after the election, those barrel houses, juke joints, and brothels reopened, and a full panoply of whores went back to work in time for the victory celebrations.[23]

After the election, it became clear that Democratic charges of thousands of illegal black voters in southern Illinois—and as many as three hundred thousand nationwide, according to Wilson's attorney general—had been grossly exaggerated. The November 1916 election in East St. Louis seems to have been no more dishonest than usual, perhaps ironically in part because all the lies and false rumors on the front pages of newspapers alerted poll watchers of both parties and both races. After all the furor and all the challenges, the bipartisan Board of Election Commissioners ended up striking only 86 blacks from the registration rolls.[24]

Mayor Mollman himself, a Democrat with significant black support, later made peace within the bipartisan machine by downplaying his party's inflammatory preelection charges that Republicans had "imported" thousands of black voters to southern Illinois. What the Republicans actually did, he said, was work hard to register those blacks who had already established residency. As for the newcomers, most of them came looking for work but "in numbers larger than could be utilized," he said, in what may have been his first public hint that some of the employment practices of the local captains of industry might be problematic in the long term.[25]

Be that as it may, the repeated charges of "Negro colonization" in the weeks leading up to the election strengthened the feeling of many East St. Louis whites that their community was under siege by thousands of blacks who were up to no good.

CHAPTER 6

The May Riot

On the first Sunday of 1917, prodded by a disapproving visit from stiff-necked federal judge Kenesaw Mountain Landis of Chicago, East St. Louis mayor Fred Mollman and police chief Ransom Payne began enforcing the ban on Sunday drinking. What's more, Mollman closed down completely, if not permanently, about fifty of the city's more notorious saloons. More than half of those saloons happened to be places with predominantly black patrons, which could have presented the mayor with a potential problem. Angry black voters and politically powerful black saloon owners might turn against him, and he had an election against a "good government" candidate coming up in three months. But he had tried to fix that.[1]

Prior to the closings, Mollman had a quiet chat with a politically well-connected black lawyer named Noah W. Parden, and Parden passed the message on to his constituents in the alcoholic beverage, numbers, and prostitution trades, men with such names as Hophead Nelson, Red-shirt Frank, Alabama Jack, Seven Hundred Dollar Jimmie, and Long Tom Lewis. If the crucial black vote went to Mollman and he was reelected in April, Parden explained, things would "loosen up" after the election—and maybe even before then, if the saloonkeepers would keep their patrons from overt acts of criminality in the immediate vicinity of certain drinking establishments.[2]

On February 15, the *East St. Louis Daily Journal* aroused its readers with a front-page story headlined, NEGRO BRUTE SEIZES WHITE GIRL OF 19. (The girl was unharmed; the "brute" she said had grabbed her could not be found.) Four days later the three-hour epic movie *The Birth of a Nation*—which had swept through much of the country two years before, triggering small riots,

Klan marches, and sporadic picketing by the NAACP—finally opened for a three-day run at the Majestic theater in downtown East St. Louis. The theater was packed with families. Twice a day, a few blocks from black neighborhoods, the flickering white knights of a Klan-like army rescued Southern damsels on screen from the paws of blacks who, to movie patrons, resembled those men hanging around downtown in ever-increasing numbers, some of them actually sitting next to white women on the streetcar.[3]

Robert Abbott of the *Chicago Defender*, relentless promoter of black migration to the North, outdid himself in 1917 with an extravaganza of ballyhoo called the Great Northern Drive. This mass exodus of the South was set to begin on Thursday, May 15, but the *Defender* began promoting it months ahead of time, and many thousands of readers in the South were so excited about the prospects of life in what Abbott's paper referred to as the "Promised Land" that they couldn't wait. All winter the paper was full of reports of blacks leaving Tampa, Jackson, Huntsville, Birmingham, and dozens of other Southern locales, heading for points north. As the spring of 1917 and the official date of the Great Northern Drive approached, the weekly paper promoted migration even more intently, urging its hundreds of thousands of black readers to "Leave to all quarters of the globe. Get out of the South." Week after week, articles promoted the drive it characterized as the "Flight out of Egypt."

The movement succeeded beyond even Abbott's grandiose expectations. The white South watched in dismay as train after train packed with its former farmhands and mill workers headed North, leaving fields fallow or unharvested, looms still, and band saws silent. "The loss of her best labor is another penalty Georgia is paying for her indifference in suppressing mob law," opined the *Atlanta Constitution*, noting that the heaviest migration came from "those counties in which there have been the worst outbreaks against Negroes." Public officials used legal subterfuges to sidetrack trains for days and even resorted to inducing black preachers to plead with men and women waiting in stations with segregated bathrooms and drinking fountains for trains to Chicago or St. Louis. Things would be better, they promised. Stay.

TURN A DEAF EAR, responded the *Defender*. "You see they are not lifting their laws to help you. Are they? Have they stopped their Jim Crow cars? Can you buy a Pullman sleeper where you wish? Will they give you a square deal in court yet? . . . Turn a deaf ear to the scoundrel, and let him stay. Above all, see to it that that jumping jack preacher is left in the South, for he means you no good here in the North."

A poem arrived anonymously from the South, fifteen stanzas long, and Abbott printed—and reprinted—the whole thing. A sample stanza read:

> *Why should I remain longer south*
> *To be kicked and dogged around?*
> *Crackers to knock me in the mouth*
> *And shoot my brother down.*
> *I would rather the cold to snatch my breath*
> *And die from natural cause*
> *Than to stay down south and be beat to death*
> *Under cracker laws.*[4]

MILLIONS TO LEAVE SOUTH! roared a headline in the *Defender*. GOOD-BYE, DIXIE LAND exulted another.[5]

In early March of 1917, Missouri Malleable Iron Company, a large East St. Louis employer, added to the exodus by placing help-wanted ads in regional newspapers in four towns with large black populations—Vicksburg, Nashville, Memphis, and Cairo, at the lower tip of Illinois. One ad read, "Colored Labor for Foundry Work . . . wages $2 to $2.60 a day. Can earn $3 to $3.50 piecework. Steady work for steady men."[6]

There were no ads for black skilled workers.

By then, many of the illegal saloons and gambling joints and bookmaking parlors that had been closed were open again. Mayor Mollman was trying to maintain a very tricky juggling act, keeping the church vote in one hand while the other was supporting illegal activity, which for many St. Louisans, black and white, was the only economic activity available.

Layoffs at the Aluminum Ore plant continued into the early spring. On March 19, labor leaders would later charge, plant superintendent C. B. Fox and other executives of the aluminum plant met in secret with streetcar company officials and other potential employers to plan a joint campaign to lure another fifteen hundred unskilled Southern black workers to East St. Louis with extravagant promises. Fox denied that such a meeting had taken place. In any event, waves of young black men continued to arrive at the train station with empty pockets and, as the blues singers put it, "a matchbox for their clothes." Some of the untrained black men, the lucky few, got low-paying jobs replacing experienced, better-paid white men at the Aluminum Ore plant. Others ended up on the streets.[7]

In National City, by the spring of 1917, membership in the meat-cutters' union had dwindled from several thousand to several dozen. Management had intimidated most workers into avoiding the union by openly firing strikers and then, week by week, getting rid of anyone who merely spoke up for the union and replacing him with a black man. Workers were angry and frustrated, and they placed much of the blame on blacks. Although earlier labor actions against meat plants had included a significant number of blacks—the leader of the union at a smaller plant in one strike had been an African American meat cutter—by the end of 1916 nonunion strikebreakers, most of them black, had replaced about twenty-five hundred low-level white meatpacking workers. Blacks made up about 40 percent of the meatpacking work force, up from 15 percent a few years earlier. Most of the men who had been replaced in the filthy, backbreaking lower-level jobs at the meat plants were from the recent wave of immigrants to East St. Louis—Austrians, Poles, Russians, Bohemians, Greeks, Turks, and Armenians. The Irish and the Germans who had come earlier, at least those that still had jobs, had moved up the ladder into more skilled positions.[8]

Thousands of cows, hogs, and sheep were slaughtered every day in the swampy bottomlands of the National City stockyards, at 640 acres a third again as large as the Chicago yards. The stink of death and rot and animal waste spread south across St. Clair Avenue into downtown East St. Louis until it permeated the air. About 8 percent of the men in East St. Louis with jobs worked in the stockyards and the slaughterhouses. Men in the slaughterhouses, Upton Sinclair wrote in *The Jungle*, his 1904 exposé of the Chicago stockyards, "worked with furious intensity, literally upon the run," wading through blood as fast as they could move their legs.[9]

Although most of the work to be had in and around the city—in the steel and aluminum mills, in the oil refineries, in the rail yards, and in

the chemical plants—involved hard physical labor in dirty, dangerous sur-
roundings over long hours for low pay, working in the meatpacking plants
was particularly dehumanizing work, in which mass killing quickly became
either unbearable or routine. The slaughterhouses were at their worst in the
summer, when, Sinclair wrote, the killing beds "became a very purgatory":

> All day long the rivers of hot blood poured forth, until, with the
> sun beating down, and the air motionless, the stench was enough
> to knock a man over . . . The men who worked on the killing
> beds would come to reek with foulness, so you could smell one of
> them fifty feet away . . . There was not even a place where a man
> could wash his hands, and the men ate as much raw blood as food
> at dinner-time. When they were at work they could not even wipe
> off their faces . . . [W]hen the sweat began to run down their
> necks and tickle them, or a fly to bother them, it was a torture like
> being burned alive [and] with the hot weather there descended
> upon Packingtown a veritable Egyptian plague of flies . . . [T]he
> houses would be black with them . . . and whenever you opened
> the door they would rush in as if a storm of wind were driving
> them.[10]

As the summer of 1917 approached, many of the men who worked in
the slaughterhouses of National City found themselves increasingly marginalized, increasingly desperate, and increasingly angry.

The United States entered the Great War in early April of 1917. Shortly af-
terward, several hundred uniformed and armed national guardsmen from
Missouri and Illinois were placed at either end of the three main bridges con-
necting St. Louis with southern Illinois: the Merchants' Bridge, the Eads
Bridge, and the Free Bridge. And more National Guard troops were stationed
around large plants on both sides of the river, including the meatpackers of
National City just to the north of East St. Louis and the Aluminum Ore
Company on the southern outskirts of the city. Placing the militiamen
around the plants was explained by federal officials as "part of a plan being
carried out in practically every Western, Eastern, Northern, or Southern

state, to guard against property damage by persons who are sympathizers with the Germans." The troops had been ordered to keep a sharp eye out for enemy sympathizers. What the officials did not mention was that the Aluminum Ore Company and the streetcar company, both of which had gone through nasty strikes recently and were worried about more, had asked the state and federal governments for protection from disruption.[11]

Management fears were understandable. Strikes were on the rise across the United States as the war in Europe simultaneously increased industrial demand and decreased the number of immigrant workers. "The urgent need for production," remarked wartime labor mediator Alexander Bing, "gave the workers a realization of a strength which before they had neither realized nor possessed." In 1916, there were more than thirty-six hundred strikes, three times as many as in 1915. In 1917, the number of strikes rose again to more than forty-two hundred—including major strikes by copper miners in Arizona and New Mexico, carpenters in Baltimore, garment workers in New York, janitors in Chicago, cereal mill workers in Cedar Rapids, Iowa, meatpackers in Denver, Kansas City, and Omaha, oil field workers in Texas and Louisiana, shipyard workers in Norfolk and all along the West Coast, streetcar workers in Seattle and Springfield, Missouri, and lumbermen in the Pacific Northwest, to name a few of the more notable ones.[12]

Blacks continued to be used as strikebreakers across the country, as in the bitter longshoremen's strike in Seattle that began in 1916 and lasted well into the following year. For most blacks, there was little or no stigma attached to crossing a white picket line. The prevalent view among influential black leaders, such as *Chicago Defender* publisher Robert Abbott, was that the late Booker T. Washington had been right in saying said that blacks crossing white picket lines were simply exercising "their right to labor as free men." Even W. E. B. Du Bois—while insisting that "the *Crisis* believes in organized labor"—had said in 1912 that if unions whose policy was to "beat or starve the Negro out of his job" went on strike, there was nothing wrong with blacks crossing their picket lines, because the displaced whites deserved "the starvation which they plan for their darker and poorer fellows." (Ironically, in Seattle, although the waterfront strike had been marked by bloody street fighting between blacks and whites, once the strike was over, the black replacement workers were invited to join the longshoremen's union, and many did. Such poststrike interracial solidarity was rare.)[13]

After the United States entered the war, Missouri Malleable Iron in East St. Louis, like industrial firms across America, anticipated a rapid growth in its armament contracts. The ironworks again advertised for black workers in the South. Once again, over the next few months, the Free Employment office shipped thousands of men, black and white, to other cities. The streets of downtown became crowded with homeless men and women, with panhandlers and muggers. Disease broke out in the close, filthy quarters. Tuberculosis spread rapidly, and health authorities were concerned that a major cholera epidemic was just waiting to break out. The diseases struck poor people without regard to race, but once again blacks were blamed.

Opponents of Mayor Fred Mollman's campaign for reelection began spreading the rumor that Mollman's black supporters all had smallpox. In fact, there was a minor outbreak of smallpox that spring, and some blacks got it, but so did some whites, particularly men who worked in the meatpacking houses in the private fiefdom of National City.[14]

Blacks, in particular, were forced by exorbitant rents in slum properties to crowd together into shacks and tenement flats south and east of downtown, some of them on the dark sandy grit of the remnants of Bloody Island.

George Locke Tarlton

Thomas Canavan

Most of the slum properties, including the brothels and unlicensed saloons—called "blind tigers" by East St. Louisans—were owned or managed by the politically powerful real estate firm of Tarlton and Canavan.

George Locke Tarlton was the thirty-five-year-old political boss of East St. Louis, the power behind Mayor Fred Mollman. His partner was fifty-eight-year-old Thomas Canavan, a politically savvy former alderman, a member of the board of election commissioners, and Mollman's commissioner of public works. Tarlton publicly bragged that he controlled the mayor, a political hack and glad-hander whose family was in the harness business. According to reformer George W. Allison, a Baptist minister, Tarlton "owned" Mollman "boots and baggage."[15]

Tarlton was president of the East Side Levee and Sanitation District, which deposited millions of dollars in public funds in interest-free accounts in favored banks. The banks in return maintained a secret political slush fund Tarlton could use for bribery in political campaigns. A ruthless politician, he rewarded cronies with lucrative jobs and punished those who opposed him, as when he ensured the defeat at the polls of a state's attorney—a fellow Democrat—who had prosecuted a corrupt Republican mayor allied with Tarlton. Tarlton became wealthy in part through crooked dealings, such as buying swamp land for a song, having it drained at public expense through the levee district, and selling it at a large profit. Tarlton and Canavan owned or managed hundreds of slum properties, including tenements and shotgun shacks where poor blacks lived and shady saloons, dance halls, and brothels frequented by both blacks and whites.[16]

Tarlton and Canavan had been instigators in the 1916 Democratic campaign against so-called Negro colonization in St. Clair County. But the city elections in the spring of 1917 were a different matter. After Mollman had promised to add several uniformed black officers to the police department and build a fire station in a black neighborhood, Tarlton was able to work out a deal with Dr. Leroy Bundy and other prominent men in the black St. Clair County Republican League to support Mollman for mayor.[17]

Shortly before the April 3 election, Illinois attorney general Edward Brundage made the first of several visits to investigate charges of widespread sin and corruption in St. Clair County. Mollman offered to support Brundage in any way he could to clean up the city, contending that most of the problems were outside of his jurisdiction, in other towns and in unincorporated areas in St. Clair County.

Brundage knew Mollman was lying. Five private detectives hired by church groups, which were desperate to get the goods on the mayor, had supplied Brundage with extensive reports on illegal saloons, wide-open gambling joints, and dance halls with busy bedrooms upstairs, all within the city limits of East St. Louis, some of them within sight of city hall. The Reverend George W. Allison of the First Baptist Church, who had worked as a fireman on the railroad before going to divinity school, borrowed an army uniform from one of his supporters and spied on brothels, pretending to be a half-drunk and lecherous doughboy with two days' leave before he was off for the trenches. The reports Allison and his private investigators brought back from the shanties of prostitution implicated prominent East St. Louisans, particularly Canavan and Tarlton, and absentee landlords as far away as New York. According to the Reverend Allison, many East St. Louis girls of high school age and even younger were being lured into working as prostitutes after being seduced by smooth-talking pimps in lowlife dance halls. "I know one mother who had three daughters ruined in three places," he said later.

Thwarted in their attempts to get their hands on theoretically public records showing who owned a particularly noisome downtown saloon and gambling joint, Allison's plainclothes private detectives pretended to be potential buyers. They were given documents that proved that one building used for prostitution was owned by a man in New York, but all the rent money went through Tarlton and Canavan. The investigators ended up with a presale invoice listing the assets of the bar and adjoining "rooming house." The assets included the names of two women. Each had a monetary figure next to her name. The women were prostitutes, and the figures represented their weekly earning capacity.[18]

On April 3, forty-seven-year-old Fred Mollman was reelected mayor by the largest majority in East St. Louis history, managing to win a seemingly paradoxical combination—the black vote, the union vote, the gambling vote, and the church vote. He even got most of the female vote. For the first time, women were allowed to vote in Illinois, although it would be four more years before female suffrage had been extended to national elections. On election day, a reporter saw Locke Tarlton drive up to a polling place and climb out of the car with a thick stack of $5 bills in one hand. Blacks who had just finished voting began lining up in front of Tarlton. Each voter gave a small piece of paper to Tarlton, and the real estate mogul glanced at it and then handed over a $5 bill. Tarlton was overheard bragging that there was "no place for pikers in this election."[19]

Mollman announced that he considered his reelection "an endorsement of my policy of law enforcement," and he pledged that saloons would never again be open on Sunday as long as he was mayor. He threw a postelection banquet for his black supporters at a Masonic hall in a predominantly black area in the South End near Thirteenth Street and Bond Avenue. Four or five hundred blacks came by for food and drink and political speeches. Although Mollman was nominally a Democrat, one of the sponsors was the St. Clair County Republican League. The banquet stuck in the craw of many white East St. Louisans, who saw it as Mollman fawning over the very people who were destroying the city.[20]

Shortly after the election, one of Mollman's reluctant reform supporters, William Miller, head of the downtown YMCA, became alarmed at the armed gangsters—they were white—swaggering in and out of the building across the street and roughing up passersby. The building, owned by Tarlton and

Canavan, housed the Commercial Hotel, a notorious saloon, gambling hall, brothel, and den of thieves a couple of blocks from city hall. The saloon had been one of the places Mollman had closed down in the cleanup campaign earlier in the year, but now that he had been reelected it was already open again. Miller warned that there was bound to be trouble coming when there were so many young men with guns downtown, "men who never worked at all but found some way to make a living." He told Mollman, "Conditions have grown rank by degrees and they are rotten clear to the core and you sit here and can't see it, can't understand it. Your moral vision is gone . . . If you live down in this end of town, where the sentiment is rotten to the core, you think it is the sentiment of the whole world, but it certainly is not. The end of this thing is coming soon."[21]

On the evening of April 17, several hundred members of the aluminum workers union met at the Labor Temple, a downtown auditorium that was privately owned but used for meetings by workers' groups. They voted to strike the Aluminum Ore Company over a myriad of unresolved issues, including the mass firings of men friendly to the union. A large and rowdy picket line went up at the plant early the following morning.

Federalized national guardsmen were already camped nearby to help keep the plant open, and management supplemented them with professional strikebreakers from Chicago. They wielded pickaxes and shovels to protect replacement workers, black and white, as they were led through lines of union men screaming "Scab!" The company announced that the strikers were German sympathizers disrupting essential work on war materiel. The *Journal* seemed to agree, remarking on its editorial page, "When strikes are called now, there is good reason to suspect something other than the interests of workers is at the bottom of them."[22]

Other industries were in turmoil, too. The streetcar workers were also going through bitter negotiations, and they were told by management to go ahead and strike if they wanted to. The streetcars would be driven by soldiers, who wouldn't have to be paid by the company at all. And the meatpackers, who could look through the fences around their plants and see soldiers dawdling in front of their tents, simply gave up trying to organize and hoped they could hang on to their jobs. The aluminum workers' strike lasted two months, but for all practical purposes it was over a week or two after it began. Superintendent C. B. Fox refused to meet with the union's executive committee, and announced before the end of April that all strikers who didn't immediately leave the Employees Protective Association would be barred from the plant for life. He took out a full-page ad in the *Journal*, stating that the company had hundreds of openings. Strikers who quit the union and wanted to come back to work could apply for jobs, but there was no guarantee they would be hired.[23]

But hundreds of men continued to picket, sustained as much by anger and bitterness as any real hope of winning the strike, and by the opportunity to vent their anger on the replacement workers who entered the plant every day under armed guard. The aluminum plant had been stockpiling guns, and strikers were sometimes fired upon. In the most serious incident, late on the evening of May 10, a powerful searchlight suddenly blazed from a tower in the plant, blinding the seven hunderd picketers near the gate, and security guards inside the plant compound fired into the dazed crowd. Five men were seriously wounded, including a unformed policeman who had been trying to maintain order.[24]

After a rash of violent crimes that spring, including the killing of two white men by blacks, Mollman announced on May 15 that police patrols were being beefed up downtown and that acting city attorney Thomas L. Fekete had been instructed to prosecute strongly anyone caught violating the ordinance against carrying loaded guns inside the city limits. At the same time, a sign went up in the window of a pawnshop on Collinsville Avenue about half a block from city hall and the police station. It was propped up in the middle of a pile of several dozen cheap used pistols, and it recommended, BUY A GUN FOR PROTECTION.[25]

That spring, Mollman visited New Orleans to speak to the city's Board of Trade and do a little fishing. On April 26, in an interview published the next day in the *New Orleans Times-Picayune*, he said that thousands of blacks from the South had come to East St. Louis recently, and the number had grown so large it was beginning to create a problem for city officials "in regard to housing and segregation." He tied the large number of arrivals to the need for workers by companies with union troubles, including the Aluminum Ore Company. "Conditions are very bad in East St. Louis because many plants are suffering for the want of labor."[26]

The interview managed simultaneously to suggest that far more blacks were arriving in East St. Louis than the city could comfortably handle and that there were plenty of job openings in East St. Louis. The visit to New Orleans would come back to haunt Mollman. Although businessmen tended to recall that the mayor had discouraged blacks from coming, labor leaders remembered the mayor saying there were still plenty of jobs for blacks in East St. Louis.[27]

By mid-May, with the *Chicago Defender's* Great Northern Drive officially under way, more than two thousand blacks were arriving in Chicago every two days, according to a daily newspaper, and trainload after trainload of blacks arrived in other Northern cities as well, including East St. Louis. As the trains crossed into Illinois and other Northern states, the blacks would ceremoniously move from their segregated cars and spread throughout the train and fill it with the rich harmony of joyous spirituals of exodus:

> *Going into Canaan, the promise has come;*
> *Testing time is over, the victory is won.*[28]

Downtown East St. Louis, it seemed to many whites, was simply overrun with blacks, most of them young men. Some of them seemed to lose their Southern inhibitions about how to behave around white people, perhaps under the illusion that they had left racist attitudes behind. Southern Illinois whites, even those whose instincts were not implacably racist, were not used to being treated in a "familiar" manner by blacks. There were reports of black men rubbing suggestively against white women on the streetcars, or sitting so close to them they were "practically in their laps." Finally, at an industrialists' meeting at the Aluminum Ore Company late in April or early in May, one large employer admitted, "Negroes are coming in here in such quantities that it is a menace to the community." It was charged at the meeting that ten thousand blacks had moved to East St. Louis in the past year. (In fact, by the most reliable estimates, no more than five thousand blacks immigrated to East St. Louis between the beginning of 1916 and the late spring of 1917.)[29]

As for the crime rate, police arrest figures and most court records from that period in East St. Louis have long been missing, but there is little question that crime went up. Blacks—who were in the main much poorer than whites and shut out of most jobs—may well have contributed more than their statistical share to the rising crime rate. But criminals and hustlers and flimflam men of all hues were coming to wide-open East St. Louis from all over the country.

A careful reading of the *East St. Louis Daily Journal*—both large and small stories, not just the front-page headlines—for the second half of 1916 and the first half of 1917 shows that whites were committing most of the crimes.[30] The two murders that had led to Mollman's crackdown on "gun toters," as the *Journal* put it, were the only reported killings of whites by blacks in a three-month period ending July 1. And some of the black crime reported so luridly in the *Journal* did not turn out to be black crime at all. For example, on May 25, the *Journal* announced at the top of the front page that a white policeman had been shot. The story was headlined:

"LEFTY" NEVILLE SHOT
BY NEGRO HIGHWAYMAN

According to the *Journal,* James "Lefty" Neville, a veteran uniformed policeman, was shot in the left arm while trying to arrest a black man who had been pulling stickups near Second Street and Missouri Avenue, a couple of blocks from the police station. Whites, according to the story, began muttering about lynching the robber, if they could find him. The Reverend George W. Allison and W. A. Miller of the YMCA looked into the matter and came to the conclusion that Neville had been shot by a white man, probably a pimp, in an argument over kickbacks from prostitution. In any event, Neville was soon promoted to chief of detectives, bad arm and all.[31]

By then the *Journal* had used the term "race riot" in a headline, over a May 24 report of blacks and whites brawling in a neighborhood southeast of downtown that blacks were moving into. Gangs of white and black teenagers were throwing rocks at each other until the police arrived and stopped the fight by shooting a young black man. He was in critical condition.

That same week, the umbrella Central Trades Union of East St. Louis, which represented about fifty separate labor organizations, sent out a news release informing the press of a resolution approved by the organization's directors at their May 23 meeting. The fateful resolution began, "Gentlemen. The immigration of the southern negro into our city for the past eight months has reached the point where drastic action must be taken if we intend to work and live peaceably in this community." It continued in that vein, mentioning "the influx of undesirable negroes" and alleging that ten thousand blacks had arrived in the last year or two. The *Journal* reported on the resolution, noting that the labor organization's directors planned on attending the next regular meeting of the city council, on the evening of Monday, May 28, to discuss the influx of blacks with council members and the mayor. The union also placed an advertisement for the meeting in the *Journal.* Hundreds of East St. Louisans who were not associated with the Central Trades Union decided they wanted to attend that city council meeting and confront the mayor about the masses of blacks moving in.[32]

On the day of the city council meeting, East St. Louis residents were greeted at lunchtime by the first edition of the *Journal* displaying at the top of the front page a story headlined:

POLICE WATCH MANY THREATENING NEGROES

Police had been kept busy over the weekend answering frequent calls to deal with crime in neighborhoods that blacks had recently moved into, the paper reported, and many blacks were found carrying revolvers. A white man from Detroit was shot in the leg and foot when he didn't respond quickly enough to a black holdup man, and "worse trouble," the *Journal* reported, came from whites and blacks fighting at Tenth Street and Piggott Avenue southeast of downtown, where the arrival of police and the firing of a few shots "narrowly averted a riot." Below that story, beneath a small one-column headline, was a brief report that the bodies of two black boys had been found in an East St. Louis canal. It was speculated that they had drowned while fishing.[33]

The evening of May 28 was pleasant and mild. By six thirty, the temperature was in the lower sixties, and East St. Louisans had already begun arriving downtown for the meeting. The most direct route from the main downtown streetcar stop to city hall went right by the Collinsville Avenue pawnshop with the guns in the window. The shop, which had a mostly black clientele, was closed, but the window was lit.

By seven P.M. the council chamber was packed to overflowing and the meeting was moved upstairs to the auditorium, which seated about twelve hundred. Just before the meeting began, a large group of women from the waitress and laundry workers union and the retail clerks union, dressed for a night on the dance floor, arrived with a flourish. They waved and swirled their long skirts as they walked into the crowded auditorium and were cheered loudly. A labor leader explained later that the dramatic entrance was intended to make an impression on the mayor, putting a human face and figure on the dangers posed to pretty white women by the black immigrants from the cotton and cane fields of the Deep South.[34]

Outside, two white men, George Fisher and Arch Dodge, were heading up Main Street toward city hall when they ran into a couple of friends from the police department. One of the policemen warned the two not to go to the meeting. There was going to be trouble, he said, because a lot of men were going to the meeting just to stir up an attack on black people. The policemen did not seem inclined to intervene except to keep their friends away from city hall.[35]

By the time the meeting was called to order, all the seats were filled and dozens of men and women stood in the back or sat in the aisles. Mayor Mollman made a brief speech, warning against "hotheadedness" and announcing that the city council was prepared to stop the northward migration, although he was vague on exactly how that would be accomplished. He said he had recently spoken with his counterparts in large Southern cities, asking them to do what they could to stem the tide.

He stood down and the debate went back and forth, with all speakers agreeing that something must be done to prevent so many blacks from coming to East St. Louis. One repeated allegation was that much of the trouble was caused by a relatively few black holdup men who had influential lawyers and were able to get off scot-free with small fines and bribes paid to the corrupt justices of the peace. There were several reports of whites being held up twice or even three times by the same black man. People complained that black men, because they were willing to work for much less than the going wage, were stealing jobs that once had gone to white men, not just at the aluminum plant and the packing houses but all over town. Men who once were able to support their families "were now at the back door of the poorhouse," one man said.[36]

Earl Jimmerson of the meat-cutters union cautioned against indiscriminate attacks on blacks. Several other labor leaders also warned against violence, and for a time, the voices of moderation seemed to prevail. Then a garrulous, jowly sixty-three-year-old lawyer named Alexander Flannigen rose to speak. He had an office right across the street from city hall, where he dabbled in both law and real estate, and had walked over early so he could get a place up near the front. No one had invited him, labor leaders insisted later, but no one had invited most of the people in the room. Flannigen was a former city treasurer who, while in office, had made full use of his access to public funds. When he left office, the joke went, "The only thing left was a postage stamp. And that was because he didn't know it was there." Flannigen didn't seem embarrassed by such reports; indeed, he regularly referred to city hall as "the steal mill."[37]

Flannigen told a few jokes, and he laughed as he told the crowd that his friends and neighbors had paid pretty good money for their houses, and they certainly didn't want any "colored" moving in next door. But, he said, they couldn't figure out any way to keep blacks from moving into their neighborhoods. He rambled on, remarking that these blacks never seemed to get completely moved in. A lot of their furniture remained in the front yard or maybe eventually made it as far as the porch. His florid face spread in a wide grin. The crowd "began getting itchy," one man recalled.[38]

Then Flannigen said something serious. There are several versions of his exact words, but what he said in effect was that blacks couldn't move their furniture into the house they had just bought if they couldn't get to the front door. And then he said clearly, "As far as I know, there is no law against mob

Collinsville Avenue

violence." Even if there were such a law, he said (as there assuredly was), the police could hardly arrest an entire mob. Much of the crowd rose to its feet in cheers. The mayor began pacing up and down the aisles, trying to calm people down, joined by some of the labor leaders. Slowly, most of the people in the auditorium quieted down and took their seats, waiting for the meeting to continue, but fifty or a hundred men and women stayed standing and kept loudly cheering Flannigen's speech. Then, as if on cue, they turned and pushed their way down the crowded aisles and stormed down the stairs and out the front door toward Collinsville Avenue.

Another crowd of men and women stood outside, waiting for the meeting to end. They had news. A block from city hall, a black holdup man had shot a white man, wounding him superficially, and had been arrested. By the time the report had been passed on to the newcomers and had made the rounds, the story was that the victim was dead. Just then, several policeman walked by with a young black man in handcuffs. The crowd surged toward them. Shouts rose from the mob. "Get a rope!" "Lynch him!" The mayor and several city officials and union leaders had come outside by then, and they tried to calm the mob down as the accused robber was led into the police station and put in a cell.[39]

Earl Jimmerson climbed onto the high steps of the police station next to city hall and shouted, "If there is any men in this crowd that carry union cards, if you think anything of that card, if you think anything of organized labor, for God's sake go home. Don't let the public press come out in big headlines in the morning and say this meeting was called by organized labor and caused a riot."[40]

Half a block away, fifty or sixty men stood across the street from the pawnshop with the guns in the window on Collinsville Avenue, trying to work up the nerve to attack it in full view of the police station. "That's where they're getting those guns," one man shouted. A few policemen and uniformed soldiers stood nearby, and the mob hesitated and lost the moment. But as more and more people left the meeting and came down the stairs to Main Street the angry crowd grew until, in less than an hour, it numbered about three hundred, mostly men. The rumors about blacks running amok had spread and been further amplified, and now it was said that white women had been attacked by blacks, and two white women and a young white girl had been shot.[41]

One common factor in virtually every race and ethnic riot are rumors of horrible acts on the part of the despised race. Often, the rumors involve sexual atrocities. Another common factor is that the rioters generally go through a period of indecision, when the mob seems to be in motion but without focus, as if waiting for an event that will give direction to their actions, a spark to ignite an explosion.[42] That cool May evening in East St. Louis, the white mob stood milling around in front of the police station, anger rising in a gathering storm, when a paddy wagon pulled up and police emerged with another young black man in handcuffs.

Someone shouted, "That nigger shot somebody." The mob roared in fury, and the riot began. A gang of white men broke off from the mob and rushed down Collinsville Avenue, the main north-south thoroughfare in East St. Louis, and attacked black men and women. "Every time you would hear them hit a nigger or knock down a nigger, they would yell like a rabbit hound," recalled Earl Jimmerson. The union leader grabbed people around him and tried to get them to go home before someone was badly hurt. "I talked to one fellow there," he said, "and I said, 'you ought not to be doing that' and he slapped me in the face."[43]

Near the police station, someone yelled, "Let's go get those guns in that nigger pawnshop," and a gang of men rushed across the street, intent on grabbing the pistols. By then, policemen were nowhere to be seen, and the handful of soldiers just stood and watched. But the pawnbroker, Frank Marks, appeared in the doorway with a shotgun held in one hand, the butt pushed back against his shoulder.

Marks had been in a bad accident and had been in a hospital in St. Louis with a cast on his arm when he read in the morning *Republic* about the meeting that night. "There's going to be trouble," he said to a friend. He fretted until he couldn't stand it anymore, checked himself out of the hospital, called a cab, and went to his pawnshop. He could barely stand, but he held his ground and chased the mob away, and he stayed on guard until the riot was over.[44]

Philip Wolf, head of the aluminum workers union, was having a quick beer in a saloon across the street from city hall, hoping the trouble would die down, when he heard shouting and the pounding of feet just outside. He went to the door and saw a gang of men heading toward the South End. Another union man—John Simon, a veteran employee whose firing had helped provoke the aluminum strike—said to Wolf, "I sure hope none of our boys is in that gang." The two men began walking south on Main, deciding they would grab anyone they knew and pull him out of the mob. But the gang broke up into small bunches that swarmed out from the center of downtown in every direction, beating and kicking blacks until they lay bloody in the streets.

Most of the rioters were young men, but a girl of sixteen or seventeen wearing a boy's cap and a long spring coat was leading one gang. She would spot a black coming around a corner, and she would yell, "There's one. Let's go get him." In the mob of whites that followed her were two young men in soldier uniforms—they were, it turned out, on leave before being shipped overseas and were just looking for thrills, beating up blacks. Another group of rioters grabbed a black man and laid him across a trolley track and began chanting for the driver to run the car over him. "Come on, come on, cut off his head. Cut off his feet." The driver did not budge.[45]

Police arrested several blacks for carrying concealed weapons on the outskirts of the riot, but they did little or nothing to stop the rioters, who began setting fire to black homes and businesses. There was one notable exception to the laissez-faire attitude of the police. Two plainclothes detectives, Samuel Coppedge and Frank Wodley, drew their guns and stopped white rioters from burning down a row of houses in a black enclave at Third Street and Missouri Avenue.[46]

After seeing the chaos in the streets, Mayor Mollman ran back inside city hall and called Major Ralph W. Cavanaugh, who was in charge of the national guardsmen at National City and at the Aluminum Ore Company plant. Cavanaugh said there was nothing he could do without authority from above. So Mollman called Illinois National Guard headquarters in Springfield, and was bounced from office to office, trying to find someone who could order two hundred troops a mile away to come rescue the city and its black citizens.[47]

Southeast of downtown, Dr. Lyman Bluitt, a black physician, got a call about nine P.M. to go down to the police station and care for people who had been injured. He was headed north on Tenth Street when he was met by a crowd of black people trotting south. "Don't go that way," they warned. "There's trouble that way." He cut over to Seventh Street, where he was stopped by another group of a dozen blacks. "Don't go that way. They're pulling men off the street and they'll tear you to pieces." So he made a U-turn and drove back to his office and called the police station. He told the desk sergeant what had happened, and said, "maybe I better not come down there." The sergeant allowed as how that might be best. "We'll send the ambulance for you."

Bluitt had barely hung up the phone when it rang again. The sergeant told him not to wait for the ambulance but to go to a small hospital well east of downtown. Bluitt drove there, and treated two black men who had been beaten. Before he was through, another dozen or more injured black men were brought in. He worked through the night and well into the next morning as new patients kept coming in every few minutes until about midnight, when admissions slowed. Two of the men he treated were shot, but most of the patients had head wounds from being beaten and kicked, and broken arms or legs.[48]

The mob downtown apparently wearied of bloodshed by midnight, and perhaps ran out of easily caught victims. "Come on fellows, let's go home," a leader of the riot shouted. "Tomorrow we'll be ready for them. Tomorrow we'll have guns. We'll burn them out. We'll run them out of town." Most of the men left. A few stragglers went to the downtown railroad station looking for more trouble. A trainload of Southern blacks was rumored to be scheduled to arrive any time. The rumor was false. Blacks were leaving town, not coming into it. Hundreds of black men, women, and children were heading through downtown toward the Free Bridge carrying bundles or suitcases. The whites let them pass and cheered them on their way.

By the next morning, tempers had cooled. Mollman called in the entire police force of about seventy men, and announced that groups of men larger than five would be thrown in jail. Saloons, theaters, and schools were closed, and Mollman said anyone who sold guns to blacks in East St. Louis would be arrested. After a report appeared in the afternoon *Post-Dispatch* that pawnshops in the St. Louis black neighborhood known as the Chestnut Valley were doing a brisk business in firearms, Mollman called the mayor of St. Louis and asked that the sale of firearms to blacks be stopped there, too. That was done. East St. Louis detectives were stationed at the Illinois approach to bridges and ordered to search all blacks coming in and confiscate weapons. Police arrested dozens of black men carrying guns. As they were brought into the police station, the handcuffed men were jeered and threatened by crowds of whites milling around in front of the police station.[49]

That morning, Mollman was finally able to reach Governor Frank Lowden, who agreed to call out the Illinois National Guard. Lowden also freed Major Cavanaugh to send his men into the central city, if needed. National guardsmen began arriving that afternoon. By then, the riot had sputtered back to life. Shacks were burning in black neighborhoods, and whites were throwing bricks and paving stones through windows in black neighborhoods and at blacks in the streets. Black and white gangs were taking shots at one another just north of downtown. But, as the number of guardsmen grew to a couple of hundred, armed platoons were sent to trouble spots and ordered to disperse crowds, show no racial favoritism, and be ready to fire their rifles or use their unsheathed bayonets to protect life or property. As midnight approached on May 29, soldiers were rushed by truck out to the Aluminum Ore Company, where they broke up a workers' demonstration, and the riot fizzled out. By the next day, several hundred Illinois national guardsmen under the control of Colonel E. P. Clayton had the situation in hand. Major Cavanaugh and his troops remained camped on the edge of town, guarding against saboteurs.

No one was killed in the May riot. A number of people were arrested, most of them black. The *Journal* railed against a "foreign and lawless negro element" in a front-page editorial that continued:

> The lamentable transpiracies here within the past 24 hours are being attributed to an antagonism of the white against the negroes, culminating in a race riot. This is not the real case. The trouble arose over the large influx here of penal and shiftless negroes from the south who upon arriving here and finding no employment are thrown about the streets in idleness to shift for themselves. Amongst them are many lawless and violent characters who have resorted to assault upon white people . . . There is none of this feeling against the older, law-abiding and long resident portion of our negro population who are in no sense responsible for the criminality of the late negro emigration here and, hence, the trouble is not really a race one.

The black-owned *St. Louis Argus*, on other hand, knew race trouble when it saw it, and knew whom to blame. UNION LEADERS START RACE RIOTS, the *Argus* proclaimed in a front-page banner headline on June 1, and the story traced the trouble back to when the aluminum workers struck and "were displaced by Negroes."

"During these six or eight weeks of the strike," the *Argus* opined, "the Negroes were getting a firmer hold on the industrial situation; and strikers were getting weaker and hungrier each day . . . the Negro labor, honest and conscientious, was fast winning the hearts of the managers of the firm."[50]

The *St. Louis Post-Dispatch* also called the events of May 28 and 29 a "race riot," and its report led off with two blacks being shot and nine others severely beaten in the first hours of the riot. The *Post-Dispatch* noted that "five negroes had been arrested for carrying concealed weapons and one white man was arrested for throwing a brick." The *Post-Dispatch* warned that further trouble could be expected since "the negroes, in anticipation of another attack were preparing to resist [and] it was expected that a large number of additional negroes will arrive on evening trains from the South."[51]

The predicted trainloads of blacks never showed up. It seems likely that blacks in the South read and heard about what had been going on in East St. Louis—word spread fast through the underground telegraph of black railroad porters—and decided to stay home or head somewhere else, thus taking some of the pressure off the city by temporarily lessening the illusion that blacks were arriving in East St. Louis by the trainloads. It would take several more weeks for racial anger in East St. Louis to build up to a second and much more devastating explosion.

CHAPTER 7

Shots in the Dark

T
he topic of Reverend George W. Allison's sermon at the First Baptist Church in East St. Louis for the first Sunday in June was "The Race Problem."

"God has no pets," Allison proclaimed in a plea for racial tolerance. But the tough, crusading preacher also suggested that the races, at least for the time being, should live and work and study and marry and worship apart. He intoned, "The black man never had a chance until he was set out on his own initiative. It was separate schools that produced Booker T. Washington . . . The attempt to equalize the races is a sin against both the black and white man." The sermon, coming from a rare voice of moderation and tolerance in East St. Louis, suggests what small steps even the supposed racial liberals of the time were willing to take to gain racial peace.[1]

Meanwhile, East St. Louis labor leaders had sent a telegram to the Illinois Council of Defense, the state's civil defense overseer, arguing that the racial situation in East St. Louis threatened war industries and should be investigated. Two members of the council's labor committee and a staff counsel came to East St. Louis for hearings on June 7 and 8. They interviewed dozens of witnesses, including city officials, policemen, black leaders, white industrialists, and several unemployed black men who had recently come to East St. Louis because they had been told there were jobs to be had.[2]

In its report, the committee attributed the riot on May 28 to "the excessive and abnormal number of negroes" in East St. Louis. "There was resentment that the colored people, having overcrowded their quarters, were spreading out into sections of the city regarded as exclusively the precincts of the white people. The colored men, large numbers of whom had been induced there and who could find no jobs, in their desperate need were . . . threatening the existing standards of labor."

The committee charged that there had been "an extensive campaign to induce negroes to come to East St. Louis . . . a campaign [that] required considerable financing," including "extensive advertising" in Southern newspapers "setting forth the allurements in East St. Louis in the way of abundant work, short hours, and high wages, good conditions and treatment." Labor agents, the committee reported, "were also shown to have been very active in the South," sending black men North by rail. "At convenient points these agents would leave the car with the remark that they had telegrams to send, or would get lunch. They never came back, and the train pulled out without them. The negroes were thus left to shift for themselves upon their arrival at East St. Louis, to find work as they could and quarters as they might."

Although the committee stopped just short of definitively stating who was behind this anonymous campaign to import blacks to East St. Louis, it observed that "during the previous year there had been industrial troubles in several of the plants of the city," and took note of allegations by witnesses "that employers had brought about the extraordinary influx of colored men to have a surplus of labor and thus defeat the contentions of their employees."[3]

The attacks on blacks in the streets of East St. Louis that had intensified into a small riot on May 28 continued in June. Police stopped one such assault, let the whites go, and arrested three African Americans for carrying concealed weapons. An old black man was beaten almost to the point of death by a gang of young whites after he allegedly refused to give up his seat on a streetcar to a white woman. He staggered to a nearby firehouse, where police had to rescue him from a mob of several hundred whites. Black strikebreakers were beaten outside the aluminum plant so regularly that, toward the end of June, national guardsmen were ordered to escort black workers on the night shift back and forth between work and home.[4]

Strife between labor and management intensified across the city. Both the streetcar workers and the retail workers went out on strike. But street crime was down, at least for a few weeks. With hundreds of troops in town and the police on alert and under orders to brook no nonsense, criminals, black and white, were laying low. On June 15, the *Journal* gave big play to the story of a black robber who had held up a white man, noting that this was the first such occurrence in the two and a half weeks since the May riot. But rumors continued to spread through the white population that blacks were buying guns and were preparing to storm white neighborhoods and slaughter whites to exact revenge for the assaults of May 28.

Some blacks *were* buying guns, despite the mayor's ban on East St. Louis gun and pawnshops from selling weapons to African Americans. Policemen and national guardsmen stationed at the bridges from St. Louis would regularly stop blacks coming into East St. Louis and confiscate any weapons they found. Whites were waved on through, and a few very light-skinned blacks supplemented their income by buying several guns a week in St. Louis and passing for white as they toted them across the Free Bridge. Black funeral homes with hearses traveling between the two cities sometimes stashed a few guns in coffins. Still, despite a public statement by Mayor Mollman that "colored people . . . had made no individual retaliations to defend themselves," the rumors of black aggression against whites persisted. Blacks tried to avoid giving the impression that they were plotting aggressive action. For example, since 1909 the local black chapter of the Odd Fellows lodge had held weekend parades in military formation on Bond Avenue, wearing lodge uniforms and carrying ceremonial swords, but without guns. The rumor spread that Dr. Leroy Bundy, who lived on Bond Avenue, was drilling the Odd Fellows for battle in the streets. After the May 28 riot, the parades ceased.[5]

Still, Thomas G. Hunter, a black surgeon, recalled, "Things grew worse and worse. The colored people were greatly terrified. We sent committees to . . . the governor, to the mayor. Some of us went down to see the mayor, and the mayor's secretary, Mr. [Maurice] Ahearn, stopped us and asked us what we wanted." Hunter told Ahearn that he and assistant county supervisor Dan White, a black man, recently had been stopped at the Free Bridge by soldiers armed with rifles and told to put their hands in the air. While the soldiers were searching them and poking through the tool box in Dr. Hunter's car, an automobile passed by carrying two large trunks. The car, driven by a white man, was waved through the check point.

"Why don't you search that?" Hunter had asked, lowering one hand to gesture at the passing automobile. "It looks more suspicious than I do."

A soldier poked him with a rifle and snarled, "If you don't shut up your beefing, I'll fill you full of lead." Hunter thrust his hands high and kept his mouth shut.[6]

Early in June, a committee headed by Bundy and Dr. Lyman B. Bluitt responded to telephone calls from the Central Trades Labor Union and met with the regional labor organization. The union leaders, including Earl Jimmerson of the meat cutters, wanted to talk about organizing blacks. A biracial committee was appointed to look into the matter, but nothing was done beyond that. Bundy and Bluitt also warned Mayor Mollman, whom they had supported for reelection, that eventually some black man would get mad enough to retaliate against white attackers, and perhaps trigger a riot, unless the police stopped standing by while whites assaulted blacks. The mayor said he was surprised to hear their concern—he thought relations between the races had improved considerably since the end of May. But he told Bundy and Bluitt that their complaints would be thoroughly studied. He called in police chief Ransom Payne, who furiously denied that his officers were practicing any favoritism and insisted the police were doing a fine job of enforcing the law with an even hand.[7]

As spring crept toward summer, tension between the races in East St. Louis tightened even more, like a powerful spring under increasing pressure. At Fifteenth Street and Boismenue Avenue in Denverside, a neighborhood blacks had been moving into in recent years, three white national guardsmen in their summer dress khakis overpowered a city detective, stole his service revolver, and went on a rampage. They already were carrying Army 45s, and with their impressive arsenal they robbed three black men at gunpoint and wrecked a saloon in a black neighborhood after drinking a considerable amount of the whiskey on hand. Outside the saloon, they were subdued by police and national guardsmen before, as the *Journal* put it, "They started a race riot." The three young men were said to be from wealthy Springfield, Illinois, families.[8]

At the beginning of the last week in June, attorney Maurice V. Joyce introduced a resolution to the chamber of commerce urging companies to stop importing blacks to East St. Louis and calling on city officials to "employ every legitimate means to prevent the influx of negroes into East St. Louis, and thereby take every precaution against crime, riot and disorder." The resolution was tabled.[9]

As attacks on blacks increased, a committee of blacks headed by Dr. Leroy

Bundy went to the mayor again asking for help. Once again, the mayor tried to calm them, saying things were not as bad as they thought. On June 28, the aluminum workers' strike whimpered to an end. The number of pickets had dwindled, at times, to a handful. A union spokesman said the strike was being called off for "patriotic" reasons. Very few of the strikers were ever rehired.[10]

Meanwhile, as the *Post-Dispatch*'s relentless Paul Y. Anderson reported, East St. Louis had once again stopped enforcing Sunday closing laws as well as the ordinances against prostitution and gambling. After the Reverend George W. Allison, a source for Anderson's stories, complained to Mayor Mollman about growing lawlessness, the minister was summoned to a meeting with Mollman and political baron Locke Tarlton at city hall. Mollman shut the door to his office and the three men talked for three quarters of an hour. Allison said he felt that he had been betrayed after working hard to get Mollman elected, and, his anger building, mentioned by name a bar owner who was illegally open on Sunday, selling drinks and, it appeared, the services of prostitutes. Allison said he had confronted the man and told him he was going to report his activities to the mayor, and the man had laughed and said the mayor already knew all about it and had no intention of honoring his campaign promise to enforce Sunday closing laws.

Tarlton sighed deeply and said, "Reverend, the trouble about it is, the damn city is just like it has always been." The mayor heaved himself out of his well-cushioned desk chair and said, "Locke, you don't mean that?"

Tarlton replied, "Yes, mayor, it is just like it has always been."

"Why Locke," said the mayor, "didn't I run those penitentiary birds out from the rear of the police station here?"

Tarlton laughed and said, "Yes, mayor, you ran them out of *here*, but they are still in town. Your old friends are all here, mayor, they are all here."

And Mollman, his long, thin face and balding scalp turning red from barely stifled laughter, sat back down and said, "Well, I'll be damned if I don't believe I'll join the Third Artillery and go to France." Tarlton and Mollman shared a long, hearty laugh.

Allison, a tough, righteous Texan who had seen a lot of sin in his life, ended the meeting by telling Tarlton he had five days to close down one particularly notorious "hotel" or Allison and his supporters would shut the place down themselves and nail the door shut so no business of any kind could be conducted there for a year. "If you don't clean this town and get rid of this idle thug crowd you've got here," he said, "you will have a riot here one of these days and that little thing you had in May will not be a patching."[11]

As summer arrived, East St. Louisans stayed in the streets later and later. Even without daylight savings time, darkness didn't fall until about eight o'clock, and by then the temperature had usually gone down to the low eighties. Holdups increased, and so did assaults on blacks. But blacks in East St. Louis had not retaliated for the frequent attacks on them.

On Sunday, July 1, the temperature hit ninety-one degrees at ten in the morning, and hovered around ninety until late afternoon, typical of a summer day in East St. Louis. The air was blanketed with moisture, as usual. The coming together of the Mississippi and the Missouri, the two largest river systems in America, cranks up the humidity that hangs palpably in the miasmic summer air of St. Louis and East St. Louis.

Out-of-work white men had taken to hanging out near the eastern end of the Free Bridge, harassing blacks verbally and sometimes shoving and hitting them. The crowd of whites was larger than usual that Sunday, perhaps

The Free Bridge facing east

in anticipation of the Fourth of July. The whites drank, boasted, and flourished guns—many East St. Louisans of both races routinely fired guns into the air in lieu of fireworks to celebrate the Fourth. Some blacks who were unlucky enough to be caught alone at the East St. Louis end of the Free Bridge were beaten. Reports of the beatings quickly spread to the black neighborhoods a few blocks away, adding strength to a rumor that whites planned on killing everyone—men, women, and children—at a black Fourth of July celebration in a city park in the South End. A similar rumor—blacks were planning to attack white Independence Day festivities—spread among whites.

About seven o'clock Sunday evening, in a South End neighborhood near Tenth and Bond Avenue—the intersection near the approach to the Free Bridge was a focus of black street life—a black man was attacked by roving whites. He pulled a gun and fired, possibly wounding one of his attackers. The story of the shooting, much magnified by rumor, made its way into both the black and the white communities. Shortly after that, a black woman in the same neighborhood ran crying hysterically onto Eleventh Street, where a group of black men stood at a corner waiting for the cool of the evening finally to descend. The woman screamed that she had been attacked by three white men a block to the west. "Let's go to Tenth Street," a black man shouted.[12]

About the same time, black plainclothes policeman John Eubanks reported to duty at police headquarters and saw a white railroad security officer with three men in custody—two white, one black. "I want them booked," the security officer told the police lieutenant in charge. "This negro was running and these two white men were running after him up the railroad tracks." It turned out the two white men had been in the vanguard of a mob of fifty or more chasing the black man through rail yards near the Free Bridge. The lieutenant asked the white prisoners what had happened and they said the black man had insulted them and they had hit him in retaliation and he had taken off running. The lieutenant told the black man to go home and ordered that the two white men be held and booked. Normally, a booked suspect was held at least overnight, but Eubanks checked later and found out the white men were released and back on the street by ten thirty P.M.[13]

A little after nine P.M., a veteran black policeman named W. H. Mills finished a relatively uneventful twelve-hour shift in the northern part of downtown and took a streetcar out to Seventeenth and Bond on his way home. A couple of black men he knew asked him what the trouble was downtown. None that he knew of, said Mills. One of the men said with agitation, "Why, two colored women just came by and said that the white folks down at Tenth Street and the Free Bridge were rocking every nigger they could see." Mills gathered some details and ran across the street to a garage that had recently been opened by Dr. Leroy Bundy, who operated several small businesses in the neighborhood, and used the telephone to call police headquarters. He reported that whites, some of them drunk, were attacking blacks and pulling them from automobiles around Tenth and Bond. Then he walked to his home on Market Avenue and went to bed.[14]

Later that evening, nearby on Bond at Nineteenth Street, the day's last services ended at St. John American Methodist Episcopalian Zion Church. A bishop from St. Louis had given a guest sermon. Dr. Thomas G. Hunter, who lived across the street from the church, saw the bishop outside the church and offered to drive him back to St. Louis. Two other men, a minister named Oscar Wallace and a teamster named Calvin Cotton, came along for protection: Hunter had heard of the attacks near the Free Bridge, and he was concerned for the bishop's safety. While they were across the river, they found out later, a black Model T Ford full of white men had sped through their neighborhood firing into houses. The streets in that part of town were unpaved or in poor condition, and Model T Fords have minimal suspension systems, so the car would have bounded down the street from pothole to pothole, with the men firing wildly, unable to aim. But if the purpose was intimidation, it didn't really matter what they hit—homes, cars, people.

They also found out that some of the men who had lingered in front of the AME church, holding on to the evening, heard the shots about a block away and went home and got their guns.

Hunter, Cotton, and Wallace made the trip back and forth across the river without incident, and returned to the neighborhood after eleven thirty. A couple of blocks southeast of the AME church, Dr. Hunter stopped at Twentieth Street near Market to let Cotton off at his house. As they were standing on the street, chatting about the evening, a black automobile— Hunter could not ascertain the make—sped up from the south on Twentieth Street with its lights out, made a screaming left turn, and headed west on Market. As it accelerated, men leaned out of both sides of the open car and fired into the houses on either side of Market.[15]

At his home at 1914 Market, black lawyer N. W. Parden was awakened by a fusillade of gunshots that sounded "like firecrackers popping." He ran out into the yard in his pajamas in time to see a carload of white men firing with pistols. Then he heard the crack of rifle fire and the boom of shotguns. Although he could barely see anyone in the shadows, it was clear from the flashes of light from either side of the street that blacks along Market Street were returning fire. The white men stopped shooting as the car sped west into the darkness.

Parden's next-door neighbor, policeman W. H. Mills, was exhausted from his long shift and was pulled from a deep sleep by the gunfire from the street. Urged by his wife to get out of bed and see what was going on, he ran to the front door. Parden was standing in the front yard with a pistol in his hand, and a young man named Harry Sanders who lived nearby shouted that a car had gone through full of men shooting guns—"a gang of white fellows," Sanders said.[16]

Mills immediately thought of the brutal beatings of blacks on May 28, and the fires that had been set. He was worried about his wife—she was sick in bed—and he was afraid she wouldn't have the strength to escape if a mob of whites attacked. He wasn't sure what to do, but finally he went back in the house and lay down next to his wife. A bit later, he heard what sounded like a gun battle somewhere in the direction of downtown, but the carload of nightriders did not return to his neighborhood—probably got scared off, he thought, with some satisfaction—and he finally drifted into a fitful sleep.[17]

A block away on Bond, Dr. Hunter and Reverend Wallace, who were next-door neighbors, were too jittery to go to bed so they sat on Hunter's darkened front porch and waited nervously to see if anything else happened. A little after midnight they saw flashes of light from the west, toward downtown, and heard a long, sustained volley of shots. For a moment, it sounded as if a war had started. Then the firing stopped, and left an ominous hole in the night. They went into their houses and locked the doors.[18]

Shortly before midnight, police began receiving reports that armed black men were assembling in the South End. Night police chief Con Hickey was on the phone talking to one of the callers when another line rang and cub reporter Roy Albertson of the *St. Louis Republic* picked up the receiver. A grocer named James Reidy, who lived on Eighteenth Street south of Bond Avenue, said more than a hundred armed blacks had gathered in his neighborhood, summoned by a church bell. "It's ringing now," the grocer said. "If you listen, you can hear it."[19]

Albertson, who was only eighteen years old, couldn't hear any bell. But he sensed a story, particularly after the grocer—thinking he was talking to a policeman—added, "If you get some men down here right away you can disperse them before there is trouble." Albertson passed the report on to Con Hickey. Earlier phone calls reporting blacks being beaten and shot at and pulled out of their cars by whites had elicited little or no official reaction, but this time it sounded like the long-rumored armed black rebellion had finally begun. Hickey told two plainclothes detectives, Samuel Coppedge and Frank Wodley, to "get out there and see what's going on."[20]

Coppedge, who was playing gin rummy with Robert Boylan, a *Globe-Democrat* reporter, laid down his cards and he and Wodley headed to their assigned car, an unmarked, black Model T Ford. The Ford was just like at least one other car that had recently driven through black neighborhoods in the South End carrying white gunmen firing into homes. Wodley and Coppedge were hoping to get their business over with by one thirty A.M., when their shift ended and they could go home. Albertson asked Coppedge if he could ride along. The detective nodded.

The two detectives, in summer suits and straw hats, sat in the front with the driver, police chauffeur William Hutter. The forty-nine-year-old Coppedge, a sergeant, was next to the door. His twenty-nine-year-old partner, Wodley, sat in the middle. Two uniformed policemen, Oscar Hobbs and Patrick Cullinane, sat in back. The top was up. The car was crowded with bulky men, and Roy Albertson stood on the running board on the driver's side, holding on to the door. The farther they got from the heart of downtown, the fewer streetlights broke the darkness. The temperature had dipped into the upper seventies, although the high humidity persevered, as usual.[21]

The police car headed east to Tenth and then turned south through a predominantly black area close to white neighborhoods. As the police car reached Tenth and Bond, the driver slammed on the brakes to avoid plowing into a mob of black men who were dimly lit by the weak headlights of the Ford. The mob parted as the car came to a halt, and most of the men ended up on the sidewalk near the passenger side of the car, where Coppedge sat. There was no streetlight within fifty feet of that spot.[22]

Albertson later recalled that, in the dim light, he could see that the black men were heavily armed with revolvers and automatic pistols, rifles and shotguns. Some held large sticks or clubs. There were 125 to 150 of them, Albertson said, mostly young men, some in their teens. The men, it turned out, were headed toward the Free Bridge, where several white men working at a service station had beaten a black man with no apparent provocation. But Albertson and the police did not know that.

Albertson, Cullinane, Hutter, and Hobbs all later testified that Coppedge identified himself as a policeman and exchanged words with the men. In Albertson's version of the confrontation, Coppedge yelled out the window, "What's doing here, boys?" and someone shouted in reply, "None of your damn business." Coppedge said, "Well, we're down here to protect you fellows as well as the whites. We are police officers." Someone shouted at Coppedge, "We don't need any of your damn protection," and the crowd began guffawing.[23]

Coppedge, according to Albertson, turned to the driver and said quietly, "Let's get the hell out of here." The driver put the Ford in gear but he hadn't traveled more than a few feet when there was a loud, explosive pop. Albertson was not sure if one of the tires had blown—tires were always blowing on Model T Fords—or if someone in the crowd had fired a shot. In any event, Albertson said, the explosion triggered a volley from the black men. The front tires blew flat, then the rear ones, and the bullets kept coming, punching into the metal with loud clangs and pops, shattering the windshield and plowing into the flesh of three of the men in the car. "It looked like they turned loose and tried to empty their guns as fast as they could," said Albertson, who threw himself down on the wide running board on the driver's side away from the gunfire as soon as he heard the first bullet. One or more of the policemen may have fired back, but without apparent effect.

The startled driver jammed his foot down on the gas pedal and drove hard into the middle of the crowd, banging men aside as he pushed east down a long dark block of Bond Avenue, running on his rims, with sparks striking from the pavement and metal howling. By the time he had driven to Eleventh Street and the next streetlight, the shooting had stopped. The driver slowed briefly, looked to his right, and said, "Sam is shot." Coppedge had taken a bullet to his jugular vein and died almost immediately in a spurt of dark blood.[24]

Coppedge's partner, Wodley, had been shot in the abdomen, probably more than once, and he was moaning with pain, critically wounded. He died two days later. Hobbs, on the right side in back, had been hit in the right arm. The other uniformed policeman, like Albertson and the driver, remained unhurt. The driver headed for Deaconess Hospital, only four blocks away at Fifteenth and Bond. Just before he got there, he passed a fire station, and Albertson told him to slow down. The reporter hopped off the running board and ran in to call police headquarters.[25]

Albertson's call came into the police station at about twelve twenty-five A.M. He reported to Con Hickey that Coppedge was almost certainly dead, and Wodley was gut-shot and dying. And he said a mob of black men, "armed with everything in the way of portable firearms," was heading for downtown. The general feeling around the police station, Boylan recalled, was that the mob had already killed a couple of policemen, and they were heading for the station to kill some more. Instead of rushing out to confront the mob, the handful of police on duty at that hour on a Monday morning stayed at the station to protect it and the adjoining city hall. Hickey called Mayor Fred Mollman, who was already awake. A machinist named Fred Peleate had called him about twelve thirty to report that a policeman had been shot on Bond Avenue near his house. The mayor got dressed and headed downtown.[26]

Meanwhile, on Missouri Avenue about a block from the police station, at the YMCA, director W. A. Miller was awakened by the sound of a car skidding to a stop in front of the Commercial Hotel across the street. The hotel, saloon, brothel, and boardinghouse for hoodlums was managed for New York absentee landlords by political moguls Thomas Canavan and Locke Tarlton, and its denizens enjoyed a considerable amount of official protection.

Miller got up and went to the window in time to see four white men get out of the car. Two of them stood on the street, pacing back and forth, apparently looking for someone. One of them was walking strangely, as if he had a hurt leg. The other two ran quickly into the hotel. In a moment, another car drove up, with bullet holes in the radiator and the rear. The driver and passengers, Miller recalled later, "looked like a bunch of outlaws. I gathered [from their conversation] that they had been driving through that section of town where the policeman had been shot, and they were fired on by Negroes."[27]

Mayor Mollman arrived at the police station between one and one thirty A.M. Boylan was standing out front, between the police station and the downtown fire station, nervously scanning Main Street for the black mob he had heard was coming. Mollman got out of his car and walked up. He said, "Looks awful bad, don't it?"

"Yes, it does," said Boylan.

"Do you think we're going to have trouble?"

"Yes, but you better talk to Roy. Albertson was in the machine and got first-hand information and he can tell you better than I can, but it looks bad to me."[28]

By then, Albertson had arrived back at the police station, and he joined Mollman and Boylan on the sidewalk. He gave the mayor a quick summary of what he had seen and said, "As soon as these morning papers get on the streets in East St. Louis you're going to have trouble. As quick as people find Coppedge has been killed and Wodley is dying . . . there's going to be trouble around here. You had better get the troops. You had 600 or 700 soldiers down here on May 28 for that riot. It will take double that number to even try to handle what is going to turn loose today."

Albertson may have been trying to goad the mayor into saying something interesting, something quotable. The reporter had a two A.M. deadline to get his stories into the *St. Louis Republic*, a morning paper that was due to hit the streets by five A.M. But Mollman did not say a word. Albertson ran inside the police station and called the *Republic*, dictating his first-person account to a rewrite man. It would, of course, be the main front-page turn story that morning.[29]

Boylan had a similar deadline for the *St. Louis Globe-Democrat*, and his main morning competitor knew a lot more about what had just happened than Boylan did, so he tried another tack. "All right, Mr. Mayor," he said, "come on over to my office where you can be quiet and we'll work the telephones." That way he could listen to the mayor's calls.

"Well," Mollman replied, after a moment of thought, "I might as well go to my own office." Boylan nodded. The mayor left to make some calls. Mollman tried several numbers in Springfield and got no answer before he reached Dick Shinn, an assistant to the adjutant general of the Illinois National Guard. Shinn had been in East St. Louis during the May riot, and he had kept in touch with the situation, although he had been assured by Mayor Mollman that things had settled down. Shinn began calling National Guard officers in towns all over southern Illinois, telling them to assemble troops and head for East St. Louis. By then, off-duty policemen had been called in, and there were about a dozen uniformed patrolmen and several plainclothes detectives—all white—waiting inside the station for police chief Ransom Payne to tell them what to do. More were on the way.

A call came in that a mob of whites had assembled in front of a chili parlor a block or so away, on Collinsville Avenue. Some of the men had been drinking, working up the nerve to storm a nearby building and wreck the dental office of Dr. Leroy Bundy. There was a light on in the window of what they thought was his office, and finally the mob surged across the street, led by a couple of army enlistees who were waiting to be sent to basic training. One of them had a rifle, and he led the crowd up to the second floor and smashed the butt through the opaque glass door to Bundy's office. There was no one there, but an electric fan was running and a light was on, so they decided the dentist must be nearby and began searching the building. They found no one. A few policemen walked over and broke up the crowd, but some of the men were reluctant to go home. So a small gang milled around in front of the police station for hours, waiting for something to happen.[30]

At about two in the morning, a neighbor with a telephone knocked on the door of John Eubanks, a black policeman who lived on St. Louis Avenue just north of downtown East St. Louis. She told Eubanks that a policeman had called and asked that he come to the station at once. The woman was unclear about what the trouble was. Eubanks quickly dressed and headed on foot for the police station, just a few minutes away. When he got there and saw a surly crowd of whites milling around in front of the station, he pulled out his badge and pushed his way through, ignoring the curses and threats and racial epithets.

There were about seventy policemen on the East St. Louis force, six of them black. The blacks all worked in plainclothes, perhaps on the theory that a black man in a uniform would offend or outrage the white majority. Inside the station, Eubanks noticed that most of the white policemen were there, but none of the other blacks. A lieutenant told him, with great agitation, "John, Coppedge was killed a short time ago, Sergeant Coppedge. Down in the South End, at Eleventh and Bond." Eubanks was shocked and saddened. Coppedge was married with a couple of children, one of them now a young soldier training in Florida to fight in the Great War.

"How did it happen?" asked Eubanks.

"He was killed by an armed crowd of Negroes," was the reply.

"Well, we better get on down in there, hadn't we?" said Eubanks.

"No, no," said the lieutenant. "Wait until your boss comes in. I have sent a machine [an automobile] out for the chief of detectives, and he will be here in a few minutes." Chief of police Ransom Payne was there, too, but he said nothing to Eubanks.

Chief of detectives Anthony Stocker arrived a few minutes later. Eubanks went up to him but was waved away, and Stocker and Payne went into the chief's office. The two men spoke heatedly about something, and Eubanks sensed through the office window that he was among the topics of conversation. At one point, the mayor walked in and joined the discussion. Finally, the chief came out of his office.

"What are we going to do?" Eubanks asked impatiently.

Chief Payne spoke very carefully, watching for Eubanks's reaction. "Owing to the circumstances," he said, "it is not safe to attempt to go down in there now with the little handful of men we have. It seems there is a very large body of Negroes armed in there, and it isn't safe for us to go in." And that, it seemed, was that. Eubanks was dismayed, but he stopped himself from asking why they had called him in the first place. He walked back home to try and catch a few hours of sleep. He figured he would be busy later that day.[31]

At about three in the morning, in Springfield, Illinois, Dick Shinn of the Illinois adjutant general's office phoned National Guard colonel Stephen Orville Tripp. He asked Tripp to come over to his office immediately. Tripp put on a summer suit rather than his colonel's uniform and hurried to the adjutant general's office. Tripp was the assistant quartermaster general for the Illinois National Guard, a slight man of late middle age who had been a deputy United States marshal, a policeman, and a deputy sheriff—as well as a lumberyard foreman. One man in the state capital who had seen him in action said sarcastically, "Tripp is an excellent man as an office clerk."[32]

Shinn told him that a policeman was dead in East St. Louis and the situation had the makings of a riot. Several National Guard units had been contacted and would be arriving in the city in a few hours. Tripp would be in command of them. Less than two hours later—still in his business suit and carrying only a briefcase—Tripp was on the train to East St. Louis with orders to meet with the mayor and cooperate with him "in the matter of enforcing the law."[33]

About four thirty A.M., Earl Jimmerson, the East St. Louis labor leader who was also a member of the county board of supervisors, was awakened by a phone call. It was a white woman he knew in the South End, and she told Jimmerson that Coppedge was dead. Coppedge had been a friend, and Jimmerson was stunned. He went downstairs and opened the front door and was a little surprised to see that the *St. Louis Republic* had already been delivered.[34] It was as if it had been rushed into print, and he would later realize that the paper's error-ridden stories reflected that haste. He picked up the paper, went back inside, and turned on a lamp. The story was spread across the front page:

POLICEMAN KILLED, 5 SHOT IN E. ST. LOUIS RIOT

NEGROES, CALLED OUT BY RINGING OF CHURCH BELL, FIRE WHEN
POLICE APPEAR

OUTBREAK FOLLOWS BEATING OF WATCHMAN BY BLACK
SATURDAY NIGHT

Roy Albertson's first-person account of the fatal shooting of Coppedge reported that the "pre-arranged signal" for the armed blacks to gather was the ringing of a church bell at an African American Methodist Church at Sixteenth and Boismenue Avenue, deep in the South End and six blocks south of Bond Avenue. There was no mention of a carload of whites, much less two carloads, speeding through black neighborhoods firing out the windows. The story said, "What caused this latest break on the part of the blacks cannot be told now. There was no trouble of a serious nature in the black belt today. The only trouble came early Saturday night, when a railroad watchman was man-handled by a negro, who escaped."

At the top of the story, in bold type, was a list of five men wounded the night before. Among the wounded, identified as a patrolman, was a man named Gus Masserang. The story said Masserang was shot in the leg, which was true—he was hit many times in the legs, the back, and the neck with shotgun pellets—although the wounds were superficial. However, he was not a policeman but a petty crook who was known to hang out at the Commercial Hotel in downtown East St. Louis.

There were numerous other mistakes in the story, many of them tending to cast a favorable light on the police, who were credited with a whirlwind of activity in the South End when in reality they had stayed close to the station after the shootings of Coppedge and Wodley.[35]

Although Albertson's story reported that Coppedge had identified himself and his companions as police officers, the *St. Louis Argus*—after interviews with African Americans in the South End following the riot— contended that there had been no exchange of words at all before the shooting. The black weekly reported that the policemen in the unmarked police car were "mistaken for rioters" making another attack on the neighborhood, and "the Negroes immediately fired upon" the black Ford, "thinking this was another machine with lawless occupants whose purpose was to repeat the act of the preceding one."[36]

On the morning of July 2, a black Model T Ford shot full of holes sat next to the Commercial Hotel. Very few East St. Louisans took notice of that particular machine. Most of the interest focused on another black Model T Ford riddled with bullet holes, all four of its tires flat and shredded, that was parked a block or so away, across the street from the police station.

CHAPTER 8

The July Riot Begins

Whand Paul Y. Anderson of the *St. Louis Post-Dispatch* arrived in downtown East St. Louis at eight A.M. July 2, seventy-five or a hundred white men were standing on the street and sidewalks in front of city hall and the police station, loudly cursing blacks and vowing revenge for the attack on the police. Their attention was focused on the black Model T Ford with flat tires and smashed headlights that sat across Main Street from the station. Anderson pushed through the mob to get a closer look. Blood was splashed across the front seat and bullets had punched holes all along the body of the car.[1]

Anderson, who was twenty-four, had been assigned to the East St. Louis beat about three years before. He moved to the small city to get to know it better, and the corruption he discovered astounded and infuriated him. A superb and tenacious reporter, the feisty son of a tough Tennessee marble quarryman, Anderson was not afraid to write about what he knew, nor, like some of his older colleagues, had he surrendered to the fatalistic view that nothing he wrote would make a bit of difference. Banned from the city hall–police station complex on Main Street because of his muckraking stories, Anderson now worked out of the *Post-Dispatch* offices in a building nearby. But he was not afraid to walk into city hall or the police station and pin down a public servant until someone made him leave. He was stubborn and bold, but not a fool. In the spring of 1917, after persistent threats on his life, he moved back to St. Louis. He continued to cover East St. Louis.

Anderson was emotionally erratic, tough but brittle, given to bitter moods but refusing to sink into the cynicism so many of his colleagues used as protection against the harsh imperfections of the world of city politics. He found another escape. Anderson was already drinking heavily, which was hardly unusual in the newspaper business for most of the twentieth century, but he went about it with a relentless lack of joy. He was relentless in his reporting, too, and in a few years he would win the Pulitzer Prize for exposing the Teapot Dome scandal and would be one of the best-known correspondents in Washington.[2]

That July morning, Anderson stood with a couple of other reporters and watched the crowd of white men gathered around the bullet-shattered, blood-stained Ford grow larger and more belligerent. Some of the men had heard about the shootings when leaving saloons early in the morning, and had not been to bed. Some were still drinking, clutching brown paper bags or openly sharing bare brown bottles.

A well-dressed man named John Seymour, one of a group of lawyers who hung around the city buildings looking for clients, approached the mob and said he would be happy to defend anyone who would "avenge the murders of the two policemen." The crowd cheered. Policemen standing nearby bantered with the angry white men, and it became apparent to bystanders that they were making it clear, intentionally or not, that they would do nothing that day to stop white men from killing blacks.

Another reporter, A. B. Hendry of the small *St. Louis Star*, arrived at the police station about that time. He had just finished driving through black neighborhoods and described the mood as "a general gala day among the blacks." Hendry regaled his colleagues and police with fanciful stories of blacks playing banjoes and singing, celebrating the uprising. The white mob hanging around the car on Main Street heard the stories and grew even angrier. Reporters hurried to the phones and called their offices, warning that trouble was coming and asking for legmen to help cover it.[3]

Police told reporters that they suspected that Dr. Leroy Bundy had, in the words of the *St. Louis Republic*, "inflamed the negroes and formed the mob which killed policeman Coppedge." Police were searching for Bundy, who could not be found. The *East St. Louis Daily Journal* speculated that he had "left the city."[4]

Colonel Stephen Orville Tripp, who was supposed to be in command of the National Guard troops expected momentarily, finally made it to the East St.

Louis city hall about eight A.M. His train had arrived at the downtown depot about seven A.M., but he apparently had not heard the conductor announce the stop and had stayed on the train as it crossed the wide river and rolled into downtown St. Louis. When he discovered his mistake, he caught a local streetcar back into Illinois. Tripp was fifty-six years old, a quartermaster—essentially a military storekeeper—with little experience in commanding troops and not much of a knack for it. Tripp had enlisted in the Illinois National Guard at the age of eighteen, and had become a cavalry officer in the army in the Indian wars of the late nineteenth century, but most of his military career had been in the quartermaster corps of the National Guard, in charge of supplies. At the time of the riot, he was assistant quartermaster general of the Illinois Guard.[5]

Robert Boylan of the *Globe-Democrat*, a former soldier, met the colonel shortly after he had finally found his way to East St. Louis, and sized him up immediately. "Colonel Tripp was not in uniform. He wore an ordinary business suit and was one of the most lady-like officers I ever saw. He was a perfect gentleman, so far as he talked with me, but soldiers need to be told, they need to be pointed out. I saw him daily when he was here, several times a day, and I never saw him with any insignia of his rank. He wore a dark gray business suit." Other witnesses said the gray summer-weight suit was seersucker, decidedly informal battle gear for a commanding officer soon to be in harm's way. They reported that Tripp tried to give orders to troops and push his way into the middle of enraged mobs with a banded straw boater perched on the top of his head.[6]

Tripp found the mayor and the police chief in city hall and identified himself, telling Mayor Mollman he was in town "for the purpose of cooperating with him in the matter of enforcing law." The mayor replied that he was not feeling well, and probably would not be much help. Mollman was uncommonly pale, his blue eyes were watery, and he seemed surprisingly inattentive, as if his mind was elsewhere. Mollman added that he had been "advised not to go out in the open." Because Mollman had courted black leaders and had taken the bulk of the black vote in his two successful campaigns for mayor, he and some of his advisers were afraid he would be attacked by vengeful whites—like the mob growing on the street outside, staring in fury at the bloody wreck of an automobile at the curb and cursing blacks. For most of the day, the mayor stayed indoors.[7]

Mollman said he would designate Thomas L. Fekete, the young acting city attorney, as his representative. And before retiring into his office, the mayor told Tripp that troops should be positioned on several key streets—Market, Walnut, and out front on Main. Fekete seemed full of pep, ready to do whatever was needed.[8] About that time, another high-ranking military officer arrived at the city hall command post. Lieutenant Colonel E. P. Clayton of the Illinois National Guard's Fourth Infantry had been visiting St. Louis and had read about the riot in that morning's papers. He, too, was in civilian clothes, but immediately called for his uniform to be sent from Springfield. Clayton had much more experience at commanding troops, and he had been in charge of closing down the May 28 riot. But Tripp outranked him.

There is a great deal of confusion about who was actually in charge of the troops in East St. Louis on July 2. Tripp recalled later that he had told Clayton, "Assume command of the military organizations upon their arrival and co-operate with the mayor in all matters for the enforcement of law." But Clayton said Tripp personally took command of the troops and made decisions on the movement of men without consulting or even informing Clayton. Other observers insisted that the chain of command was never clear, and Clayton himself was overheard at the height of the riot to complain that he could do nothing because his authority had been "superseded" by Tripp.[9]

Young attorney Thomas Fekete, the mayor's designated representative, seems to have been in a similar position to Clayton. He was given lots of responsibility (and the potential for lots of blame) but very little actual power. Essentially, no one was in charge in East St. Louis but the rioters.

Illinois national guardsmen began arriving shortly before nine A.M., beginning with Company G, at about half-strength with three officers and twenty-seven men.[10] "They came as they could," Roy Albertson recalled. "They didn't come fully equipped as soldiers. Some were in overalls, some merely brought their rifles . . . They weren't organized in any way, they were just raw recruits, farmer's boys. And what they saw that day just overwhelmed them—amazed them."[11]

Crates of ammunition arrived all day by train, and they were unloaded and stacked to the ceiling in vacant offices in city hall and the police station.

By evening, there were dozens of crates of bullets in the city hall complex, and dozens more at the army camp northeast of downtown, at Tenth Street and St. Louis Avenue. Most of the soldiers had loaded rifles or at least cartridge belts with bullets in them, and most soldiers had bayonets affixed to their rifles, even if they didn't have full military uniforms. "They could have quelled the riot with bayonets alone if they had wanted to," an observer remarked.[12]

Calvin Cotton, a black teamster who attended the AME church at Nineteenth and Bond and had seen the white men in the Ford shoot up his neighborhood the night before, was downtown about nine in the morning chatting about the incident with a friend, when a large, muscular white man walked over and stood practically on Cotton's toes, listening to what the black men were saying. Cotton and his friend stopped talking and stepped back. A policeman came around the corner, and the big white man said to him, "You better get these niggers off the street, because we're going to kill every one of them in a minute." Cotton recognized the white man, but couldn't recall his name. Later, he identified him as Richard Brockway, a security guard for the streetcar company.

Brockway, a strong, bulky man in his mid-forties, was well known as a tough guy and a brawler. The policeman listened to Brockway rail for a minute or two, threatening to kill blacks if they didn't get off the street immediately, and then he just turned and walked away.

Cotton quickly crossed the street to a real estate office. About ten minutes later, he heard shooting. He went to the window of the real estate office and saw a black man lying on the sidewalk near where Brockway had been standing. He wasn't moving. Brockway had disappeared. Cotton walked quickly out the side door, which opened onto Main Street, and caught a streetcar across the river to St. Louis.[13]

Brockway had gone to a meeting at the Labor Temple. He and several hundred other angry whites met for about an hour. Fairly quickly, control of the meeting was taken by Brockway. The security guard and a few like-minded men stirred up the crowd with inflammatory speeches, calling for whites to form a "home protective league" to defend themselves and, if necessary, to strike out at blacks. He recommended that everyone go home immediately after the meeting, get a gun, and come back downtown, ready for battle.[14]

Black plainclothes policeman W. H. Mills read about the shooting of Coppedge and Wodley in the morning papers and went to police headquarters. Mills and his partner, W. Green, were at the station when a report came in by telephone. "They were killing a Negro up on Illinois and Collinsville Avenue," Mills recalled. Mills and Green were sent out to the South End to "instruct all the Negroes to stay off the streets" and then go home and look after their families. The other four black policemen were told the same thing. By late morning, there were no black policemen—and very few white ones—on the streets of East St. Louis.[15]

Earl Jimmerson, the labor leader and county supervisor, also came downtown that morning and was horrified to see the shattered and blood-spattered police car across from city hall. He found the mayor and the police chief inside the city hall complex and said, "If I was you fellows, I would move that Ford away from in front of the police station. Take it some place where people can't see it." Eventually, the city officials took his advice, but by then thousands of East St. Louisans had seen the car and absorbed its enraging message.[16]

Walking across the street to a cigar store in the Illmo Hotel, Jimmerson encountered a porter he knew—"a very nice little colored fellow, got a family," he later recalled.

"Herb," Jimmerson said, "if I was you I would take my family and go across the river. It looks like trouble here."

The young man replied, "Mr. Jimmerson, I haven't got any money to go across the river and no place to take them when I get over there."

"Well, go over and get under a bridge if you have to," Jimmerson said.

A crowd of white men walked by, talking angrily and cursing blacks. The porter drew back into the shadows and watched them for a moment and then, when they had passed, he slipped away.

The Reverend George W. Allison was in a lawyer's office on the fifth floor of the Metropolitan Building on Missouri Avenue when he heard shots. He hurried to the window. Two or three black men in overalls had been working on the streetcar tracks, but they dropped their tools and began to walk quickly away. A mob of white men was rushing toward them. A black man was grabbed and attacked, but he broke free and ran. Allison rushed to the mayor's office a few blocks away. He told Mollman trouble was coming, suggested he deputize Allison and eight or ten other good men, and they would go grab the whites who were making trouble and shut them up in city hall. "Tell them, 'The first man that comes down these stairs will get killed in his tracks,' and you will break this thing up."

But the mayor said he would rather wait for the National Guard to deal with the problems.[17]

By ten o'clock, several dozen national guardsmen had been scattered around downtown. Reporter G. E. Popkess of the *East St. Louis Daily Journal* talked to a few on Main Street near city hall and they all said the same thing, "We have no orders." As he was talking to the group, one of the militiamen broke away and strolled over to a white man standing nearby, on the edge of a loud mob clearly waiting for something to happen. In a conversational tone, the militiaman asked, "Got your nigger yet?"

The white man grinned and replied, "I'll get mine by sundown today, I guarantee you that."[18]

At the Labor Temple, someone—it may have been Richard Brockway— got the crowd growling with angry assent by saying he had lived in the South, where they knew how to deal with uppity blacks. The meeting broke up when Brockway shouted, "We're going to get some niggers today," and strode out of the building to loud cheers. Most of the men went home, some to hunker down and try to stay out of trouble, others to get their guns, but a couple of dozen followed Brockway down the steps and into the street. As the small mob moved south, a black man got in the way and stumbled to the ground. Brockway pulled out a pistol and shot him, pumping the trigger five times as if to be sure the man was dead.[19]

Another black man got in the way, and several white men grabbed him, but someone from the crowd yelled, "Let him go. He's just an old barber-shop nigger." The white men left the old black man lying half-conscious on the sidewalk.

By then, the streetcars that ran every few minutes down Broadway and across the Eads Bridge for St. Louis were packed with blacks, and blacks who were unable to jam themselves onto the cars began walking south and west through the perilous downtown, toward the Free Bridge. Several dozen men in the white mob near city hall joined the gang from the Labor Temple, and they

Blacks fleeing East St. Louis

all began marching raggedly down the middle of Collinsville Avenue south toward Broadway and the main east-west streetcar line. When they reached the
streetcar stop, they smashed their way in the doors of the cars, pushing in
against the weight of the mass of black bodies until the doors crumpled and
they could drag people out. One black man was shot almost immediately. Others were beaten unconscious, or kicked and smashed with huge paving stones
until their heads were bloody and pulped. Whites stood and watched and
cheered as each black man or woman was pulled from a car and hurled to the
ground.[20]

The white onlookers, said one observer, "were in good humor," as if they
were "waiting for a circus parade." Fewer than one hundred white men were actually attacking blacks, and most of them, according to later testimony, were
"bar-flies" and petty criminals, but as word got around town, the crowd of onlookers along Broadway grew to thousands of people—all of them white. The
riot was under way. Some onlookers cheered the rioters on, but most of the mob
that packed downtown just watched, their silence and lack of interference—as
in most race riots—seeming to give the mob encouragement to do its worst. At
first, a few whites tried to stop the beatings, at least with words, but men booed

and cursed and women hissed through their teeth and in some cases stabbed out with hatpins or penknives until the peacemakers gave up.[21]

The riot moved across downtown East St. Louis with startling swiftness, like a fire on a wind-blown prairie. At least three black men were already dead from bullets or beatings and several others critically wounded by ten fifteen A.M. when a white man was killed, the first since Coppedge, in an accident that typifies all the things that can go wrong in the blur of a riot. A drunken white man shot at a black man in front of the Illmo Hotel on Collinsville Avenue. The bullet either missed the black man entirely or passed through his body and killed a white man standing behind him. A policeman, one of the few in evidence, ran over and grabbed the wobbly shooter before he killed anybody else. He started to drag him off to jail and a large crowd shouted to turn him loose. The crowd pressed in closer and became more threatening, and finally the policeman shrugged helplessly and let the man go and walked away. Then another streetcar full of blacks hoping to get across the river came in from the east and the mob turned again to pulling black men, women, and children onto the street and beating and kicking them into unconsciousness.[22]

Lyman Bluitt, the black doctor who worked part-time for the city, one of the civil rights leaders who had repeatedly urged the mayor to do something about the growing racial violence, arrived at the city hall dispensary a little after ten o'clock. By then, most of the white mob had gone from Main Street near city hall toward the streetcar lines and the South End, but Bluitt was shocked to see that the few who remained were gathered around the bloody and battered Model T Ford in which a white policeman had died. "How foolish that is," he said to himself. "You may as well put a red blanket in front of a bull." He went inside city hall and was at his desk talking to a supervisor when he heard loud, belligerent voices from outside. The supervisor, a white man, said to him, "I will tell you, I'm going to take my wife and get my buggy and go out to the country. I believe that would be a good thing for you to do, as well."

"Mr. Ross, I have come to that conclusion myself," said Dr. Bluitt. He stood up, put on his hat, and drove home. He had been there for about two minutes when the telephone rang. There was an emergency. Victims from the rioting were already coming in to both main hospitals, Protestant Deaconess and Catholic St. Mary's. Both were, under usual circumstances, segregated, and blacks needing hospital care either had to make do with makeshift clinics or be driven to the city hospital for blacks across the river in St. Louis. But the

hospitals did accept blacks in emergency situations, and it was quickly determined that this was an emergency situation.

Bluitt went immediately to St. Mary's, at Eighth and Missouri. He arrived about ten thirty. There were two wounded men there, but by the time
he had finished treating them, more had arrived. And they kept coming, until the treatment rooms were full and badly injured men and women were lying on blankets in the hallway and in the operating room. Some of them were
dead, or dying. By then, several white doctors had arrived. The victims kept
coming in. Bluitt worked in the emergency room at St. Mary's hospital until
six o'clock the next morning, treating whites as well as blacks.[23]

Around ten thirty, Mollman and Tripp met with a group of fifty or sixty businessmen in the chamber of commerce offices near city hall. The businessmen
were demanding that Mollman and Tripp do something before rioters burned
down the business district. Mollman reluctantly had decided it was time to ask
the governor to declare martial law. Colonel Tripp disagreed, and insisted that
his soldiers could stop the riot without suspending civilian authority. At that
point, Tripp had about fifty mostly untrained National Guard troops spread
out all over the central core of East St. Louis, and nothing they had done so far
had accomplished anything but give the mobs of whites in the streets the feeling that the riot was somehow justified, or at least permissible. One soldier
seemed to sum up the attitude of most of his comrades when he said loudly he
wouldn't shoot a white man for killing a black, not after what had happened
the night before.[24]

Mayor Mollman later said that he "didn't know what martial law
meant . . . but I had a kind of an idea that it would be much more drastic
and . . . firmer and have a moral effect on the community." Without coming
to an agreement, the two men got Governor Frank Lowden on the phone in
Springfield. Colonel Tripp took the phone and told Lowden that he had the
situation well in hand.

"Just a minute," sputtered the mayor. "Let me talk to the governor."
Mollman grabbed the phone and told Lowden the situation was not in hand;
several men were dead already and the riot was just getting started. The phone
went back and forth between the mayor and the colonel, with the mayor arguing for more force and the colonel arguing for "moral suasion." Finally, the

governor, reluctant to admit that civilian authority had failed, decided to leave Tripp in charge, and to delay declaring martial law. He told Mollman that declaring martial law would not make things any better in the riot zone. Be patient, he advised. Many more National Guardsmen were on the way.[25]

By eleven o'clock, the rioting had spread, and blacks were being beaten and shot over a square mile of East St. Louis, from the southern parts of downtown to as far north as St. Clair Avenue, which formed the boundary between East St. Louis and National City, home of the stockyards and the large meatpacking plants. Thousands of workers crossed into National City six days a week, and dozens of prostitutes patrolled the "Whiskey Chute," the row of rowdy saloons and cheap hotels that lined the East St. Louis side of St. Clair Avenue, but the official population was less than three hundred. The residents were mostly poor people, black and white, who lived in shacks with outhouses in the back and who voted as they were told (and paid) to do.

On St. Clair Avenue in front of the stockyards, white men were running after blacks "like boys chasing rabbits," recalled Robert Boylan of the *Globe-Democrat*, who had driven up from downtown. "There were some women dressed in silk stockings and kimonos, with last night's paint still unwashed on their cheeks, chasing negro women. [White prostitutes] were chasing a nigger woman that had a little boy by the hand. She dragged the little boy as she ran, and finally the little boy couldn't keep up, and she grabbed him into her arms and ran into a shanty. These women stood about and threw chunks of coal at the shanty."[26]

As the rioting grew more intense, scattered fires sprang up in downtown and in the South End and railroad shanties on the bottomland west of downtown on what had once been Bloody Island. Whites had begun firing into shacks where blacks lived, or setting them ablaze, shooting the men, women, and children when they ran out the doors.

Thomas Hunter, the black surgeon, was stopped at a gas station at Fifth Street and Illinois Avenue late that morning when the white proprietor rushed over to him and said, "Doctor, my God, flee for your life. They are killing niggers all over town. They have just killed two niggers up on Summit Avenue and they're taking them off the streetcars down on Collinsville Avenue, and on Broadway and on Missouri Avenue."

Hunter said, "I'm not going to run any place." Then he looked the white station owner directly in the eyes and said, "You're a man of influence, you should get together with other white men of influence and go to Mayor Mollman and pressure him to protect law abiding Negroes. The good people in this city shouldn't suffer for the depredations of the criminals."

"Doctor, we can't do anything," the man said.

"If Negroes were killing and beating up white men in this city here, you and many other men would see that the disturbance was stopped at any cost," Hunter replied.

The white man shook his head slowly and said again, with apparent sadness, "I'm sorry, but there's nothing we can do."[27]

About noon, a black husband and wife from St. Louis, Edward and Lena Cook, and her teenage son were brutally attacked on Collinsville Avenue in the middle of downtown East St. Louis. The man was beaten to death. The boy was shot and mortally wounded. The woman was knocked unconscious. All three of them were picked up off the street and laid in the back of an ambulance that, at this point, was picking up the dead as well as the living. Mrs. Cook regained consciousness, wiped the blood out of her eyes, and realized that she was lying on top of a dead man. Horrified, she scrambled to the front of the ambulance to get away from the bodies. It was then that she looked back and saw that her husband and her son were both lying there dead. The Cooks had been visiting East St. Louis and had been trying to get back across the river to St. Louis when they were dragged off the streetcar by a white mob. It was the first time that they had been on the eastern side of the river. They were trying out a new fishing spot, a lake north of East St. Louis. Their thirteen-year-old daughter was with them, and she was saved from the mob by a white storekeeper, who pulled her into his shop and protected her.[28]

At noon, Colonel Tripp left city hall for lunch. At that point, he had fifty or seventy-five troops in the city. Even he was not sure of the total. But he knew that the young soldiers were outnumbered by the rioters 20 or 30 to 1. Most of the militiamen carried loaded Springfield rifles with bayonets fixed to them, and many wore belts holding forty .30-30 caliber cartridges. But Tripp insisted that firing on mobs that were killing innocent men, women, and children would result in more deaths than it would save. The soldiers were told not to use their guns unless they were under attack.

Tripp and assistant city attorney Fekete, the acting mayor, drove a cautious and circuitous route to a restaurant about six blocks from city hall, on Collinsville Avenue. At that point, they were north of the riot zone. By the time they had finished lunch and drunk their coffee and paid the bill, it was almost one thirty P.M., and the riot was practically outside the front window. While Tripp and Fekete were lingering over dessert, a white man was killed nearby when whites broke into a pawnshop, presumably to steal guns and valuables, and shot the proprietor. What were Tripp and Fekete doing all morning and during that long lunch? Tripp was asked that question in October by an incredulous congressman at hearings investigating the riot.

"Planning," Tripp replied. The congressman remarked that he could have planned the battle of Verdun in that time.[29]

Troops continued to trickle into the downtown rail station. By one thirty, when Tripp and Fekete got in Fekete's car and headed back downtown, there were about a hundred troops under Tripp's command, although he had seen very few of them. Tripp and Fekete were stopped by a raging mob blocking Collinsville Avenue near the Labor Temple. Tripp, in one of the moments of almost foolhardy bravery that seemed to overtake him in the midst of timidity and indecision, walked right up to a soldier—one of only a few at the scene—and grabbed his rifle. He held the Springfield out in front of his body like a horizontal bar and pushed into the mob, shouting for the "unlawful assemblage to disperse in the name of the laws of the state of Illinois." Tripp was "tossed round and round," he recalled, but he was not harmed and, to the apparent surprise of some onlookers, the mob grudgingly gave ground and broke up and scattered down the street. As Tripp drove away, he could see the mob reassemble, like spilled fluid converging at a low point. If his relatively easy if fleeting victory suggested to him that the riot could be stopped with a small but resolute show of force, it was several hours before he would act on that notion.

Tripp found an open drugstore that had a telephone and called city hall and the police station and asked that "all available men" be sent to Collinsville Avenue. Tripp also called the mayor's office from the drugstore and asked that the saloons be closed. Mollman told him the order had already gone out.

In a report that was alarming, false, and probably malicious, a policeman told Tripp over the phone that there was bad trouble up on St. Clair Avenue near the stockyards—that black vigilantes were on the march. Tripp rushed to the scene. The few blacks who remained in the area were running for their lives. By the time Tripp had returned downtown after chasing those phantom vigilantes, another black man had been killed, bringing the death toll for the day to more than half a dozen.[30]

The official order to close the saloons had come from the mayor at about noon, but it took an hour or two to shut them down and empty all of them out. Ironically, closing the saloons—a reasonable, perhaps inevitable step, and one of the few decisive acts the mayor took that day—may have backfired. According to Robert Boylan of the *Globe-Democrat*, the drunks and "floaters" and petty criminals who spent their days in nickel-a-shot barrelhouses, "men who would do something, legal or illegal, to get a little money and then drink . . . men who didn't want to work," some of them drawn from St. Louis by the cheap liquor and lax law enforcement of East St. Louis, were forced out onto the street in the heat of the early afternoon. He estimated that ten rough saloons within a couple of blocks of Fourth and Broadway contributed about a hundred people to the melee. Boylan called the area "the storm center."[31]

As the afternoon wore on and the temperature rose into the middle eighties, four soldiers came at a kind of ragged march down Main Street toward the city hall complex, half-guarding, half-escorting two black men, one of them with a bloody head. Following close behind them were dozens of white women wearing garish blood-red lipstick and slathered-on makeup and mascara. They were dressed in kimonos or short dresses or cheap oriental pajamas or filmy slips, shouting and gesturing obscenely at men on the sidewalk. Some of them were chanting "Left, right, left, right," like drill sergeants leading a march.[32]

By then, dozens of blacks had been pulled off of streetcars on Collinsville Avenue and beaten, hit with bricks and paving stones, and shot. Sparks flew as rioters yanked the overhead trolleys loose from charged wires so the streetcar could not move as they attacked the passengers. From time to time some of the rioters would step aside and rest while others took their place. The men taking a break stood next to soldiers, and the two groups chatted and joked. The soldiers did nothing to stop the mayhem.

The only time Paul Anderson saw a soldier do something halfway decent came later in the day, after a black man had been beaten to the ground and was lying unconscious on his side, curled up like a baby. Several men stood over him, one of them with a pistol. A young soldier held his hands out, in an imploring gesture, and said "Now, boys, you've done enough to this man. Leave him alone. He's all in now." One of the rioters then knelt on the pavement and shot the black man in the back of the head.[33]

To at least one observer in the middle of the East St. Louis massacre, many of the rioters seemed in an odd way almost calm as they did the most horrible things. It was "not a wild riot," not an emotional catalyst, said James Kirk, editor of the *East St. Louis Daily Journal*, who watched the brutality for hours from his window above Collinsville Avenue. He recalled that men and, shockingly to him, women "stood around there and you wouldn't know they were agitated at all, and that's what made it even more heinous" as they attacked black men and women and children, knocked them down and hit them, shot them and left them dead in the street. Kirk said, "As quick as a Negro would show up, maybe a young man or a boy, they would say, 'there's a nigger,' and immediately they would all start for him, to perform their execution, let him lie there, and then go and stand on the corner again and hobnob with the police and militiamen."[34]

By refusing to intervene in the slaughter of blacks, the militiamen, supposed authority figures even if beneath the uniforms they were frightened farm boys, along with the police, became part of the complex synergism of mass violence. In effect, their inaction gave the rioters permission to do their worst. The crowd of whites was turning into a mob, a group willing and even eager to commit atrocities that most of them as individuals would shy away from. Sociologists describe what happens in violent mobs as an "emergent norm" situation. As a new norm of behavior emerged in East St. Louis, the mob became, in a sense, a radical ad-hoc community with its own rules and rituals and uniformed guardians of order. As the terrible day wore on, the guardians became more permissive, the rules less restrictive, and the rituals increasingly brutal.[35]

CHAPTER 9

"This Was the Apocalypse"

About two P.M., rioters began torching flimsy railroad shacks on the Mississippi River bottomland west of the South End, near the Free Bridge. The scattered fires, fanned by a light wind from the west, slowly licked eastward into rickety, overcrowded rows of flats and small industrial buildings and warehouses.

Charles Roger looked to the west from the chemical plant he ran at Sixth Street and Walnut Avenue south of downtown, and he could hardly believe his eyes. The fires were about two blocks away, and the smoke was dark with creosote from railroad ties. As he looked down Walnut toward the railroad yards and sandy bottomland along the river he saw half a dozen white men emerge through the smoke. The men were jeering and throwing bottles and stones at the blacks who ran out of the buildings to escape the fires. For the moment, the whites seemed content to see the homes destroyed and let the blacks escape with their lives. Roger saw no guns, although he could hear sporadic gunfire from other parts of the city. An hour or two later, he saw the first soldiers, not that their arrival did anything to stop the rioters.

Roger had been born and raised in Scotland but he had spent half of his forty-nine years in the United States, the past seven managing a chemical plant and freight company in East St. Louis. He thought he knew the place well, but he had never expected to see anything like this, and it shocked and frightened him.[1]

In front of his building, three or four black men huddled on the sidewalk along Walnut and watched the jeering whites. Suddenly, another black man came running toward them from the east, gripping a pistol in his right

138

hand. He yelled something as he approached and waved with the pistol toward a small gang of white men who were chasing him. They were less than a block behind him, shouting racial curses.

The black men all began running south toward the Free Bridge. Roger figured they could escape across the river, if they could fight their way through the whites who, Roger had heard, were massed at the bridge, beating blacks and forcing them at gunpoint to jump into the deep, churning Mississippi. It was a plunge few could expect to survive,

Roger turned away for a moment, horrified at what he had seen that day, fearful of what would happen to the businesses he had been put in charge of—$300,000 worth of plant and warehouses—and worried about the lives and homes of the people who worked for him. The plant had its own hauling company that delivered freight by horse-drawn wagons, and one of his teamsters was black. Understandably, that man had not reported to work that morning, and Roger could only hope that he was safe.

An old African American pensioner who did odd jobs around the company's horse yards and stables had come in early, as usual, but as soon as Roger learned that blacks were being yanked off of streetcars, beaten, and shot just a few blocks to the north, he managed to get a cab to come to the plant and take the terrified old man to St. Louis. Then the taxis stopped running.

Most of his other employees had gone home, or never came in. A half dozen remained. They had blankets and fire extinguishers and hoses and their main task was to protect the plant, wooden sheds, outbuildings, and equipment. Roger was thankful that he had gotten the horses out of the stable and headed across the river with the teamsters first thing that morning, after he had driven to work from his house north of downtown and seen the angry men in the streets. He had expected trouble, but the chaos in East St. Louis was worse than anything he could have imagined. It was like war.[2]

A few blocks north, in the heart of downtown, Colonel Tripp received a report that blacks, some of them armed, had holed up in a nearby two-story brick house after a black man had been shot in the street. The house was surrounded by a small mob of whites, who were gearing up for an assault. Tripp turned to Fekete, the young assistant city attorney, and said "The thing to do is to go to that building and get the colored people out." Tripp and half a dozen troops walked down to the brick house. The soldiers held the whites at rifle point until they surrendered their guns. The blacks were finally coaxed

out of the building and Tripp confiscated their revolvers. There were no policemen in sight.[3]

The soldiers escorted the blacks to city hall. A few said they would not
stay in East St. Louis for any amount of money, and Fekete drove a carload of
them across the river to St. Louis, which, at the request of the St. Louis chapter of the NAACP, had opened its Municipal Lodging House, a shelter
for the poor and homeless, to refugees from East St. Louis. Hundreds of
NAACP members and other volunteers took refugees into their homes.[4]

By midafternoon, more than one hundred soldiers had arrived in East
St. Louis, and Tripp had spread most of them across downtown with vague
orders to "maintain order." Despite the smoke rising from the South End,
there seemed to be a lull in the rioting downtown and Tripp and Fekete had
reason to believe, at least for a while, that their limited show of force and the
mere presence of scattered troops had begun to calm the riot down without
any further killing. It turned out they were merely in the eye of the storm.
The colonel went to another meeting with city officials and businessmen at
the downtown offices of the chamber of commerce. The meeting lasted for
almost three hours as Colonel Tripp and Mayor Mollman once again went
back and forth about the wisdom of declaring martial law. As the arguments
rolled on, fires set by men carrying torches made from oily rags spread to the
south and east of downtown, and the beatings at the streetcar stops along
Collinsville Avenue resumed after rioters saw that the soldiers who had recently arrived were standing around with their rifles slung on their backs doing nothing. A block from city hall, a black man who had been yanked off
a streetcar tried to run away and a mob of about five hundred whites surrounded him and fought each other to get close enough to beat and kick the
man and hit him with cobblestones and pipes and anything they could get
their hands on. He was knocked to the ground and unable to get up. The
crowd closed in, and he was kicked unconscious, and then kicked some more,
even after it appeared that he was dead.[5]

About three o'clock, a white mob downtown began chanting, "Get the mayor!
Get the mayor!" The chant would rise and then die down and then rise again,
sometimes with a variation, "March to city hall! March to city hall!" Several
thousand men now were surging through the downtown streets, some of them

haranguing the others, urging them to take the city back from the "nigger-loving politicians." Many just watched. Reporter G. E. Popkess couldn't find anyone preaching tolerance and sanity. At this point, the peacemakers and the fearful had gone home. Popkess heard a rumor that someone had been beheaded. He was not able to confirm that, but he knew that at least a dozen blacks were dead by late afternoon, including at least one woman.[6]

Paul Y. Anderson called the *Post-Dispatch* office around three P.M. and told rewrite man Carlos Hurd what he had seen. When he had finished with the horrifying details, he left the drugstore where he had used the phone and waded back into the riot. He saw a pawnshop with a broken window and a kicked-in door. Inside, white men were grabbing guns off the shelves and running out with them. One man had a satchel full of cheap pistols and was handing them out. Anderson heard a national guardsman cheering on a white rioter who was holding a revolver. He didn't like black people either, the guardsman said.[7]

Across the river in downtown St. Louis, in the creaky old *Post-Dispatch* building on North Broadway, Carlos Hurd hung up the phone and looked out the window to the east in dismay. The Free Bridge was jammed with people fleeing East St. Louis on foot and by car, and clouds of black smoke rose above the city.

Hurd, who was the top rewrite man on the evening shift, had been in the office for a couple of hours. He had seen the smoke above the river from his house forty-odd blocks to the west in the comfortable residential area called the Central West End. Hurd's wife was out of town, and he was eager to get the news, so he came in early. Already one of the best-known reporters in America at a time when print journalists could be stars on a national level, Hurd had scooped them all five years earlier when his first interviews from sea with the survivors of the *Titanic* shipwreck appeared in Joseph Pulitzer's two major dailies—the *New York World* and the *St. Louis Post-Dispatch*. The survivors had terrible tales to tell, and Hurd interviewed them in secret aboard the rescue ship, the *Carpathia*, defying the ban on interviews by the Cunard steamship company. His wife hid the notes in her corset, and he wrote the story in his cabin, wrapped it in oilcloth, and, in New York harbor as the *Carpathia* was hooking up to tow boats, he tossed it to Pulitzer employees in a speedboat.

Hurd had covered natural disasters, murders, major fires, and bitter labor battles, but had never seen anything like the horror that reporters were

Carlos Hurd and his wife in Venice, Italy, in 1912

breathlessly describing to him over the telephone from East St. Louis. Every hour or so, Anderson or one of his legmen would call in with reports of the latest atrocity, and Hurd would incorporate the news into the expanding story that would dominate the front page of the next day's paper. Hurd, an Iowa Congregationalist minister's son, had what a friend described as "a tidy mind," and finally he decided he needed to see the riot for himself to comprehend it fully. When Hurd had begun work at the *Post-Dispatch* in 1900, he had sped to assignments on a bicycle, and once, in his early years, he had been arrested in East St. Louis for "scorching"—speeding—on his bike. Now forty years old, he was still in a hurry, but he rode the streetcar. After telling managing editor O. K. Bovard what he was doing, and getting Bovard's approval, he left the office about six fifteen P.M. By then, about 160 National Guard troops had arrived in East St. Louis.[8]

About five P.M., in a spectacular conflagration, four rickety old houses where blacks lived in an area of warehouses and stores near the downtown East St.

Louis railroad yards seemed to burst into flames simultaneously, as if from the coordinated actions of several men. The houses were at Main Street and Brady Avenue, about three blocks south of city hall. Half a dozen black men tried to run out of the torched houses. Armed rioters fired at them, hitting several. The wounded men were picked up by their arms and legs and thrown back into the burning buildings. A half-dozen soldiers were leaning against a wall across the street, watching. They held rifles, and had full cartridge belts, but the men did nothing. They were leaderless and seemed "overwhelmed," observed Roy Albertson. Even if they had wanted to stop the riot—and nothing in their posture suggested they did—without leaders they were "like lost babes in the woods," decided Albertson.[9]

By then, the mob had broken up into amoeba-like clusters that were moving through the streets of downtown, with the center of the riot in the heart of the city at Fourth and Broadway, about two blocks south of city hall. At five forty, another fire alarm sounded, this time signaling a new fire on Walnut Avenue, a block south of Broadway, and the siren kept blowing and was echoed from other parts of town. There were many more fires than East St. Louis had firemen or trucks or water pressure to fight, and sirens sounded unheeded into the night.

As the smoke from the flames rose into the air above East St. Louis, and thousands of blacks fled across the Mississippi River to Missouri, large crowds of St. Louisans, black and white, came down to the levee to watch the exodus. Among them, barely able to believe her eyes, was an eleven-year-old girl named Freda Josephine McDonald. Many years later, after she had become internationally famous as Josephine Baker, she wrote down what she had seen and heard that horrible day.

She and her family lived in a tiny shack near downtown St. Louis. Her father was on relief, and she often woke up hungry, as she did on Monday, July 2. That afternoon, she wrote:

> An ominous humming sound filled the air. It seemed to be drawing nearer.
> "Is there a storm coming, Mama?" my brother Richard asked.
> "No, not a storm, child, it's the whites."
> "Wait, Mama, I have to get my babies."
> Two tiny black-and-white puppies shared the bed in which

we children huddled together for warmth. I had discovered them half dead in a trash can while I was sorting through garbage. They barely had the strength to whine . . . Gathering my babies up, I hurried along behind Mama, who had picked up little Willie May and was pushing Richard and my sister Margaret out the door.

What I saw before me as I stepped outside had been described at church that Sunday by the Reverend in dark, spine-chilling tones. This was the Apocalypse. Clouds, glowing from the incandescent light of huge flames leaping upward from the riverbank, raced across the sky . . . but not as quickly as the breathless figures that dashed in all directions. The entire black community appeared to be fleeing.

A precocious child budding into womanhood, Josephine had already been planning on leaving St. Louis and heading for Broadway, and the riot made St. Louis even less bearable, as mistrust increased between the races and the color line became even more rigid. Two years later, the thirteen-year-old stepped onto a train at Union Station, just a few blocks from the ghetto where she lived, and headed east. Before Josephine Baker was out of her teens, her singing and dancing, her wit and her beauty, her powerful ambition and the unstoppable desire never again to live anywhere remotely close to racist East St. Louis—even, it would seem, in the same nation—had made her a star in New York and then in Paris, where she remained.[10]

All afternoon and evening in East St. Louis, huge crowds of black men, women, and children, some of them carrying battered suitcases or large shopping bags filled with clothes and other belongings, some of them with little more than the clothes they wore, were also fleeing to the east out Illinois and Cahokia avenues, away from the Mississippi River. Dr. Thomas Hunter, the black surgeon who had left downtown when the rioting had intensified, was standing with his wife and others at Nineteenth Street in his mostly black, middle-class neighborhood well east of downtown watching the mass exodus. He recognized a patient and asked what was going on downtown. "Oh, doctor," the man said, "they are killing and beating our people. And they are burning everything down there at Fifth and Broadway."

"My god," said Hunter. "What about my office?"

"It's gone," the man replied. "Burned down."

Hunter was unnerved by the news. He had heard rumors that "business Negroes"—Bundy and other influential men in the black community—were going to be targeted by rioters, and he feared that his house would be attacked as well. "I think we had better get in the machine and take to the tall weeds," he said, but then he had second thoughts. There were too many people, including a druggist and his family and two female schoolteachers, to fit in his car, and he didn't want to abandon anyone to the riot. He decided they would be safer staying where they were as long as they kept away from his own home. They found shelter at a neighbor's house. "I guess it will be just about as safe there as any other place," Hunter said, "and we will all be together."[11]

Mayor Mollman and Colonel Tripp stayed at the meeting at the chamber of commerce into the late afternoon, arguing with each other and chamber members, seemingly at a loss as to how to stop the destruction and murder going on around them. Lawyer Dan McGlynn told the mayor that "two or three determined men" could stop the riot in its tracks. He said later, "I remember there were four or five of us there that said if we didn't get proper assurance from the Mayor that we would do something . . . We could go over to a hardware store and get some shotguns and rifles and get out and undertake to save the town from being burned up. [But] the mayor assured us that Colonel Tripp was here and that everything would be all right in just a little while."[12]

At about that point, Colonel Tripp left the meeting. He received a report from police he felt he couldn't ignore. Armed blacks were forming a mob in a saloon "out in the colored districts" around Seventeenth and Bond and were preparing to attack whites wherever they found them. Tripp and the chief of police and a couple of soldiers headed east, with assistant city attorney Fekete driving. They were followed by an army truck intended to hold prisoners. They found about fifteen black men sitting in the saloon, taking it easy. "Beer was on the table," Tripp reported later, "but there was no disorder. I told them if they lived there they had a right to remain, but if they had any arms to surrender them." Nobody said anything. Tripp asked the bartender if he was "organizing any forces of colored people." He said he wasn't. Tripp and Chief Payne began searching people, and they found that one man was holding twelve or fifteen shotgun cartridges. They had been split with a knife. The effect of cutting the cartridge would be that all of the tiny lead balls would tend to explode from the barrel in a single lethal lump, like a bullet fired from a big-game hunting rifle. The man was arrested. In a cubbyhole in the saloon, where a bartender might reach for it if there was trouble, they found a loaded rifle. The rifle and shotgun shells were confiscated, and the other men were told to go home.

The saloon adjoined a garage owned by Dr. Leroy Bundy. Tripp was told by the men in the saloon that they hadn't seen Bundy all day. A search of the black leader's garage by the soldiers revealed nothing but auto supplies and stationery. On a tip by the black bartender, Tripp and Payne searched a saloon across the street that had a white clientele. They found and confiscated another gun. The white men said they hadn't seen Bundy for a couple of days. Tripp and his military escort walked down the street to Bundy's house. His wife said she hadn't seen him for about twenty-four hours.[13]

Late that afternoon, black policeman John Eubanks got a call at his home northeast of downtown from the chief of detectives asking him to come down to the police station. Eubanks kissed his wife good-bye and told her to stay away from the windows and head east at the first sound of gunfire. He walked downtown by Missouri Avenue, staying well clear of now-embattled Broadway, and went up to the detective bureau on the second floor. The chief of detectives said, "John, I tell you things are in an awful condition. They've been rioting all over town. It seems like there's a dozen mobs working in the city. I've got to leave the office, and I want you to stay here and take charge and answer any calls that come in." Eubanks remained on duty in the police station until the next morning, and then was sent to city hall to help with the hundreds of refugees from the riot being sheltered there.[14]

Nearby, at Broadway and Collinsville, members of the Illinois National Guard leaned on their rifles as blacks were beaten and kicked. One older black man on his way home from work ran from the mob, his lunch pail swinging in his right hand, and tried to protect himself by heading for a line of national guardsmen. Several of the militiamen held the man off with bared bayonets, and forced him back into the arms of the mob. He was beaten until he fell down, and then kicked in the head. He tried to shield his face, but soon was unconscious, and the kicks continued. An ambulance pulled up, but a white man standing over the body threatened to kill the driver if he picked up the black man. The ambulance driver, an agonized look on his smoke-streaked face, stood silent for a moment, staring at the white man, and then turned and drove away. The next day, the old black man lay dead in a black funeral parlor that was crowded with bodies. His arm, stiffened from rigor, still shielded his face.

The ambulance driver drove off toward the downtown railroad station, where another black man had been reported lying in blood, badly injured or dead. Behind him, siren blaring, was a fire engine heading in the same direction. New fires were springing up all around downtown.[15]

Standing on Broadway, Baptist preacher George W. Allison heard the sirens scream past him, rising and falling in pitch. He could see the fires nearby in the Black Valley and a mob of white men, as he later put it, "hunting for Negroes [who] were not armed or could not defend themselves." The whites carefully stayed away from the most dangerous section of the Valley, the so-called Bad Lands along Walnut, until fires had spread into that area and sent blacks scattering. At that point the whites could shoot them down and then advance like foot soldiers entering enemy territory after an artillery barrage.[16]

On Sixth Street, in the midst of all the chaos, Charles Roger was standing outside of his chemical plant when a man in a passing mob of whites gestured with his thumb at the building and said, "There's a place that would make a good fire." But another man looked over at Roger and grinned. "Leave that place alone," the man said. "He's no nigger lover. He don't have any niggers." Roger employed two blacks, but was immensely relieved that the men did not know that. The man who had spared his plant looked only vaguely familiar, and Roger was struck with how few of the rioters he recognized, even though he had spent so many years and so much time in the midst of the working men of East St. Louis. He had even seen a couple of strangers wearing what looked like brand-new blue cotton work shirts and pants, as if they had bought them to blend in with working men. He wondered where they came from.

The men walked on by, heading east, and the fires spread in that direction until Roger's plant and warehouses were covered in dense smoke. Although small fires sprang up from time to time on the building, Roger and the few employees who stayed with him were able to extinguish them. By the next morning, his plant was the only building standing in four square blocks.

Later, Roger was asked if there were any soldiers around when the men were torching buildings.

"One," Roger replied.

"What was he doing?"

"Shooting niggers."[17]

CHAPTER 10

A Drama of Death

The sun loomed ominously large and low in the western sky, glowing deep orange through the black smoke that rolled up from downtown East St. Louis. Sundown was an hour away, but the light was already dimming as darkness came early to East St. Louis on July 2.

The State Street car stopped at Broadway and Collinsville Avenue, a couple of blocks from city hall, and at about six thirty P.M. Carlos Hurd stepped down into what he later described as "a drama of death." A fire engine screamed past him heading east, where fires burned along Broadway as far as he could see. A light west wind—and, he soon discovered, men with torches and oily rags—pushed the flames eastward. Then he heard shots, and shouts of "They got him! They got him!" and Hurd ran toward the intersection of Fourth Street, shoving his way through a milling mob of men and a surprising number of women who were shouting and running about excitedly, drunk with murderous exhilaration. He reached the intersection and saw hundreds of people looking south at a row of burning buildings on Fourth Street between Broadway and Walnut Avenue.

Smoke and flames were rising from two- and three-story frame and brick buildings where blacks lived above and in the rear of storefronts. Flames grabbed at the rickety wooden rear stairs—the "fire escapes"—and leaped to the flimsy outbuildings. The fires lent an eerie glow to the scene, and Hurd saw a circle of rioters around the body of a black man who had been shot. His head was bleeding profusely. He tried to rise up, and a boot smashed into his face.

"Don't do that, I haven't hurt nobody," the man screamed hoarsely, but another kick came. The black man kept struggling with his attackers. A young man dressed for the office, the only person Hurd recalled seeing among the rioters who looked like a business or professional man, lifted a broken chunk of curbstone and hurled it down at the black's head, silencing him. The natty young man turned and walked away from the now-still body, past a seemingly unconcerned National Guard sergeant and several militiamen, all of them holding rifles. The sergeant strolled over to the circle of rioters around the body and peered down at the black man whose head was in a growing pool of blood.

"This man is done for," he said. "You men better get away from him." The sergeant walked away. Hurd asked if he couldn't call an ambulance. "The ambulances quit coming," the sergeant replied, seemingly without much interest. Another shot pierced the babble of voices and sirens and the suck and roar of fires, and Hurd was horrified to see two men with revolvers taking aim at blacks as they ran one by one from the blazing buildings.

"It was stay in and be roasted, or come out and be slaughtered," he wrote later that night.

Hurd stayed in East St. Louis for two hours, never getting more than a couple of blocks from where he had stepped down from the trolley car, and then he hurried back across the river to the *Post-Dispatch* headquarters to write with seething anger that what he had seen in the streets of downtown East St. Louis was not so much a riot as a "massacre," "a man hunt" conducted "on a sporting basis" where "a black skin was a death warrant."

"I have read of St. Bartholomew's night," he would write in a report that is remarkable for its personal fury. "I have heard stories of the latter-day crimes of the Turks in Armenia, and I have learned to loathe the German army for its barbarity in Belgium. But I do not believe that Moslem fanaticism or Prussian frightfulness could perpetrate murders of more deliberate brutality than those which I saw committed, in daylight, by citizens of the State of Abraham Lincoln." Somehow, he wrote, he could not call what he saw "mob violence":

"A mob is passionate, a mob follows one man or a few men blindly; a mob sometimes takes chances . . . The East St. Louis men took no chances . . . They went in small groups, there was little leadership, and there was a horribly cool deliberateness and a spirit of fun about it. I cannot allow even the doubtful excuse of drink. No man whom I saw showed the effects of liquor." A few men shouted at the mob to stop, and Hurd shouted too, but he concluded, "Only a volley of lead would have stopped these murderers." The police were nowhere to be seen, and straggling soldiers stood around and watched, leaning on their rifles, some of them with bayonets bared as men shouted "Get a nigger" and earned a chorus of replies, "Get another!"

"It was," he judged, "like nothing so much as the holiday crowd, with thumbs turned down, in the Roman Coliseum, except that here the shouters were their own gladiators, and their own wild beasts."[1]

Robert R. Thomas, owner of the Hill-Thomas Lime and Cement Company south of Broadway on Sixth Street, was eating supper at his home in Landsdowne, about four miles northeast of downtown East St. Louis, when the telephone rang. He knew it would be bad news. "The air was full of lightning that day," he said later. The distraught foreman of the plant's stables told him a building just north of the company's stables had been set ablaze. The foreman said he was going to move the horses and mules, and Thomas said he would come right back down. When Thomas arrived at the cement company, the flames had spread to the stables and the main plant. A large mob of men stood around, and some of them fired rifles and pistols into the building, which was just beginning to burn. Thomas feared that some of his black teamsters—there were a dozen of them in all—were still in the building, where they had hoped to be safe from marauding mobs, but he decided there was nothing he could do without help. He drove five blocks to city hall, past a couple of dozen soldiers, talking and smoking cigarettes, watching as the riot raged around them.

Jumping from the car at city hall, he asked a group of loitering soldiers who was in charge. He was directed to Colonel Tripp, who was talking to a small group of soldiers, seemingly without urgency. Thomas later recalled:

> It took me some little time to get his attention. I butted in once and he told me if I would just wait until he got through with what he was doing, we could probably get along a little faster. I made it so insistent that he finally took notice of what I wanted. I told him some of our men were down there and they probably would be burned up if he didn't get some help. He finally called, maybe, eight soldiers, and it is my recollection that he called them by their

first names—didn't give an order to anybody, but called them over to him and told them to go down there and see what they could do.

One of them said, "I haven't had my supper yet," and another said, "I just got off duty." They seemed to know him very well, and he finally persuaded them to go down there. He persuaded them finally to get in a truck. I don't think he put an officer in charge of them.

"There were several hundred soldiers right around city hall, coming from upstairs and different rooms around there," Thomas said. "I am satisfied there were enough soldiers there to at least have made a showing if they had had somebody to show them what to do [but] nobody seemed to be in command."

Thomas drove back south, past dozens of loitering soldiers, and watched his plant burn to the ground. If the soldiers in the truck ever arrived at the burning plant, they left immediately. A mob of a hundred men surrounded the blaze, Thomas said, "shooting at anybody that would show their head, and shooting at random when there wasn't anybody to shoot at."

Then he saw several black teamsters run out of the flames without being shot. At this point, the mob seemed more interested in watching the buildings burn down than in taking shots at men fleeing from the fire. It later turned out that two of the company's black teamsters had been wounded in the riot and one man, a twelve-year employee named Moses Keefe, simply disappeared. He is not included in the official death toll—by that point, at least two dozen people were dead—but, according to Thomas, there was enough evidence that he had been killed for an insurance company to pay off Keefe's brother on a $300 life policy.

One of the wounded men was shot trying to get horses away from the fire; the other was ambushed about three blocks south of the plant by a gang of young men firing at blacks fleeing down a main route to the Free Bridge. The man was so badly wounded that he lay immobile in a ditch and was assumed to be dead. At four P.M. the next day, he regained consciousness and was taken by ambulance to a city hospital in St. Louis.[2]

Charles Roger stood in the doorway of his Walnut Avenue chemical plant, keeping an eye out for fires while trying to avoid getting himself killed, his anger growing into rage as he watched militiamen in khaki uniforms standing around joking as a gang of five or six white men set fire to the shacks and flats all around him. A building nearby burst into flames and several blacks dashed out the door and ran east. Half a dozen white men stood and jeered but let the blacks run. One rioter shouted that the soldiers couldn't shoot them if they tried. A soldier replied, "The hell I can't. I'll show you."

The soldier put the rifle to his shoulder, aimed at the small group of blacks running away—they were now perhaps a hundred yards down Walnut Avenue—and squeezed the trigger. One black man fell to the street. The others kept running.

When Roger recited the incident three months later to the congressional committee investigating the riot, Congressman Ben Johnson asked if Roger had gone to see if the man was wounded or dead.

"No, I didn't," Roger said. "You know, there were a great many instances where really common humanity would urge me to go ahead and interfere, but what were you going to do? You know well enough you would get killed yourself."[3]

By then, Carlos Hurd had walked a block or so south of Broadway, to where rioters were chasing blacks down a railroad spur, firing at them with rifles and pistols. Then he heard more shots coming from Fourth Street, and when he ran there he saw two more blacks lying in the street, apparently dead. Railroad shacks along the street—shacks used by black prostitutes—had been torched, and black women ran from them. A gang of white women began chasing them, cursing and hurling stones. The white women, Hurd wrote that night, were "of the baser sort . . . I do not wish to be understood as saying that these women were representative of the womanhood of East St. Louis. Their faces showed, all too plainly, exactly who and what they were." They were prostitutes, and professional jealousy may have had as much to do with their rage as racial hatred.[4]

Hurd wrote:

> One frightened black girl, probably 20 years old, got so far as
> Broadway with no worse treatment than jeers and thrusts. At
> Broadway, in view of militiamen, the white women, several of
> whom had been watching the massacre of the negro men, pounced
> on the negress . . . [T]hey were the heroines of the moment with

that gathering of men, and when one man, sick of the brutality he had seen, seized one of the women by the arm to stop an impending blow, he was hustled away, with fists under his nose . . . "Let the girls have her" was the shout as the women attacked the young negress. The victim's cry, "Please, please, I ain't done nothing," was stopped by a blow in the mouth with a broomstick, which one of the women swung like a baseball bat. Another woman seized the negress' hands, and the blow was repeated as she struggled helplessly. Fingernails clawed her hair, and the sleeves were torn from her [shirt]waist, when some of the men called, "Now let her see how fast she can run." The women did not readily leave off beating her, but they stopped short of murder, and the crying, hysterical girl ran down the street.[5]

A block or so away, fellow *Post-Dispatch* reporter Paul Y. Anderson walked up Broadway and saw mobs all the way to Eighth Street, burning homes and shooting blacks. Two black men tried to save themselves by walking slowly with their hands on top of their heads in a gesture of surrender. Rioters shot both of them.[6]

The Reverend George W. Allison was at the railroad station downtown when eleven or twelve white women and men—he thought they were all drunk and looked like whores and pimps—rushed into the station and attacked a black woman waiting for a train to take her out of East St. Louis. The station, crowded with men, women, and restless children, turned into bedlam. Allison and a couple of other men tried to protect the woman, getting between her and her attackers, but the terrified black woman darted out from the corner where she was huddling and the white women ripped her clothes off, leaving her in her corset. Allison went immediately to the police station but the mayor wouldn't let him have a policemen to go back and arrest the assailants. One of the officers said, "The truth is that there is no damn town big enough for the two races."[7]

Barely two blocks from the police station, Carlos Hurd heard a cheer go up behind him, and when he turned he saw a black man with his head laid open by a paving stone being dragged down an alley toward Fourth Street. Someone looped a thin rope around his neck. Someone else shouted that the rope was not strong enough, and the men circling around the prone man began laughing and making jokes. The rope was thrown over a cable box low on a light pole, and several men hauled on the rope, pulling the unresisting black man to his feet, where he stood wavering for a few seconds, held like a puppet, until the rope snapped. The victim and one of the men holding the rope tumbled to the ground. An old white man wearing a black, shiny-billed cap ran out of a nearby house, one that had not yet begun to burn, and shouted, "Don't you hang that man in the street. I dare you to!"

The men accepted the dare. The old man was shoved aside, and someone ran up with a stronger rope. "Right there," Hurd wrote, "I saw the most sickening incident of the evening. To put the rope around the negro's neck, one of the lynchers stuck his finger inside the gaping scalp and lifted the negro's head by it, literally bathing his hand in the man's blood.

" 'Get hold, and pull for East St. Louis' called a man with a black coat and a new straw hat, as he seized the other end of the rope. The rope was long, but not too long for the number of hands that grasped it, and this time the negro was lifted to a height of about seven feet from the ground."

Hurd dashed up to Broadway, where he had spotted a small group of militiamen. He pled with them to stop the lynching, but they ignored him and stood and watched as the men hauled the victim to his feet and then pulled him in the air. They held him there until he had stopped kicking, and then tied off the rope. Several of the guardsmen traded gory jokes with the rioters as the man hung in the air, dead.[8]

At least two other black men were hanged from light or telephone poles in downtown East St. Louis. One survived the hanging and was sitting on the steps of Bader's drugstore, the rope still around his neck, when a white man walked up to him and, without saying a word, shot and killed him. The second also lived through the hanging, but died four days later of internal injuries from being beaten and kicked and dragged through the streets.[9]

And what were white citizens of East St. Louis, the thousands who were not locked in their houses or actively participating in the riot, doing on those downtown streets lined with stores and businesses? Watching. Mostly, observers said, with approval. The majority of East St. Louis whites, said G. E. Popkess of the *East St. Louis Daily Journal*, were "in sympathy with the rioters."[10]

Roy Albertson of the *St. Louis Republic* left the paper's East St. Louis office,

in the Arcade Building across from city hall, about seven P.M. His three tem-
porary legmen had already been dispatched to scenes of violence, and he
watched in front of a saloon at Fourth and Broadway as three white women in
flouncy dresses and gaudy makeup—he recognized them and knew them to
be prostitutes—shoved and beat a young black woman who was desperately
trying to escape their blows. She huddled over a tiny baby wrapped in her
arms.

"Have mercy on my baby!" she screamed, but one of the white women
balled up her fist and slammed it into the bundle in the black woman's arms.
The black woman wailed, "Leave my baby alone." The whores followed her
as she ran from one side of Broadway to the other, falling down several
times, and they ripped most of her outer clothing off before she was able to
struggle to her feet and run up Broadway in her shredded underwear, still
clutching the baby. The whores jeered at her as she ran. Albertson learned
that the whores had already beaten up two or three other black women that
night.

Albertson decided Fourth and Broadway "wasn't a very safe place for
me," and headed back to his office. On his way, Albertson saw Lieutenant
Colonel E. P. Clayton and told him, "Colonel, you won a reputation for
yourself in the first riot. It is time to be taking this situation in hand, and not
be trying to handle it with kid gloves the way a certain other man is."

The colonel laughed bitterly, and shook his head. "Well, this time I'm
superseded."[11]

It seemed to Albertson that Clayton's superior, Colonel Tripp, instead of
trying to stop the violence, was busy grabbing news photographers and trying
to prevent them from taking pictures of the riot. Some of the rioters as well
as policemen and soldiers were more direct in trying to conceal evidence of
the atrocities being committed in East St. Louis. Police and soldiers confiscated cameras and bared the film to the light, and at least three newspaper
photographers had their cameras smashed by rioters, which is the main reason so few photographs remain of the riot.[12]

After a quick supper at the Illmo Hotel, Colonel Tripp and Fekete walked
over to city hall and met with Colonel Clayton. Mayor Mollman put in an
appearance, and city controller James M. Kelley ran over from the fire area

and asked the mayor if anything could be done to stop the torching. Mollman said the firemen had been there, but had retreated when it became clear that no one would protect them from the mob.[13]

"Well," said Tripp, "we think they are a little thin-skinned. They ought to be able to protect their hose." Kelley angrily replied that the firemen themselves should be protected so they could do their jobs and save the city from burning to the ground. Tripp did not reply, and the mayor did not seem to be interested in the conversation. Just then, a man ran up to report that a huge, out-of-control mob had gathered at Fourth and Broadway, about two blocks away. Fekete, Tripp, and a major named William Klauser jumped into Fekete's car and rushed to the scene. They saw two black men lying dead in the streets, and a body still hanging from a light pole.

Tripp could locate only three or four soldiers, scattered on the edges of the mob of fifteen hundred men and women, doing nothing. Apparently horrified at what he saw, with black men coming under fire while running from the burning buildings, Tripp jumped out of the car in his summer suit and straw boater and tried to disperse the mob himself. "In the name of the law of the state of Illinois and the governor of Illinois," he shouted into jeers and catcalls, "I am ordering you to disperse this unlawful assembly, go to your homes and discontinue the rioting." The mob laughed and screamed obscenities, and a few men rushed Tripp and began pushing him. Deciding the odds were impossible, Tripp and Fekete returned to city hall, where a fresh contingent of troops had been scheduled to arrive a little after seven P.M.[14]

The arrival of Company B of the Illinois National Guard, with three officers and sixty-six men, brought the total number of troops in East St. Louis to about two hundred thirty, widely scattered through the central city. Tripp ordered Colonel Clayton to "take personal command" of the new troops "and such additional men as he could find" and return to Fourth and Broadway. Clayton loaded the soldiers into trucks and accompanied them to Fourth and Broadway, two blocks away. Tripp followed in an automobile. Tripp insisted later that the chain of command never changed, but either Tripp said something he hadn't said before or Clayton chose to interpret Tripp's orders in a new and more forceful way. For whatever reason, at around seven P.M. on the night of July 2, with hundreds of buildings in flame and more than two dozen people dead, Colonel Clayton, a battle-tested, professional soldier, took charge.[15]

On Broadway between Seventh and Eighth streets, black policeman Otto Nelson saw the fires moving eastward toward the two-story frame-and-brick house where he and his wife lived. They were in their thirties, with no children. He had come home at noon to be with her. He told her to leave, to go to St. Louis, but she had refused to go. If he was going to stay, she said, so was she. White men had fired into the building several times in the afternoon and early evening, and the Nelsons were sitting on the floor in the middle room of their second-story shotgun flat, keeping away from the windows. About seven P.M., a white man threw a brick through the front window and Nelson raised his head enough to look out and see a half dozen white men in the street, some holding bricks or paving stones.

Just then, half a dozen militiamen came into view. Mrs. Nelson, thinking she would be protected, ran to the front of the house, but when she appeared in the front window several white men fired into the house and she dove to the floor. The soldiers did nothing. Nelson yelled to his wife, "Let's try and get out the back way," and they ran to the rear of the house. But the rickety wooden back steps were already beginning to burn.

With his wife hanging on to him, Nelson walked out the back door and down the steps into the flames. The bottom of her dress caught fire, and she let go of her husband and backed up the stairs. He turned and they both slapped at the flames on her dress until they turned to smoke. Then the two of them jumped half a flight of stairs through the flames to the ground.

The neighboring houses to the west were already burning. Nelson and his wife ran out of the back yard and started up Eighth Street, toward Broadway. A white man Nelson had never seen before was standing nearby, watching the fires, and when he saw the Nelsons heading toward Broadway, he waved them back. "Don't go that way," he said, "go this way." He waved toward the alley at the rear of the houses. Across the alley, near Eighth Street, was a large vacant lot that was covered with a jungle of weeds and low saplings. Holding hands, the Nelsons ran across the alley and threw themselves down into the weeds. They hid and watched for ten or fifteen minutes, catching their breath, as East St. Louis burned around them. Only then did they discover the painful burns on the palms of their hands.

More white men with guns came down Eighth Street, firing into the flames, driving blacks back into the burning flats. But most of the rioting was on Broadway. And the Nelsons could see flames to the south as well, toward Walnut Street. There was no place to run, and by now it was almost completely dark except for the light of the fires around them. The Nelsons huddled all night in the weeds half a block from the scorched remains of their home.[16]

A half-dozen blocks south of downtown, as night fell, a diminutive black woman named Katherine Kennedy decided it was time to leave the house on Piggott Avenue where she was raising her nine children without a father. Earlier in the day, white men passing by had fired into the house, and now flames from buildings that had been torched were spreading toward the wooden structure. She had been warned that white mobs were attacking blacks at the eastern end of the nearby Free Bridge, so she and her younger brother, Eddie, gathered together the six boys and girls who were at the home and headed west across the nearby railroad yards for the river.

They carried with them stockings and long strips of cloth and lengths of clothesline. As they went, sometimes ducking into the shadows to hide from rioters, they gathered scrap lumber from shanties that had been torn down. At the river's edge, they built a raft.

When they first launched the raft and everyone began paddling with planks, the clumsy vessel just kept turning around in circles, but eventually they figured out how to divide the paddlers so the boat would head west across the river. The Missouri shore was five hundred yards away. After a long struggle, with the relentless current carrying the boat downstream as they fought their way across, they landed on the western shore of the Mississippi well south of downtown St. Louis. Seven-year-old Samuel Kennedy looked back across the river toward East St. Louis. He would never forget what he saw. It looked like the whole horizon was on fire.[17]

From his large home in suburban Alta Sita, politically powerful real estate mogul Thomas J. Canavan could look to the west toward the South End and

Mississippi River and see smoke rising. Concerned about what was happening to his property, he and his grown son decided to drive downtown and look around. For reasons that remain unexplained—perhaps their wives had left the house—they took Canavan's younger son, who was thirteen, and Canavan's two-year-old grandson with them.

At about seven twenty, they climbed in the car with the older son driving and the children in the backseat and headed west from Twenty-sixth Street along the main thoroughfare, Bond Avenue. At Fourteenth Street, in the midst of a black enclave, they stopped when they saw a mob two or three blocks ahead, moving their way. A car sped ahead of the mob and jammed on its brakes as it came up alongside the Canavans. The white driver waved at them to turn back and then rolled down his window and shouted, "Turn around quick, you will be killed. They are shooting at me."

The man jammed his foot onto the accelerator and was gone. Canavan looked again to the west and saw that the black mob had gotten closer. It was led by six or eight men, several of them armed with pistols and seemingly firing at random. Suddenly, with a scream of tires, a Ford came speeding through the mob, scattering the men. The Ford pulled up next to Canavan's car.

A man rolled down the driver's side window. It was Dr. Albert B. McQuillan, who worked at the Aluminum Ore Company. His wife was with him. He told the Canavans that he had just escaped from the mob, and that they all needed to flee. McQuillan headed east and the Canavans followed.

McQuillan and the Canavans had gone a block or so when they saw two white men in work clothes, walking eastward on Bond. Suddenly, black men jumped out of the head-high weeds of a vacant lot and shot both of them—one fell where he was shot, and the other stumbled away and tripped over the curb. The doctor later found out the white men were George Hare, who was badly wounded, and Robert Murray, who died several hours later. The two men had been walking home from work in the Southern Railroad yards.

The Canavans and McQuillan realized they were trapped, with one hostile gang a block or two behind them and the other just ahead. McQuillan turned his wheels to the right, stepped on the gas and, bouncing over the curb, smashed through the high weeds of a vacant lot, heading for Market Avenue, a block south of Bond. The Canavans started to follow him, but they stopped when they saw armed black men run through the edge of the lot to get ahead of McQuillan. The men were so close that Canavan could see the mad fury on their faces and hear them shout, "Get the white bastards."

McQuillan's car, engine racing, bottomed out in the tall weeds and slid to a halt against a telephone pole. More blacks appeared in the waist-high vegetation, and several of them were carrying rifles or shotguns. McQuillan and his wife climbed out of the Ford and were trying to run south to safety. The black men ran after them, firing. Canavan saw McQuillan fall to the ground when a man with a pistol shot him in the head from close range. Mrs. McQuillan grabbed the gun and tried to tear it from the man's hands, pleading with him and the other armed blacks to spare her husband.

The Canavans took the opportunity to speed away. "I could look in many directions, and everywhere I saw a colored house, they were shooting out of it," Canavan recalled. With bullets flying around them, the Canavans turned north on Fifteenth Street. They spotted the white men who had been shot earlier lying on the curb. "One of those men is alive," Canavan's older son shouted. "I'm going to pick him up." He stopped the car and the Canavan men opened the door and dragged George Hare into the car, putting him in the backseat. They took the wounded man to the closest hospital, Deaconess, seven or eight blocks to the north at Fifteenth and State streets. It was nine P.M. before the Canavans got home. None of them was hurt.[18]

Back on the vacant lot, Dr. Albert McQuillan was still alive, bleeding heavily from a superficial bullet wound to the scalp. His wife was alive but bleeding, too. One black man jammed a revolver against the doctor's head while the mob searched his car for weapons. Mrs. McQuillan screamed and tried to grab at the pistol. "A life for a life," one man shouted, shoving Mrs. McQuillan away. Another man smashed McQuillan in the chest with the butt of a shotgun, breaking a rib.

Desperately, McQuillan looked at the faces of the men around him and recognized one as a worker he had treated at the Aluminum Ore Company. "Don't you know who I am?" he gasped. The man—his name was Joe Black—looked closely and shouted that he knew the white man, he was the doctor from the aluminum plant. "He treated me square when I was hurt. He's alright."

The doctor seized the opportunity. "Now, you are a fine bunch of fellows," he said. "Here I take care of one of you when you are hurt, and you are going to kill me."

The mob backed off. With blood pouring down his face and into his eyes, the doctor gestured at his automobile. "Help me and push my machine off that post," he said. After a moment's hesitation, four or five men stood at the front of the car and half pushed, half lifted it away from the telephone pole.

McQuillan climbed in, and one of the black men helped Mrs. McQuillan get into the passenger seat. McQuillan drove to his home in suburban southeast East St. Louis, where he treated his and his wife's wounds. Neither of the McQuillans was seriously injured.

McQuillan said later that he did not think that the blacks who had attacked him and then set him free were organized rioters, but were reacting to the white rioters. The blacks, he decided, must have decided they needed to protect themselves when they realized that the soldiers standing everywhere would do nothing to protect them. He said, "Had they been deliberately out to murder us, nothing would have stopped them."[19]

As is suggested by the attacks on the Canavans and McQuillans and the shooting of the two railroad workers, by the afternoon of July 2 armed blacks patrolled some of the African American enclaves in the South End. Their focus was Tenth Street, which not only was the western border of the neighborhoods blacks had been moving into in recent years, but led to the Free Bridge, the escape route for thousands of East St. Louis blacks. As a result, relatively little killing and burning was done by whites west of Tenth Street. The *Republic* reported on one border confrontation:

> The [white] mob, with the characteristic bravado of mob spirit . . . threatened to go toward Tenth Street, where the blacks were ambushing the roadway. They started, halted, each one looking out of the corner of his eye for men who would go to the front. None moved up to the perilous position.
>
> The crowd hesitated, halted, and then milled back. A shot now and then from the negro dwellings whizzed toward them. Then someone set up the shout. "Let's go back and clean up Third Street."
>
> And they turned in the other direction.

Or, as the black *St. Louis Argus* put it, "The scene of the destruction of life and property was not in the thickly populated district, the mob was too cowardly to invade it."[20] Blacks like Dr. Thomas Hunter and his friends, who had decided to stay together in their middle-class neighborhood at Nineteenth Street and hope for the best, were safe as the white rioters were driven back by armed blacks protecting their homes.

Back downtown, as Carlos Hurd roamed through the center of the riot area, he saw militiamen stand and watch the killing and beating and torching and even "fraternize," as he put it later, with the rioters. Finally, at seven thirty, he did see "instances of what National Guardsmen, in reasonable numbers and led by worthy officers, can do."[21]

As he looked to the east along Broadway, a platoon of soldiers under the command of Colonel Clayton slowly appeared out of the billowing smoke. They had formed a hollow square, and inside the protection of the square were black men, women, and children, most of them with their hands raised as if in surrender. At the front of the blacks was a frightened boy not more than six years old.

The mob parted with shouts and curses as the phalanx made its way without hesitation up Broadway. A few rioters tried to dash past the soldiers at the rear, but at the command of an officer those men turned with fixed bayonets and held the rioters back. The platoon marched around the corner to the police station, where they protected the refugees as they ran inside the building. Then the platoon marched at quickstep back up Broadway. Another group of soldiers appeared out of the smoke, a smaller group protecting perhaps a half-dozen blacks, and marched to the police station. Black refugees were being protected at both the police station and city hall.

Hurd followed this group down Broadway and around the corner to the police station. For the first time, he saw Colonel Tripp, in his gray summer suit and straw hat. Hurd assumed he had just arrived in East St. Louis. Tripp had assembled a platoon of guardsmen in formation, barked a quick order, and the men marched up to Broadway, where he ordered them to change to a quickstep.

"Get those men," Tripp shouted, and pointed ahead, where a dozen white rioters were hauling on a rope. The other end of the rope was around the neck of a black man with a bloody head. Every time he managed to struggle to his feet, the rioters heaved on the rope and his feet flew out from under him.

The guardsmen's bayonets were bared, and they rushed toward the rioters, who dropped the rope and scrambled out of the street onto the sidewalks on either side of Broadway. On the south side of the street, the guardsmen held the men prisoners with their bayonets. On the north side, one soldier yelled at the men on the sidewalk, "Move on!" "No!" Tripp shouted. "Don't let them get away. Make them prisoners." Colonel Clayton and the troops grabbed two of the men who had been pulling the rope. The others scattered into the raucous crowd.[22]

Paul Anderson, who had been in the streets of East St. Louis since eight in the morning, recalled that moment as "the first time that day I had seen any adequate effort made by the soldiers. By that time, most of the killings had already occurred." By using 200 soldiers to round up and arrest what turned out to be 198 men—several of them blacks who simply may have been swept up with the mob—Clayton "broke the back of the riot," Anderson later testified. "That was the turning point of the riot," said reporter Robert Boylan, a veteran of the Indian Wars. "Our troubles were practically over then. Of course, it continued for several more hours."[23]

Assistant city attorney Fekete peeled the rope off the badly wounded man's neck. He helped the man to his car and drove him to a hospital. Back at the police station, Tripp made certain the rioters were being booked while Clayton marched his troops back up to Broadway to make sure the riot did not get started again. As many as half of those rounded up may have been onlookers, Boylan estimated, but the show of force had its effect, scattering the crowd. After that, Boylan said, "It was guerilla warfare"—organized bodies of soldiers fighting small groups of men.[24]

There were not enough cells in the jail, which was in the basement of city hall, to hold the rioters, so many of them simply had been shoved into the basement without being locked up. They then discovered that the windows could be opened, and many merely crawled out and ran away. Tripp ordered soldiers to guard the windows and exits. Guards were placed on rioters in the basement, as well as rioters in a locked room on the second floor. Tripp spotted two men he had seen dragging on a rope wrapped around the neck of a black man and ordered that they be locked in a separate cell.[25] Martial law still had not been declared, but there had been a noticeable change in attitude, in the level of tolerance for acts of violence. Carlos Hurd gave full credit to Tripp. "The temper of the men in the street showed a change after the first encounter with Tripp methods. It began to seem the situation had found its master." At this point, seemingly after he had turned over full authority to Clayton, Tripp also acted aggressively and bravely to stop the riot.

The death and destruction were not ended, and some fires burned through the night, but almost all of the killing was over. Around eight P.M., Hurd wrote, "One negro ran the gauntlet on Broadway. Several shots were fired at him, in a reckless fashion that explains the number injured by stray bullets earlier in the day. But it appeared that he got away." Shortly afterward, Hurd began walking west on Broadway toward the streetcar stop. City officials had stopped the cars from bringing passengers into East St. Louis at seven P.M., but a few cars were continuing to take passengers across the Eads Bridge to St. Louis. An ambulance pulled into Fourth Street just ahead of him to pick up the bodies of three black men. They had been lying in the street for almost an hour.

Downtown was quieter now, with small groups of men standing around. And though the large mobs had been broken up by military action, shots could still be heard to the south and west, and fires still burned all around. Hurd watched the attendants lift one of the dead bodies in the ambulance— now also a hearse—and then climbed onto the waiting streetcar. A man who came aboard a few minutes later, just before the car began lurching to the east, said that a small posse of armed white men in the street had prevented the removal of one of the bodies. The men said that the black man was not dead. They said he must lie there until he was. The ambulance left with only two bodies aboard, the man told Hurd.

"I did not verify this, and I do not state it as a fact," Hurd carefully noted in the harrowing story he wrote when he returned to the office. "Everything which I have stated as a fact came under my own observation. And what I saw was, as I have said, but a small part of the whole."[26]

As Hurd was returning to the *Post-Dispatch*, rioters torched a small, two-story frame building across the street from the main public library at Eighth and Broadway. It held a café and a hairdressing salon patronized by blacks. G. E. Popkess, who was standing in the shelter of the library, watched as a black woman and a small child who appeared to be about four years old ran screaming from the building. They had not gotten ten feet from the front door when a gang of about two dozen whites swarmed over them and beat them both until they lay still on the ground.

Two white men picked up the tiny child by his arms and legs and hurled him back into the building, the small body arcing through the doorway and into the flames to the cheers of the rest of the gang. One black man and then another tried to run from the blaze. Both were shot instantly—by a squad of militiamen, Popkess would later testify under oath—and fell back into the flames. The badly burned bodies of the men who were shot were found the next day in the rubble of the building but not the body of the child, and Popkess concluded that his remains were consumed by the fire. The child was not part of the official body count.[27]

Dr. Lyman Bluitt had been working nonstop in the emergency room at St. Mary's hospital for ten hours. Finally, woozy from fatigue, he forced himself to take a breather. He stretched his muscles and walked to a window and looked out. Half a block away, at Seventh Street and Missouri Avenue, a row of flats was on fire. As he watched, the roofs began to collapse and black men, women, and children ran out onto Missouri Avenue. A gang of white men, women, and, Bluitt could swear, children threw rocks and sticks at them, as if to drive them back into the murderous flames. Bluitt heard gunfire. The whites scattered, and the blacks ran away from the blazing buildings. Bluitt didn't see anyone fall to the ground. It appeared that all had escaped.

Wearily, Bluitt returned to the emergency room and went back to work. Electric power had been lost during the day, and he worked through the night by the illumination of flashlights and candles. By the morning, he had treated seventy men and women, mostly blacks.[28]

Downtown, at the National Guard command post near the police station, someone ran up and breathlessly passed on one of the persistent rumors that continually misled and misdirected soldiers. About two hundred armed blacks were massing a few blocks away, at the old city park at Sixth and Bond, a predominantly black area. Colonel Clayton sent a major and a company of soldiers down that way. They found two black men with guns. They took them into custody.

Shortly after that, another alarming report came in. Another large mob—this time of whites—was forming at Third and Missouri, just a block away. Company F of the Illinois National Guard was just reporting for duty, bringing the total of men available to Colonel Clayton to a little over three hundred, some of them by then from as far away as Chicago. Before the grocery clerks and farm boys had a chance to take off their packs and bed rolls, they were ordered to trot double time to the scene. They broke up a gathering of perhaps two dozen whites, a much smaller crowd than had been reported, and told the men to go home. By that point, probably because of decisive action by the National Guard after many hours of ineffectiveness, rioters no longer massed in heavily armed groups of many hundreds. But small groups of whites continued to attack blacks and to set fires in the South End well into the night.[29]

In the city room of the *St. Louis Post-Dispatch*, Carlos Hurd finished writing his story at about one thirty A.M., several hours before his early morning deadline for the first edition of the paper, which would hit the streets in the late morning. The final paragraphs read:

> I must add a word about the efficiency of the East St. Louis police. One of them kept me from going too near the fire. Absolutely the only thing that I saw policemen do was to keep the fire line. As the police detail marched to the fire, two of the men turned aside into Fourth Street, apparently to see if two negroes lying on the pavement within a few stops of Broadway were dead. These policemen got a sharp call into line from their sergeant. They were not supposed to bother themselves about dead negroes.
>
> In recording this, I do not forget that a policeman—by all accounts, a fine and estimable policeman—was killed by negroes the night before. I have not forgotten it in writing about the acts of the men in the street. Whether this crime excuses or palliates a massacre, which probably included none of the offenders, is something I will leave to apologists for last evening's occurrence, if there are any such, to explain.

The story was more than three thousand words long, exceptional for daily news reportage at any newspaper. O. K. Bovard, the tough but soft-spoken managing editor of the *Post-Dispatch*, so stressed brevity in news stories that he had a printed motto hanging on the walls of the city room: TERSENESS. ACCURACY. TERSENESS. But he trusted and respected Hurd. Bovard's first important act after becoming a top editor at the paper in 1900 had been to hire the reporter away from the *St. Louis Star*. Given the importance of the terrible events on the other side of the river, he let Hurd write the story the way he wanted to, even giving him permission to put his account in the first person, which Bovard normally would have considered a great sin against journalistic standards of integrity and objectivity. "Reporters are not news" was a byword at Bovard's paper. But putting the story in the first person helped humanize the account, and endowed it with a deep and palpable sense of righteous rage at the almost unbelievable acts of senseless cruelty and injustice men are capable of.[30]

The headline read:

POST-DISPATCH MAN, AN EYEWITNESS, DESCRIBES

MASSACRE OF NEGROES

Carlos Hurd, before he left the office, also would have written the bird line—a short phrase or quip accompanying the drawing of the *Post-Dispatch* mascot, the Weatherbird. Half bird, half man, dressed like a dandy and always in the latest fashions, the pop-eyed bird was drawn anew every day by staff artist Carlisle Martin to reflect the main news of the day. The bird and his comment on the news accompanied the front-page weather forecast. Hurd had a poetic touch, and almost always it was he who wrote the bird lines, and earned a dollar for each one, enough to buy a round or two for his colleagues at one of the newspaper bars nearby.

When Hurd was finished, since his wife was out of town on vacation, he went to the Maryland Hotel near the paper and collapsed into bed. He slept deeply for five hours, and then his eyes popped open. It was a little after seven. There was no chance he would be able to go back to sleep.[31]

On the front page of the July 3 *St. Louis Post-Dispatch*, a grim Weatherbird in a seasonally appropriate polka dot shirt frowned beneath the prediction that the weather was going to be partly cloudy and warm for the Fourth of July. Carlisle Martin's Weatherbird looked simultaneously enraged and deeply sad. In the set of the Weatherbird's jaw and the sternness of his visage, he called to mind photographs of the sixteenth president of the United States in moments of angry despair over a war he hated but that he had thrown the nation's young men into, a war over America's treatment of blacks. The Weatherbird was perched next to Hurd's extraordinary three-thousand-word moral diatribe, and Hurd's bird line read:

AND LINCOLN CAME FROM ILLINOIS

Legacy of a Massacre

Adjutant General Frank S. Dickson, the veteran commander of the Illinois National Guard, reached East St. Louis shortly after midnight on July 3. In full uniform, he went straight to city hall through crowds milling around almost aimlessly. He heard occasional shouts, but no shots, and the crowds, he was told, were much smaller than they had been at the height of the riot. There was a sense of lassitude, even of exhaustion, among those who remained. But Dickson, who had commanded troops in riots before, knew the violence could erupt again, particularly if control of the streets was not clamped down by uniformed men carrying guns, men who were willing—reluctant but willing—to shoot rioters.

At city hall, after threading his way down corridors packed with hundreds of black refugees lying exhausted on the floor or lined up for one of the few toilets in the building, Dickson discovered that Mayor Mollman had gone home to bed. He strode into the mayor's empty office, picked up the telephone, and called him. When Mollman had cleared the sleep from his voice, he told the general, with great relief, "I'm very glad you are here. Take charge of the situation and restore order in East St. Louis." The mayor said he would "be down in the morning," hung up, and went back to bed.[1]

Dickson took a quick automobile tour of the devastated riot area. Fires still smoldered in the remains of gutted buildings across fifteen or twenty square blocks of downtown East St. Louis. Bodies lay in ditches and deep gutters and shadowed alleys, in the high weeds of vacant lots, and in the stagnant water of Cahokia Creek. And the smell of rotting and burned flesh was

Adjutant General Frank S. Dickson

unmistakable in the acrid smoke that still hung stubbornly over the bottom-lands of East St. Louis.

The general found it worrisome that the fires and mayhem had been spread over such a wide area, an area that was almost impossible to patrol effectively with a few hundred troops. At that point, he had about seventeen officers and two hundred seventy men under his command. However, troops were arriving at the East St. Louis railroad station every hour or two. By sunup, which officially came at four forty A.M., his troops would number about five hundred, although most of them were green as new hay.[2]

Dozens of somewhat more experienced soldiers, federalized members of the Illinois National Guard who had come in response to the May riot, were still camped just outside of town, on a field near the slaughterhouse village of National City, with vague orders to "protect assets vital to national security in a time of war." They had never joined the main body of militia under the command of Tripp, Clayton, and now Dickson. Instead, they continued to guard bridges and keep rioters away from industrial plants. Declaring martial law might have brought them into the fold, but Governor Frank Lowden could never quite bring himself to do that, in part perhaps because the two men supposedly in charge at the height of the riot—the mayor and Colonel Tripp—had so vehemently disagreed on whether it was necessary. Dickson, however, inspired confidence that he could control the situation without martial law.

A former Illinois congressman, Dickson had been a professional soldier for twenty-one years, fighting in the Spanish American War as an enlisted man and working his way up to the top ranks. Dickson had been in command in the brutal riot a few years earlier in his hometown of Springfield, Illinois, and in two smaller flare-ups in the deeply Southern river town of Cairo at the tip of Illinois. Unfortunately, when the riot broke out in East St. Louis, he had been on a train returning to Springfield from official business in Washington.

"In all riot situations, there are one or more particular danger points," Dickson would explain later. "In order to handle more effectively a mob situation, your troops should be unified as much as possible." Soldiers should never be scattered throughout a riot area, he said, but should be concentrated at a few trouble spots. And if there was a shortage of troops, sometimes the best thing was to keep them all together and attack the riot at its core.

"In my experience," Dickson said, "in almost all activities the difficulty is with officers and not with individual men." The average soldier, he believed, would carry out his orders "if he has clearly in his mind exactly what the instructions are. Much of the haziness comes from haziness on the part of the officers."

After tours of East St. Louis, Dickson met at city hall with top subordinates and went over a detailed map of downtown. He showed the officers where he wanted troops to be concentrated, and told them to begin by forming a "flying squad" of a dozen or so trusted men to go immediately up to Broadway and Collinsville and disperse the crowds Dickson had seen there. The general ordered that the remainder of the troops be broken up into five or six groups, and sent to other points where people were congregated and fires still burned.

"No one man starts a riot," Dickson stressed. "It is only when two or three or four get together that things begin . . . to snowball." Soldiers were to be ordered to keep their rifles loaded and their bayonets bared.

As the light of the rising sun came dimly through the lingering smoke and the haze of morning, black policeman Otto Nelson and his wife cautiously rose from their hiding place in the tall weeds near Broadway. Well over two hundred buildings—homes, stores, cafés, barber shops, schools—had been destroyed. Most of them were in black neighborhoods downtown and in the South End, but rioters also attacked and looted areas where many whites lived. The Nelsons' old tenement flat was smoldering rubble now. They stretched aching muscles and brushed themselves off and looked around at a scene that, for several blocks in several directions, looked like the aftermath of house-to-house fighting in the Great War. The Nelsons didn't see any white people around, and no soldiers, and so they began walking slowly to the east, away from downtown East St. Louis. They hoped to pick up a ride a few blocks along at the home of a friend with an automobile, but when they got there the car was gone, and so was the house. Soon they found themselves part of a stream of black refugees leaving East St. Louis. The Nelsons walked nine miles that day and did not return to East St. Louis for two weeks.[3]

The last lethal outburst of the East St. Louis riot took place in broad daylight on the morning of July 3 in a rough and remote part of town that had once been part of Bloody Island and was still called the Island.

Black workmen from a railroad freight house near the Mississippi levee regularly gathered in the rear of a saloon to drink beer for breakfast. About seven thirty on the morning of July 3, several men were gathered in the usual spot. They felt safe, half a mile or more from the fringes of the riot, which seemed in any event to be over. They were boisterous, as usual. Someone reported to police that blacks were creating a disturbance in the area, and that the saloon was open contrary to the mayor's order of the previous day. Three policemen went down to check the report out, two patrolmen and a sergeant named Cornelius Meehan. They were accompanied by seven or eight national guardsmen. When the black men saw the approaching soldiers and police they jumped up from their stools and wooden boxes and started to run away. Meehan, according to two of the soldiers, ordered the soldiers to fire.

The soldiers fired, killing one of the workmen, wounding another, and blowing off at the elbow the right arm of a black girl named Mineola Magee who was just emerging from an outhouse. A black porter heard the shots, ran inside the saloon, and tried to hide in the walk-in icebox, but a soldier tracked him down, dragged him out, and beat him badly.

Paul Y. Anderson remarked of the killing of the unarmed workman, who was shot in the back, "It was entirely murder." Meehan, who was later indicted for murder, denied that he had given any orders at all.[4]

Most city police, including several black policemen, reported to duty at their usual times on Monday, July 3. Two teams of detectives—one white, one black—were sent on to the area of Tenth and Bond, where Coppedge and Wodley had been shot fatally, to look for evidence and talk to potential witnesses. The white policemen, who had been told to look for evidence while the black policemen interviewed black residents, found several used shotgun shells mingled with a considerable amount of trash in the gutter. The waxed paper shells were slit by a sharp blade—apparently altered to deliver a more deadly blow.

Meanwhile, a black policeman, John Eubanks, discovered that no blacks remained near Tenth and Bond. Walking farther afield, he finally found a man willing to talk if his name was never revealed. Eubanks promised to keep his identity secret, and subsequently refused to reveal the name or the race of his informant, even under oath.

To the policeman's surprise and sad dismay, the informant told Eubanks that a young man named Nathaniel Peebles had been in the crowd of shooters on July 2. Eubanks had known Nathaniel Peebles "since he was a boy in knee pants," he said later, and had never known him to make trouble. Eubanks and another black policeman went to the young man's house and searched it. They found a shotgun and a half-empty box of shells. The shells were identical in make and gauge to the shells found at Tenth and Bond, and the sides had been slit to deliver a more deadly blow. Eubanks arrested Peebles. Investigations by Eubanks and other black policemen led to the arrest of several other young black men, including George Roberts, whom Eubanks had also known for most of the boy's life. "I never knew him to commit a crime of any kind before," Eubanks said later. "That boy worked continuously. I never knew him to loaf a week in years." Neither Peebles nor Roberts had criminal records. Eventually twenty-one blacks were indicted for murder in the deaths of the policemen, many of them young men with no criminal records. Some of the indictments were later dropped.[5]

Eubanks also looked into the charge that blacks had rallied to the ringing of a church bell. The dearth of willing black witnesses, Eubanks said, made it difficult for him to say for sure whether or not a church bell had rung shortly before the police were shot. His impression, however, was that a bell rang at a church in the South End to signal the end to Sunday evening services, not as a rallying call. But he also conceded that blacks believed so strongly that an invasion by an armed white mob was imminent that the bell could have served as an alert whether it was intended that way or not.

When asked his opinion on why a mob of blacks with guns were standing at Tenth and Bond around midnight, Eubanks said, "Well, my opinion is that they got together for the purpose of protecting their neighborhood."[6]

City police also arrested and jailed several black leaders on riot charges, although the man who was widely accused of being the leader of the blacks who had shot Coppedge and Wodley, Leroy Bundy, was nowhere to be found. Among those arrested (although he was later released) was Dr. Lyman Bluitt, who, along with Bundy, repeatedly had warned city officials that the wave of attacks on blacks could well lead to racial violence, and who had worked through the night of the riot at St. Mary's hospital to save the lives of both whites and blacks. According to the *East St. Louis Daily Journal*, federal agents were questioning black leaders like Bluitt about suspicions that the "uprising" by blacks had been part of "a well-organized plot" by German agents, working with a "clique" of the radical Industrial Workers of the World, "to bring about a revolution . . . which would materially affect East St. Louis industries manufacturing war supplies." In fact, the Justice Department's Bureau of Investigation—later known as the FBI—did look into suspicions that enemy agents or nationally organized political radicals had played a role in the riot, and found no evidence to support the allegations.[7]

The death of Wodley, who never regained consciousness, would bring the toll of the dead to at least forty-eight, including thirty-nine black men, women, and children. But that figure was widely considered to be absurdly low. There had been many reports of blacks being chased onto the Free Bridge and forced over the side into the swift and deep and muddy waters of the Mississippi. There were also reports of black corpses being thrown off the bridge. No bodies were recovered from the river, which means little. Not just drowning victims and suicides but horses, steamships, automobiles, and, in modern times, even helicopters and their occupants have been known to disappear after plunging into the treacherous Mississippi at St. Louis.[8]

Because thousands of blacks had arrived in the city in the past three years, many of them undocumented, and thousands had fled during the riot, many of them never to return, it would have been virtually impossible to determine who was missing and presumed dead. The NAACP and the *Chicago Defender*, both of which had investigators on the scene interviewing survivors shortly after the riot, estimated the death toll at between one and two hundred. Reporters for the black weekly, the *St. Louis Argus*, and several reporters for white dailies agreed that the death toll exceeded one hundred. The St. Clair County grand jury that would later convene would set the death toll at close to one hundred.[9]

On the morning of July 3, as John Eubanks was rounding up and arresting the sons of his friends and neighbors, the smoldering riot would, from time to time, burst again into flame. Reverend George Allison had been called to city hall to help with the roughly twelve hundred refugees camped in and around it, and occasionally he heard reports of another attack on blacks, or another building torched. "They were burning property as late as three o'clock in the afternoon of the Third," he said later.[10]

The Red Cross was trying to help the displaced blacks, providing emergency food and medicine and taking as many as practicable to larger emergency centers across the river in St. Louis. Husbands were separated from wives and mothers from children and didn't know whether they were dead or alive. Allison kept track of some of these cases of missing relatives, and decided a few weeks after the riot that the death toll was one hundred at the absolute lowest, and could have been as high as three hundred. After many tours of the riot areas, he decided that many black bodies, particularly those of small children who were still missing, simply had been cremated. Allison bemoaned the fact that there had been no systematic checking of missing people with police reports from other cities and states. (After some study, the state fire marshal remained unconvinced that any bodies, no matter how tiny, had completely gone up in smoke.)[11]

On July 3, the East St. Louis chamber of commerce met and formed, basically from its own membership, the Committee of One Hundred to help the city recover from the riot. There were only two members from labor groups, and no blacks. There were, however, plenty of men with close ties to the Aluminum Ore Company and to Swift and Armour, as well as to railroads that later admitted luring blacks North with false promises. There were many with ties to the thoroughly corrupt bipartisan political machine and its farcical legal system as well. The membership of the group included lawyers who would represent accused killers and policemen in trials growing out of the riots.[12]

Early that afternoon, in response to prodding from an editor, reporter Roy Albertson of the *St. Louis Republic* drove out to Tenth and Market, near where the two policemen had been shot fatally, and asked about numerous reports of carloads of white men joyriding through the neighborhood shooting into homes. Albertson called his editor and told him he had checked out the rumor, which had been reported in other papers, and it was untrue. No one he talked to said they had heard or seen anything like that. It was later revealed that he had only interviewed white people.[13]

Three hundred miles to the north of East St. Louis, the Chicago morning papers on July 3 were full of news about the riot. The Negro Fellowship League met in a packed library on State Street at nine thirty A.M. and passed a resolution condemning the rioters and calling for a biracial conference to try and breach the terrible gulf that had opened up between the races. At the end of the meeting, Ida B. Wells-Barnett, who had presided, said the participants could sing "America" or "The Star Spangled Banner" if they wished. No one sang a note. A total of $8.65 was collected to send Wells-Barnett to East St. Louis as an investigator. She left the next day.[14]

On the afternoon of July 3, Governor Frank Lowden arrived in East St. Louis and toured the city. The next day, he said, "I have been weighted down since I visited those hospitals last night, since I saw those charred ruins of homes, since I saw the havoc this riot wrought . . . A stain rests upon Illinois— a stain that will remain . . . We in the North have been in the habit of frequently criticizing our Southern friends for their treatment of the Negro . . . I tell you that I know of no outrages that have been perpetrated in the South that surpass the conditions I found in East St. Louis, in our beloved state."[15]

More than one thousand troops were in place by the evening of July 3, enough to insure that rioters and arsonists were dealt with swiftly and decisively, and, except for very minor incidents, the riot was over. A stunned peace came over the city, and for the next week or so there was very little crime.

On the evening of July 4, Ida B. Wells-Barnett took an overnight train from Chicago to East St. Louis. She arrived early the next morning and quickly was in the streets, despite a warning by a black conductor in her Pullman car that she might be killed. A short, matronly looking woman in her mid-fifties with four children, Wells-Barnett was a fearless veteran of the fight for federal antilynching legislation who had documented the murder of blacks in some of the most virulently racist regions of the South. Refusing to be intimidated because of her gender or race, she had withdrawn in anger from the NAACP after it became clear that she and other outspoken blacks were considered too radical for leadership positions by the white men and women who dominated the organization in its early years.

In the three-block walk up Missouri Avenue from the rail station to city hall through what was once a lively black urban neighborhood and now was a burnt-out wasteland, she did not see a single black person. She asked a young white soldier standing on a corner how things were. "Bad," he replied. What, she asked, was the trouble? "The Negroes won't let the whites alone," he said bitterly. "They killed seven yesterday and three already this morning."

Wells-Barnett met dozens of black female refugees at city hall, and helped them with their few belongings as the Red Cross and other relief agencies carried them across the river in St. Louis, where thousands of black men, women, and children stood and sat and lay in and around the Municipal Lodging House, where food and medical treatment were available.[16] Many of the stories she heard were devastatingly similar. The victims were ordinary black housewives and mothers whose husbands had low-paying jobs, or were looking for work. Many of the women took in laundry or worked as maids. Wives and children had been separated from their husbands on July 2, and they had survived by hiding in basements and garages and sheds and open fields, sometimes—but rarely—helped by white neighbors. Most of them had scrimped for years to be able to afford such necessities as a bedstead or a dining room table, and now everything was gone.

"Every which way we turned there were women and children and men, dazed over the thing that had come to them and unable to tell what it was all about," Wells-Barnett wrote later. "They lined the streets or were standing out on the grassy banks of the lawns that surrounded the city hall or stood in groups discussing their experiences . . . these people who had suddenly been robbed of everything except what they stood in."[17]

At the end of a long, exhausting, and embittering day going back and forth between the two cities, Wells-Barnett discovered there was no place in East St. Louis for her to stay. She picked up her suitcase and took a streetcar to St. Louis, where, despite her protests, she was swept up in a group of East St. Louis blacks who were taken in a police wagon to the Municipal Lodging House for mandatory vaccination against smallpox. A teacher from Chicago who was working as a volunteer at the vaccination center recognized her, believed her when she said she had already been vaccinated for smallpox in considerably more sanitary conditions, and helped her get out of the lodging house and to a home in a black neighborhood where she could spend the night.

In her riot report, Wells-Barnett quoted extensively from Carlos Hurd's first-person account of the hanging in the middle of downtown to illustrate the horror of the events of July 2. She returned to Chicago on July 8, and she and a number of black and liberal leaders in that city and across the country joined in a plea to the president of the United States to initiate a federal investigation of the riot in East St. Louis. The White House and the office of the attorney general were inundated with telegrams and letters calling for a federal investigation and federal action, at long last, on antilynching legislation.

The East St. Louis race riot also triggered a national debate about race and the labor movement after it came up on July 6 at Carnegie Hall, where former president Theodore Roosevelt got into a ferocious argument with Samuel Gompers, the head of the American Federation of Labor. The occasion was an official greeting of a delegation from the revolutionary Provisional Government of Russia.

"Before we speak of justice for others," said Roosevelt, "it behooves us to do justice within our own household. Within a week there has been an

Samuel Gompers

appalling outbreak of savagery in a race riot at East St. Louis, a race riot for which, as far as we can see, there was no real provocation." Gompers reacted to Roosevelt's remarks by insisting that there had been plenty of provocation. He blamed the violence on "reactionary" employers who had imported black strikebreakers from the South. "The luring of these colored men to East St. Louis is on a par with the behavior of the brutal, reactionary and tyrannous forces that existed in Old Russia," he declared.

Roosevelt stirred restlessly in his chair as Gompers spoke, and when the labor leader was through the former president jumped up and shook his fist in Gompers's face and condemned him for trying to justify the riot. He thundered, "I am not willing that a meeting called to commemorate the birth of democracy in Russia shall even seem to have expressed or to have accepted apologies for the brutal infamies imposed on colored people."

Much of the large crowd, which had initially cheered the popular ex-president, booed and hissed as his fist came so close to Gompers that it appeared to many that he had punched him in the mouth. But then another part of the audience began cheering, and the call and response of boos and cheers went back and forth as if the event was a college football game.

The *New York Times*, in a long, page-one story, noted, "It was not a mere quarrel between Roosevelt and Gompers, it was a division in the crowd— a crowd gathered together from all the friends of new Russia—Socialists and workmen who saw chiefly the economic provocation of the riot, and members of other classes who had more feeling of the horror."[18]

Several miles north of Carnegie Hall, at the Metropolitan Baptist Church in Harlem, Hubert H. Harrison, who just the month before had broken with the Socialist Party to found the militant Liberty League of Negro Americans, called for blacks to arm themselves for protection in the wake of the East St. Louis riots. To repeated applause and cheers from a black audience of about one thousand, Harrison declared that the time had come to stop violence with violence.

"They are saying a great deal about democracy in Washington now," he proclaimed, "but while they are talking about fighting for freedom and the Stars and Stripes, here at home the whites apply the torch to the black men's homes, and their bullets, clubs and stones to their bodies . . . We intend to fight, if fight we must, for the things dearest to us, for our hearths and homes. Certainly, I would encourage the Negroes in the South or in East St. Louis or anywhere else who do not enjoy the protection of the law to arm for their own defense, to hide those arms, and to learn how to use them."[19]

Closer to home, the *Chicago Tribune* looked to the atrocity in southern Illinois and judged that "the blood of victims spatters the state." And the *St. Louis Globe-Democrat*, in a raging editorial headlined THE SHAME OF ILLINOIS, called the East St. Louis riots "a disgrace to that city, a disgrace to Illinois, a disgrace to America [and] a disgrace to humanity . . . The often condemned mobs of the South have always had as their purpose the quick and effective punishment of crime . . . composed of determined men who thought that the law was too slow and too uncertain . . . Such acts are in violation of fundamental principles of orderly government and as such should not be tolerated, but in comparison with the unspeakable outrages in East St. Louis, they are righteousness itself."[20]

In the South, many politicians and newspapers were less judicious in comparing the East St. Louis rioters unfavorably to lynch mobs. And they saw one lesson above all others. It was time for blacks to come home to the Land of Cotton, where white people knew how to treat blacks. Some Southerners seemed barely able to restrain themselves from gloating as they proclaimed that the riot proved that keeping the races separate was the only way to avert racial warfare. Some even strongly suggested that an occasional lynching helped keep unruly blacks in line. In Georgia, a state representative introduced a resolution sarcastically bowing to the "superior judgment" of Illinois in its dealings with blacks, but "earnestly recommended that they do select their victims one at a time and be sure of their guilt before they act."[21]

Somewhat more elegantly, the *Atlanta Constitution* editorialized:

> Others may disconcert the negro by painting before his eyes a roseate picture of broadened rights and racial equality to be enjoyed in the North, but in the South a negro never yet was killed simply because he wanted to work and earn a living for himself and family by honest toil! And it looks as though, by employing their own methods, those rapid solvers of the negro question in Lincoln's state have set for themselves a more perplexing race problem than the South ever thought of. Before they get through with it, it is probable that they will become convinced that our way is the best way of all.

As to those colored folk who have escaped with their lives, they had better come back home, where they were well off. And those who have not gone North can thank their lucky stars that they have stuck in the South, where every man is safeguarded in the right to work—and to live in peace and security if he works and leads the life of a decent respectable citizen.

The *Constitution* did not touch on the facts that lynch law still ruled the South and that only the most menial and low-paying jobs in the region were open to blacks.[22]

Among those calling for a federal investigation, despite a history of allegiance to "states rights," was the notorious racist Senator Benjamin R. Tillman of South Carolina, who gloated on the floor of the Senate that the East St. Louis riots had demonstrated the truth of his tireless contention that the North was not all that different from the South in its hatred of blacks. And more riots could be expected, he said, as long as the doomed policy of granting legal equality to inferior blacks continued. "The average Yankee," he said, "has no love of the negro, except for political reasons . . . The North is now beginning to understand the South, and to understand the race problem . . . The more the northern people know of the negro, the less they like him. I have epitomized it by saying 'they love him according to the square of the distance.' The further off he is, the better they like him."

When resentment at losing jobs to "foreign-born competition" was added to the hatred of blacks, he said, "The white blood, once aroused, grows savage and very cruel." The black man, he contended, "must remain subordinate or be exterminated."[23]

"Pitchfork Ben" Tillman, now ill and feeble in his seventieth year but still simmering with demagogic passion, had made his political reputation as a young man during Reconstruction in the so-called Hamburg Riots. He led a white supremacist paramilitary group that wore cavalry sabers for show but also carried guns. They shot and killed six black militiamen who were deemed to be flaunting their freedom by parading through a small South Carolina town.

Social worker Roger Baldwin, who earlier that year had moved from St. Louis to New York and founded the organization that became the American Civil

Liberties Union, had spent the past five years as secretary of the St. Louis
Civic League, a reform agency that worked with the NAACP to fight segregation and racism. Baldwin knew East St. Louis far too well, and, although he
did not deny the effect of "uncontrolled race prejudice in a labor struggle," he
had no doubt where to lay the major share of blame for the riot. In the national social work journal the *Survey*, he wrote:

> East St. Louis is probably the most finished example of corporation-
> owned city government in the United States . . . East St. Louis's fail-
> ure to control the recent outbreak of race violence is only her
> long-standing failure to control every form of violence and law-
> lessness. It is due directly to the exploitation of the East St. Louis
> city government by selfish business interests . . . All that the busi-
> ness interests need is a city government that will give them the priv-
> ileges they want, and then let them alone. The politicians and the
> underworld can have the rest.[24]

A number of black writers and artists were moved by the East St. Louis
riot. Outraged and saddened by reports of the black child being thrown into
a burning building, Lola Ridge, a Harlem poet, wrote a bitterly ironic poem
called "Lullabye" that concluded:

> *Rock-a-by baby—higher an' higher!*
> *Mammy is sleeping and daddy's run lame.*
> *(Soun' may you sleep in yo' cradle o' fire!)*
> *Rock-a-by baby, hushed in the flame.*[25]

In East St. Louis, a jittery peace prevailed despite persistent rumors that mobs
of blacks were on their way from Brooklyn, Illinois, or Chicago or somewhere to exact revenge. On the evening of the Fourth of July, a motorcyclist
in police uniform rode like Paul Revere through some white neighborhoods,
warning of an imminent black invasion, and some residents prepared to flee.
But word of the false alarm reached the National Guard headquarters downtown and General Dickson immediately sent soldiers to protect and calm the

neighborhoods. No attack came—indeed, at that point very few black faces were visible in most of East St. Louis.[26]

The emptiness and devastation of once-lively black neighborhoods was overwhelming to visitors like Oscar Leonard, head of a St. Louis Jewish charity, who called the riot "the East St. Louis Pogrom" and observed, "It was a distressing sight to see block after block where peaceful homes had been located burned to the ground. The innocent suffered with the guilty. Thrifty black folk, who were doing their bit by raising vegetables, were murdered. I saw the ruins of their homes, into which had gone the labor and savings of years. The little thrift gardens had escaped the flames and orderly rows where seeds had been planted gave the plots the appearance of miniature graveyards."[27]

As the days passed and a few blacks returned to jobs in downtown East St. Louis, meat cutter Earl Jimmerson began to worry about the young black porter he had warned to leave town at the Illmo Hotel the morning of July 2. The man he knew only as "Herb" had disappeared that morning and had not reappeared. Then, one day in mid-July, Herb was back, working his usual spot in the lobby of the hotel. Jimmerson asked if he and his family were okay. Herb smiled and nodded and thanked Jimmerson, but would not tell him where they had been during the massacre.[28]

St. Clair County state's attorney Hubert Schaumleffel, a political crony of Mollman, announced that indictments of rioters would be difficult to get out of a grand jury. For one thing, he suggested, most people likely to be on the grand jury—"respectable white men" was the implication—thought the riots, despite the terrible toll in life and property, were not necessarily a bad thing. Besides, he didn't have any witnesses, at least none who would name names. Some East St. Louisans complained about Schaumleffel's attitude to Governor Frank Lowden, and Lowden dispatched assistant attorney general C. W. Middlekauf to prosecute the important cases. "Think of it," Middlekauf told the East St. Louis chamber of commerce. "The greatest crime in the history of the state and the state's attorney told me he had no witnesses a week after the riot." Middlekauf took charge of the grand jury investigation. Ten investigators were dispatched from around the state to interview witnesses.[29]

On July 8, W. E. B. Du Bois took the train from New York to East St. Louis along with social worker Martha Gruening to investigate the riot on behalf of the NAACP. They assembled a staff of more than two dozen investigators, both paid and volunteer, setting up offices at the St. Louis headquarters of the black Knights of Pythias, a fraternal lodge.[30] Initially, Du Bois and Gruening interviewed Mayor Mollman and other civic and business leaders, and grew increasingly infuriated as the white men affixed much of the blame to a few black agitators like Dr. Leroy Bundy. Thenceforth, they concentrated most of their efforts on interviewing ordinary witnesses, black and white. They stayed for about a week. Aflame with anger after hearing dozens of tales of horrible abuse and murder, Du Bois began writing about the riot as soon as the train had pulled out of East St. Louis. The words continued to spill out of him during the trip to New York, and long afterward:

> Yesterday I rode in East St. Louis. It is the kind of place one quickly recognizes—tireless, with no restful green of verdure; hard and uneven of street; crude, cold, and even hateful of aspect; conventional of course in its business quarter, but quickly beyond one sees the ruts and hollows, the stench of ill-tamed sewerage, unguarded railroad crossings, saloons outnumbering churches and churches catering to saloons; homes impudently strait and new, prostitutes free and happy, gangsters in paradise, the town 'wide open,' shameless and frank; great factories pouring out stench, filth and flame . . . I rode in this city past flame-swept walls and over gray ashes; in streets almost wet with blood and beside ruins, where the bones of dead men new bleached peered out at me in sullen wonder.
>
> Across the river, [St. Louis] is larger and older and the forces of evil have had some curbing from those who have seen the vision and panted for love; but eastward from St. Louis there is a land of no taxes for great industries; there is a land where you may buy grafting politicians at far less rate than you would pay for franchises or privileges in a modern town . . . always there was theft and rumors of theft until St. Clair county was a hissing in good men's ears.[31]

In a passionate and painfully detailed report of more than eight thousand words in the September issue of the *Crisis*—accompanied with photographs, the coverage spread over twenty-four pages—Du Bois blamed the riot

on the labor unions as well as the capitalists and the crooked politicians who
served them. He quoted extensively from Carlos Hurd's first-person account
in the *Post-Dispatch*. Estimating the death toll at "between one and two hundred human beings who were black," including a dozen or more men,
women, and children who had sought shelter in the basement of an old opera
house that was subsequently destroyed by fire, Du Bois recounted the results
of his team's interviews with dozens of survivors:

> One dares not dwell too long on these horrors. . . . Mrs. Luella
> Cox (white) of the Volunteers of America . . . had gone over to
> East St. Louis on that memorable day and . . . saw a Negro be-
> headed with a butcher's knife by someone in a crowd standing
> near the Free Bridge. The crowd had to have its jest. So its mem-
> bers laughingly threw the head over one side of the bridge and the
> body over the other.
>
>   A trolley car came along. The crowd forced its inmates to put
> their hands out the window. Colored people thus recognized were
> hauled out of the car to be beaten, trampled on, shot. A little 12-
> year-old colored girl fainted—her mother knelt beside her. The
> crowd surged in on her. When its ranks opened up again Mrs.
> Cox saw the mother prostrate with a hole as large as one's fist in
> her head.

He told the stories of more than two dozen blacks who ran for their lives
or hid in coal sheds or cellars or under beds as their homes were looted and
burned, and men, women, and children were beaten and killed all around
them. He quoted at length a twenty-six-year-old black woman named Beatrice
Deshong, who recounted in matter-of-fact language the most horrible sights:

> I saw the mob robbing the homes of Negroes and then set fire to
> them. The soldier stood with folded arms and looked on as the
> houses burned. I saw a Negro man killed instantly by a member
> of the mob, men, small boys, and women and little girls all were
> trying to do something to injure the Negroes . . . The police and
> the soldiers were assisting the mob to kill Negroes and to destroy
> their homes. I saw the mob hang a colored man to a telegraph

pole and riddle him with bullets. I saw the mob chasing a colored man who had a baby in his arms. The mob was shooting at him all of the time as long as I saw him. I ran for my life. I was nearly exhausted when a white man in the block opened the door of his warehouse and told me to go in there and hide. I went in and stayed there the night. The mob bombarded the house during the night, but I was not discovered nor hurt. The mob stole the jewelry of Negroes and used axes and hatchets to chop up pianos and furniture that belonged to them. The mob was seemingly well arranged to do their desperate work. I recognized some of the wealthy people's sons and some of the bank officials in the mob. They were as vile as they could be.

Martha Gruening talked to white soldiers who admitted they disarmed blacks of guns, knives, and razors while not bothering whites armed with rifles, pistols, knives, and clubs. "Miss Gruening," Du Bois wrote, "wanted to know if they hadn't disarmed any whites at all."

"They were doubtful. Yes, one remembered he had disarmed a drunken white man who was attacking a white woman."

Near the end of her interviews, Martha Gruening came upon a frail, elderly black woman picking through the burned ruins of what had been her house, looking futilely for anything worth saving. "What are we to do?" the old woman asked. "We can't live South, and they don't want us North. Where are we to go?"

Du Bois ended the report with the words, "And what of the Federal Government?" The question was purely rhetorical. After East St. Louis, the forty-nine-year-old Du Bois had little if any faith remaining in the white institutions of the United States of America, official or unofficial.[32]

A few months later, still obsessed with what he had seen and heard in East St. Louis, Du Bois wrote in the *Crisis* an essay entitled "The Black Man and the Unions":

I am among the few colored men who have tried conscientiously to bring about understanding and co-operation between American Negroes and the Labor Unions . . . I carry on the title page, for instance, of this magazine the Union label, and yet I know, and everyone of my Negro readers knows, that the very fact that this label is there is an advertisement that no Negro's hand is engaged in the printing of this magazine, since the International Typographical Union systematically and deliberately excludes every Negro that it dares from membership, no matter what his qualifications.

Even here, however, and beyond the hurt of mine own, I have always striven to recognize the real cogency of the Union argument. Collective bargaining has, undoubtedly, raised modern labor from something like chattel slavery to the threshold of industrial freedom, and in this advance of labor white and black have shared. I have tried, therefore to see a vision of vast union between the laboring forces, particularly in the South, and hoped for no distant day when the black laborer and the white laborer, instead of being used against each other as helpless pawns, should unite to bring real democracy in the South . . .

The whole scheme . . . of playing off black workers against white . . . is essentially a mischievous and dangerous program . . . but it is particularly disheartening to realize that it is the Labor Unions themselves that have given this movement its greatest impulse, and that today, at last, in East St. Louis have brought the most unwilling of us to acknowledge that in the present Union movement, as represented by the American Federation of Labor, there is absolutely no hope of justice for an American of Negro descent.[33]

Despite pleas for a federal investigation from dozens of prominent political, religious, business, and labor leaders, and a hand-delivered petition from the NAACP containing fifteen thousand signatures that called for an investigation and federal antilynching legislation, President Woodrow Wilson continued to ignore the riot. Prominent blacks led by James Weldon Johnson, field secretary of the NAACP, decided to catch the president's attention and perhaps force his hand with an unprecedented demonstration in America's largest city. They waited until Du Bois had returned to New York from East St. Louis and, on Saturday, July 28, Du Bois and Johnson joined eight to ten thousand blacks in marching down Fifth Avenue to the funereal beat of muffled drums in a silent protest against the riot and horrific torture lynching

The Silent Parade along Fifth Avenue in New York City

in Memphis and Waco, Texas, calling for immediate action on federal anti-lynching legislation. Some of the marchers carried signs addressed to Wilson:

MR. PRESIDENT, WHY NOT MAKE AMERICA SAFE FOR DEMOCRACY?

PRAY FOR THE LADY MACBETHS OF EAST ST. LOUIS

YOUR HANDS ARE FULL OF BLOOD

The Silent Parade was America's first major civil rights march. Du Bois biographer David Levering Lewis has written, "It seems inconceivable today that this was the first time a procession such as this had been seen in New York City . . . The Silent Parade, captured in a widely reprinted photograph, was the second impressive sign [after the picketing of *The Birth of a Nation*] that there existed an aggressive national civil rights organization representing black people." Along the parade route of more than twenty blocks, black Boy

Scouts handed out fliers that proclaimed, "We march because we want to make impossible a repetition of Waco, Memphis and East St. Louis, by rousing the conscience of the country and bringing the murderers of our brothers, sisters and innocent children to justice."[34]

The Silent Parade inspired blacks across America and, along with the riot in East St. Louis, became a primal element in the memory of a race only half a century out of slavery, a memory that persisted through the decades. In the 1930s, growing up almost six hundred miles east of East St. Louis in Lorain, Ohio, a legendary stop on the Underground Railroad, young Toni Morrison heard the stories and, like Miles Davis of East St. Louis, she never forgot what she had been told about the summer when whites slaughtered blacks in the state of Abraham Lincoln and thousands of African Americans marched in protest down white America's wealthiest avenue. The riot hovers like a dark force over her 1992 novel, *Jazz*, whose doomed central character—perhaps based in part on Josephine Baker—survives the riot that killed her parents and burned her childhood home to the ground, but never feels safe, even in the midst of America's largest black city, Harlem.

Morrison's protagonist, a girl named Dorcas, is so shattered by the experience of the riot that she cannot speak of it. She stands silently with her aunt Alice in Harlem for three hours and watches the Silent Parade, the two of them "marveling at the cold black faces and listening to drums saying what the graceful women and the marching men could not . . . It was July in 1917 and the beautiful faces were cold and quiet; moving slowly into the space the drums were building for them . . . down Fifth Avenue from curb to curb, came a tide of cold black faces, speechless and unblinking because what they had meant to say but did not trust themselves to say the drums said for them."[35]

Among the organizers of the Silent Parade was Madam C. J. Walker, who had become wealthy manufacturing and selling hair- and skin-care products for black women. She, like many others, saw the East St. Louis riot as simply lynching on a large scale, and it struck a particularly strong emotional note within her. She had lived and worked for sixteen years in St. Louis as a young woman, and had friends on both sides of the Mississippi. Two of Walker's best friends from those days worked as volunteers caring for the thousands of refugees who fled East St. Louis, and they had heartrending stories to tell.[36]

Three days after the Silent Parade, Madam Walker joined James Weldon Johnson and other black leaders in a trip to Washington. Their intention, they

Madam C. J. Walker

announced, was to meet with the president to protest "the atrocious attacks . . . at East St. Louis and other industrial centers recently," saying they represented not only "the colored people of Greater New York" but "the sentiments and aspirations and sorrows, too, of the entire Negro population of the United States." Promised a meeting with Wilson himself, they planned to urge the president to "speak some public word that would give hope and courage to the Negroes of the United States," but when the committee reached the White House they were informed that Wilson was too busy in negotiations over a farm bill to see them. They met instead with Wilson's secretary, Joseph Patrick Tumulty, who had advised Wilson in private that if he addressed the issues of lynching and the East St. Louis riot, "the fire will be re-kindled."[37]

In their petition to the president, the delegation stressed black loyalty to the United States, pointing out that a higher proportion of blacks than whites had registered for the recent draft, and they implored Wilson to use "his great personal and moral influence in our behalf." Noting that the law had not punished "a single one" of the lynchers responsible for the murder of "2,867 colored men and women" since 1885, they asked that "lynching and mob violence be made a national crime punishable by the laws of the United States," adding, "No nation that seeks to fight the battles of civilization can afford to march in blood-smeared garments."

After being assured by Tumulty that the president was "in sympathy" with American blacks, the delegation was dismissed, and Madam Walker, Johnson, and the other members of the ad hoc committee went to Capitol Hill, where several congressman agreed that an investigation should be held of the East St. Louis riot. Among them was Republican representative L. C. Dyer, who not only had been horrified by the riot but fretted that people not from his area would confuse East St. Louis, Illinois, with the city he represented, St. Louis, Missouri. Dyer had already introduced a resolution calling for a congressional investigation of the riot and began working with civil rights leaders on legislation to make lynching a federal crime. He first introduced what came to be called the Dyer Bill in 1918, although it would be several years before any congressional action was taken on it.[38]

Missouri Representative L. C. Dyer

Despite the appeals of black leaders and many prominent whites, Wilson decided there wasn't enough evidence that federal laws had been violated to justify an investigation of a riot that killed at least forty-eight people and shut down one of the nation's main transportation hubs. A majority of the House of Representatives thought differently. In response to Dyer's resolution, the Committee to Investigate Conditions in Illinois and Missouri Interfering with Interstate Commerce Between Said States was formed, and five congressmen were named to it.

In the meantime, Illinois assistant attorney general C. W. Middlekauf had been busy in St. Clair County with his riot grand jury. On August 14, 105 people—eighty white men, eight of them policemen; two white women; and twenty-three black men—were indicted on charges growing out of the riot. Thirty-two men were charged with murder. Several weeks later, thirty-nine more persons were indicted, most of them white men, including Mayor Fred Mollman, who was charged with malfeasance. Other charges ranged from arson and assault with intent to murder to "malicious mischief."[39]

In a long report, the all-white grand jury, which consisted mainly of German-American farmers and small businessmen from rural St. Clair County, traced the riot to the anger created by the importation of thousands of black workers from the South by East St. Louis industry, and particularly cited the use of black strikebreakers at the Aluminum Ore Company. "[T]he intent of employers to place the workers of one race at a disadvantage by notoriously favoring workers of another must draw down condemnation. The natural result was to precipitate a new form of aversion to the negro."[40]

The jury, which had interviewed 390 witnesses, charged that unnamed "agitators" kept race hatred stirred up among both blacks and whites until it finally exploded. Meanwhile, "as racial tensions grew, indolent public officials heard the rumblings, but, overawed by cowardly inclinations, remained inactive."

The jury reported that, on the evening before the July riot, not just one but two automobiles of white gunmen "made a number of trips" through black neighborhoods firing into the homes of blacks:

> Engendered with false fears, negroes wantonly murdered police-
> men bent on aiding them. A rival flame of passion and unreasoning

violence—all introduced into the community by intriguing ringleaders—caused white men to draw guns and clubs and shoot and beat to death some of the oldest and most respected negro citizens of East St. Louis—negroes who had lived and worked in the community for a long time preceding the period of emigration of which the community has heard so much. We further believe that the hand of a strong and fearless public official could have restrained these atrocities.

The grand jury estimated that nearly one hundred people were killed, and 245 buildings were burned down. "East St. Louis was visited by one of the worst race riots in history, a siege of murder, brutality, arson and other crimes hitherto of such loathsome character as to challenge belief. But it is now doubly so because, after hearing all evidence, we believe the riots—at least the occurrences which led up to them—were deliberately plotted . . . There is a grave suspicion that a shrewd, criminal, invisible hand directed all the moves for weeks prior to July 2, to effect the results obtained."

This was an extraordinary and shocking charge. Although the grand jury specifically blamed major industrialists in—or rather around—East St. Louis for stirring up racial hatred by bringing in excessive numbers of black workers, the panel did not identify the men wielding the "criminal, invisible hand" nor did it explain who could have benefited from the riot in the long run and thus have a motive to get it started. However, the point was made that one of the cars that drove gunmen through black neighborhoods on July 1, triggering the attack on the police car and its tragic consequences, ended up in front of the Commercial Hotel, which was "controlled by a leading politician."[41]

Nothing further was said, either directly or by implication, about either political boss Locke Tarlton or his real estate partner, Thomas Canavan. But it is worth noting that, on the morning of July 3, with smoke hanging heavy in the air and angry white mobs still in the streets, the Reverend George Allison ran into Canavan, and remarked, "Mr. Canavan, this is deplorable. This is a terrible situation."

"Yes," Canavan replied, "but my GOD, something has got to be done, or the damn niggers will take the town."

After talking to powerful citizens like Canavan, Allison said later, "I became convinced there was a concerted effort to run the negroes out of East

St. Louis"—not necessarily to kill them, he added, but to scare them so badly that they would never return.[42]

What about the widespread destruction of property owned by Tarlton and Canavan? According to both the *Post-Dispatch* and the *Journal*, the standard fire insurance policies of the period were void if the fire was caused by riot or insurrection. However, under Illinois law, the city could be held liable for damages for failure to provide protection from the rioters. Indeed, by July of 1921, the city of East St. Louis had paid $454,000 to liquidate claims growing out of the 1917 riot.[43]

The dozens of men and women indicted by the grand jury included a seventeen-year-old newsboy, a forty-nine-year-old blacksmith, a coal dealer, a railroad switchman, a baker, a bartender, and a saloonkeeper, as well as many men with no reported means of support. The predominance of Anglo-Saxon, Irish, and German last names suggests that recent immigrants from southern and eastern Europe did not play a major role in the riot. The youngest indicted were two fourteen-year-old boys. Most of the others were in their late teens or twenties, but several were in their forties—including forty-six-year-old Richard Brockway and Dr. I. H. King, a forty-three-year-old black physician indicted in the Coppedge killing. Many could not be arrested immediately because they had left town before the indictments had been issued. Some had joined the army, and those indicted on major charges who were not on a ship to France or already at the front were arrested and brought back to East St. Louis to stand trial.[44]

At least some of those who were arrested—perhaps as many as one third—lived outside of East St. Louis. None of those indicted on major charges worked for the Aluminum Ore Company, despite the role the company and its workers played in building up the white rage triggered by the riot. The rioters seem to defy classification, beyond the general observation that they tended to be men who worked with their hands or didn't work at all, at least not at anything legal.

Numerous people testified that Richard Brockway had called for and led attacks on blacks on July 2. Brockway was among the first arrested, and the hulking, headstrong security guard was injudiciously—but typically, it seems—garrulous about his role in the riot. He told the *Post-Dispatch* that he had indeed led a group of men to the Labor Temple on the morning of July 2, but that his intent was to talk them into calming down and going home. He said he had gone into the South End the day before on official business for the streetcar company and had noticed that blacks were heavily armed. He insisted he warned the crowd at the Temple that "they would probably all be killed if they went into the neighborhood." Brockway said he left the meeting and went to his home a few blocks north of downtown and had urged others to do the same. He said he did not come back downtown until the following morning. Several witnesses testified otherwise. Brockway was indicted for conspiracy to riot and assault with intent to kill, and his lawyers began a series of legal challenges that would delay his trial until mid-November.

Brockway was born in 1871 in the mountains of northern California, the son of a failed gold prospector. He lived most of his life in East St. Louis, although, according to some reports, he had spent some time in the South and publicly stated that he approved of the repressive treatment of blacks in that part of the country. He had worked with his father in the family grocery business and then sold liquor on his own for a few years, but apparently he did not succeed— at one point, he worked as a bartender for another man—and had taken a blue-collar job with a local railroad switching company. He was well known around town, a hail fellow well met, the grand vice protector of a fraternal lodge, the Knights and Ladies of Honor. He was a familiar figure at county Republican Party caucuses, but he jumped to Teddy Roosevelt's Bull Moose party in 1912 to run unsuccessfully for sheriff. He would later describe the Republican state's attorney, Hubert Schaumleffel, as a political rival who was "actively seeking his conviction" because Brockway had stood up to the East St. Louis bipartisan political machine controlled by real estate slum lord Locke Tarlton.[45]

In 1911, he became a security guard for the East St. Louis and Suburban Streetcar Company. That year, a conductor was murdered by a black man. Whites were outraged. Labor leader Alois Towers testified that "the race feeling" had been "pronounced" after the murder. More recently, the streetcars in East St. Louis had been a focus of white complaints about blacks who did not "know their place."[46]

The riot trials were set to begin in mid-August, and the prosecution had chosen its first case carefully. A thirty-two-year-old white stockyard worker named S. L. Schulz, the son of a wealthy southern Illinois farmer, was charged with several serious offenses, including brutally clubbing a white meatpacker who had come to the aid of a besieged black co-worker. Witnesses were prepared to identify Schulz as the leader of the "Stockyards gang" of rioters, accused of killing several blacks. Because of the race of the victim, Schulz's clubbing case seemed like an easy one to win, and he was one of the first to be prosecuted. After hearing jailhouse talk of harsh sentences in store for rioters—reportedly, he had overheard an official say that "hanging would be too good" for the rioters who had destroyed much of downtown—he chose to avoid a jury trial by confessing to the clubbing and pled guilty to assault to commit murder and conspiracy to riot. Other charges were dropped, but Judge George A. Crow startled him by sentencing him to fifteen years in the state penitentiary.[47] Defense attorneys who might have been considering quick guilty pleas, hoping for light sentences for serious crimes, began asking for continuances, and no case actually came to trial until October.

On August 22, Mother Jones, the radical labor leader, visited East St. Louis. She spoke to packinghouse workers at a hall barely a block from the Labor Temple, where Richard Brockway seven weeks earlier had stoked the

Labor leader Mother Jones

fires of white racial hatred. For Mother Jones the audience of 150 included twenty-five policemen, most prominently new chief of police Frank Keating and new chief of detectives Lefty Neville. The Committee of One Hundred had successfully pressured the city to get rid of their riot-tainted predecessors.

Mother Jones urged that packinghouse workers—whose union had been destroyed by bringing in strikebreakers, many of them black—throw off the shackles of prejudice and join together, black and white, to affiliate themselves with organized labor. The meeting ended peacefully and without subsequent incident, although Mother Jones did make official ears perk up, bringing a standing ovation and prolonged applause from the seventy-five or eighty meatpackers in attendance by saying, "If we can't get what we want without a riot, let's have a riot."[48]

In fact, a riot—the second major race riot of the summer of 1917—did erupt the next day almost one thousand miles to the southwest, in Houston. The riot in Houston might well never have happened had it had not been for the one in East St. Louis, which hovered like a dark cloud over Houston.

Like East St. Louis, Houston was patrolled by a police force that was considered corrupt and even dangerous by white citizens as well as blacks. Wartime pressures to clean up the vice-ridden city had resulted in racially selective enforcement of laws against prostitution and gambling, and there had been many charges in the first half of 1917 of police brutality against poor blacks. All year long and particularly that summer, according to historian Robert V. Haynes, blacks were almost routinely shot by police or falsely arrested for crimes they did not commit.[49]

In late July, a battalion of soldiers from the black Twenty-fourth Infantry, which had distinguished itself in the Indian Wars and in skirmishes along the Mexican border, was sent from the border to Houston to guard a military base under construction north of the city. The base, Camp Logan, would be used to house National Guard troops activated for the European War. The black soldiers had followed the news from East St. Louis in daily newspapers and in the *Chicago Defender* and were so horrified and saddened by what they read that they set up a fund to collect money for the victims of the riot. They were very apprehensive about the move to Houston. If something that terrible happened in the home state of Lincoln, what awful things might await them deep in the heart of East Texas? And when they arrived from the Mexican border, they found themselves in a racist bastion of the

Old South, a cotton port known for oppressive treatment of blacks, with strictly segregated, clearly labeled Jim Crow sections on the streetcars and toilets and water fountains. The soldiers objected to being treated like second-class citizens. In some cases, they objected loudly. In response, black soldiers were attacked by whites. Some were arrested on flimsy charges and beaten by police, routine treatment for men and women of color in Houston. But these men were soldiers in the uniforms of their nation, soldiers with a proud history of combat. They had been led to believe they were fighting for democracy. And they had access to weapons.

On August 17, three advance companies from the Illinois National Guard, two from Chicago and one from downstate Carbondale, arrived at Camp Logan. All three units had seen duty at the riot in East St. Louis, and it was generally known among the black soldiers that Illinois guardsmen had stood by and let rioters kill blacks, and had even shot fleeing men. Some black soldiers, it was reported later, vowed they would "fix that bunch from the Chicago slums."[50]

The coil of racial tension was tightened further over the next five days as blacks routinely were assaulted on the streets of Houston by private citizens and by police, who reportedly had decided that the black soldiers, accustomed to more liberal treatment out west and in the Philippines, were a bad influence on Houston's own blacks and needed to be taught a lesson. Particularly brutal were the mounted patrolmen, who were notorious for striking downward at the heads of blacks with heavy batons. One black soldier later recalled that his comrades had decided they would be jailed and beaten whether they did anything or not, so "they might as well fight it out."[51]

On the hot, muggy morning of August 23, a black military policeman was assaulted by Houston police after he protested their rough verbal and physical treatment of a black housewife in the city's mostly black Fourth Ward. False rumors spread that a black soldier had been shot and killed, and that a white mob was advancing on the base to kill all the black soldiers. Men from the Illinois National Guard were issued a machine gun by white officers and stationed at an entrance to the camp in case whites really were heading that way.

Seeing the white men from Illinois at the trigger of a machine gun did not inspire a sense of security in the black soldiers. Deciding they needed to act before an East St. Louis–style massacre took place, more than one hundred black soldiers grabbed rifles and marched toward Houston. Some of them may have been intent solely on repelling the rumored white mob, others on freeing one or more jailed black soldiers. But when they reached the Fourth Ward they began attacking policemen and, fairly quickly, other whites. Fierce gun battles ensued. The riot lasted barely two hours. Ironically, members of the Illinois National Guard were sent into the city to help quell the riot, and after the initial fury was expended, many black soldiers surrendered to the guardsmen rather than put themselves in the hands of the Houston Police Department.

Fifteen whites, four of them policemen, were killed. So were four black soldiers. It was the first major American race riot in which more whites were killed than blacks, and it remains one of the few such riots in the nation's history (even in most of the ghetto uprisings of the 1960s, more blacks died than whites). At courts martial over the next nine months, 110 black soldiers were found guilty of murder, mutiny, and other major wartime offenses. Nineteen were hanged, most of them in secret to avoid rancorous publicity. Sixty-three others were given life sentences. None of the participants in the East St. Louis riot, white or black, would end up being punished with anything approaching that severity.[52]

Nationally, outrage at the East St. Louis riot did much to bring blacks and whites into the fold of civil rights organizations, particularly the NAACP. Du Bois and Gruening's inflamed articles about East St. Louis boosted the circulation of the *Crisis* by many thousands, and by the end of the year, for the first time, it exceeded fifty thousand. Membership in the NAACP soared from about ninety-two hundred in 1917 to almost forty-four thousand in 1918. And for the first time, several prominent black secret and fraternal organizations, which represented a socially conservative black elite, made contributions to the NAACP. The national Urban League grew as well, and it opened a St. Louis branch in direct response to the riot. The riot also intensified and broadened the appeal of the antilynching campaign spearheaded by Ida B. Wells-Barnett and the NAACP, and played into the hands of Marcus Garvey, the charismatic black leader who used the riot as a recruiting tool for his Back to Africa movement. In a speech in New York on July 8, the eloquent Jamaican-born Garvey thundered, "For three hundred years the Negroes of America have given their life blood to make the Republic the first among the nations of the world, and all along this time there has never been even one year of justice but on the contrary a continuous round of oppression. At one time it was slavery, at another time lynching and burning, and up to date it is wholesale butchering. This is a crime against the laws of humanity; it is a crime against the laws of the nation; it is a crime against nature, and a crime against the God of all mankind." His audience leapt to its feet in cheers and applause.[53]

The Silent Parade and the presidential rebuff in Washington did not end Madam C. J. Walker's commitment to the fight for black rights and justice. Until her death in 1919, she contributed thousands of dollars to antilynching campaigns and made speeches urging the federal government to take action against the murder of blacks. At a national meeting of her sales agents in Philadelphia, the forty-nine-year-old black millionaire declared, "We should protest until the American sense of justice is so aroused that such affairs as the East St. Louis riot be forever impossible."[54]

CHAPTER 12

Judgment Days

On October 1, 1917, Circuit Court of Illinois judge George A. Crow, a crony of the East St. Louis political machine, opened the trial of the thirteen black men charged with the murder of Detective Sergeant Coppedge. The courtroom in the county seat of Belleville was packed to overflowing. About half of the spectators were black. Since this was the first case actually to come to trial—some other cases had been settled through plea bargaining—many of them shared the fear of the *St. Louis Argus*, the black weekly, that the prosecutors intended to use the trial to prove that the riot had been caused by blacks, giving them a pretext for dropping or greatly reducing charges against more than one hundred whites.[1]

The man charged as the leader of the killers, Dr. Leroy N. Bundy, was not among the defendants. The dentist and civil rights leader had left East St. Louis during the riot and finally had been tracked down in his hometown of Cleveland, where he was fighting extradition. His attorneys told the governor of Ohio he would be lynched if he returned to East St. Louis.

Several white men testified that they had seen or heard a large group of blacks on Bond Avenue late on July 1. One said the men were armed with long guns and pistols and seemed to assemble about eleven P.M. at the ringing of a church bell. Patrolman Patrick Cullinane, who had been in the police car with Coppedge and Wodley, said the mob of blacks had fired without provocation. He could not identify anyone in the courtroom as having fired shots; neither could the other survivors of the police-car shooting.

The key prosecution witness was a black iceman named Edward Wilson who testified that he had seen most of the defendants on the night of the

shooting with guns in their hands. Wilson had been arrested several days after the riot and originally had been slated to be among those tried for the police killings, but he had agreed to testify for the prosecution. The defense
contended that the iceman had actually been leading another black mob near
Tenth and Bond at the time of the shootings. According to testimony at the
trial, before his status had so dramatically changed, Wilson had told one of
his fellow defendants that he would do anything to avoid going to jail.

As the trial proceeded, blacks testified that each of the young defendants was somewhere else—home in bed, visiting his family, across the river
in St. Louis—when it was alleged that he was in the crowd on Bond Avenue.
But most of the testimony was by whites, and it was damning to the defendants. They might not individually have been seen firing at the police car,
but there was considerable testimony that each was present when the policemen were killed. In a crucial statement, a white witness testified he had
heard a black man in the crowd mutter that someone would die when the
church bell rang.

The judge allowed the prosecution to present evidence that there was a
black conspiracy to wreak vengeance on whites, but disallowed defense attempts to show that blacks were reacting to a conspiracy of terror by whites.
He cut off repeated defense attempts to get black witnesses to talk about
white gunmen driving through black neighborhoods and firing into homes.
The judge instructed the jury that just being in the crowd from which the policemen were shot, and not having argued against attacking whites, was sufficient to justify a murder verdict. It took the all-white, predominantly rural
jury fifteen hours to deliver, on October 7, a verdict of guilty for ten of the
thirteen defendants in the murder of Coppedge. They were all sentenced to a
minimum of fourteen years in the state prison at Chester, Illinois.[2]

As soon as the courtroom was cleared, the murder trial of two white men
began. Herbert Wood and Leo Keane were charged with dragging an old
black man named Scott Clark down Broadway with a rope around his neck
and trying to kill him, repeatedly, by hauling the rope over a light-pole box.
The man lived through the ordeal, but died of severe internal injuries later.
The defendants' fate was probably sealed when the much-admired Colonel
E. P. Clayton pointed out the two men in the courtroom and said he personally had seen them leading the gang that was trying to hang Scott Clark. The
final stroke came when the dead man's widow, Iva Clark, described how she

and her husband had hid from rioters in the basement of their house and finally fled when the house was set on fire. They ran to another house, but it too was set on fire, and they ran again. Rioters caught them beneath the body of a black man already hanging dead from a light pole, knocked her husband unconscious with an iron bar, draped the rope around his neck, and hauled him away as she screamed for them to stop.

The *St. Louis Post-Dispatch*'s Paul Y. Anderson took the stand and described the scene that night as "a Negro hunt," and prosecutor Middlekauf picked up that theme in his closing statement, demanding the death penalty for Wood. "If Negro hunts are considered permissible, we will have to keep soldiers in every city in this state," he said. The all-white jury deliberated for less than two hours and found Keane and Wood guilty. They too were sentenced to fourteen years in state prison.[3]

In the most dramatic trial, three white men—John Dow, a teenager who drove an ice wagon; Charles Hanna, a young adult who drove a repair truck for a tire service; and Harry Robinson, a middle-aged shoemaker—were charged with the murder of a white hardware merchant named Charles Keyser. The defendants were accused of causing the deaths of three people, not just one. But the prosecution chose to focus on the killing of Keyser almost certainly because he was white, unlike the other two victims, a black father and his black stepson, who were treated in the context of the trial as collateral damage.

Wide-ranging testimony painted a portrait of Dow and Hanna, in particular, as brutes on a bloodthirsty rampage. Witnesses testified that Hanna and Dow pulled blacks, including children, from streetcars and automobiles and beat and kicked and shot them. Each was overheard boasting about killing black men. Dow bragged about throwing the bodies of his victims in Cahokia Creek. Hanna threatened to kill an ambulance driver if he picked up a critically wounded black man lying in the street. And all three defendants were identified as being among the men who had smashed in the window of a pawnshop and taken three dozen revolvers and twelve boxes of ammunition. One of the guns, witnesses said, was used to kill Keyser.[4] The key testimony, however, came from a black woman from St. Louis whose teenage son had been the target of the bullet that had killed Keyser. Mrs. Lena Cook, her husband, her son, and her thirteen-year-old daughter were the family that had been on a fishing trip at a lake near East St. Louis and were returning home when their streetcar was stopped on Collinsville Avenue by a mob of white men who jerked the trolley from the overhead wire. Then, she testified, pointing across the courtroom at Hanna:

> That man reached through the window and grabbed my dress and tore it partly off. He said, "Come on out you black bitch because we want to kill you!" Then that other man [she pointed at Dow] came into the car and said, "All you white people get out. We're going to kill these niggers."
>
> The white people got off. I told them that we all didn't live in East St. Louis and hadn't hurt anybody there. That man [Hanna] took my husband by the collar and pulled him to the back platform and threw him off and shot him. I saw that.
>
> That man [Dow] took my boy and started to drag him out. I took hold of him. "You've killed my husband," I said. "Don't kill my boy." He jerked him away, beating him over the head with his revolver, and that was the last time I saw my son alive.

She paused, lowering her head, fighting back tears, and then she wiped her eyes and glared across the hushed courtroom. She thrust out her right hand, a finger pointing straight at Charles Hanna, and said:

> Then that man came back and dragged me out of the car, and men beat me, and kicked me, and pulled my hair out. A white man got in front of me and called out, "Don't kill the women folks." The men started beating him, and I crawled on my hands and knees into a store.
>
> Well, I fell over in this doorway, and at that time some tall white fellow came running there and said, "Please don't beat her any more."
>
> "I am not going to let them kill you," he said, "stay back there." And so he threw his arm across the door like that and I was behind him and he says, "in the name of the Lord don't kill the woman." And then some way or other they got me into the ambulance, and there was another fellow lying there, a colored fellow on the side of the ambulance, and I saw he had a big handkerchief and I took it and wiped the blood out of my eyes, and when I looked

down I saw my husband lying there and my boy right under me.
They had their eyes open and they were dead.

It was not until the next day that she discovered that her daughter had somehow escaped the mob, and had made her way to St. Louis.

Defense lawyer Alexander Flannigen, whose inflammatory rhetoric had helped trigger the May riot, subjected the woman to what the *Post-Dispatch* called "a severe cross-examination." The result, the *Post-Dispatch* observed, was that "the woman retold her story to the jury, not wavering in her identification of the two men."[5]

Dow and Hanna were found guilty of murder and sentenced to fifteen years in the state penitentiary. Robinson pled guilty to conspiracy to riot and was given five years in the state penitentiary. After the convictions in the early trials, with sentences that were considered surprisingly harsh even if they stopped well short of the maximum, white defendants began scrambling for plea bargains. The process was given more urgency when the state announced it would go to the grand jury with perjury charges against witnesses who provided alibis that were proven to be false.[6]

After two months of legal delays, riot instigator Richard Brockway finally came to trial in mid-November. Witnesses testified that the hulking Brockway had warned a crowd in front of the police station on the morning of July 2 that "niggers" would "take the town" unless they were stopped; had told a policeman, "We're going to kill every nigger in East St. Louis in a minute"; had urged rioters to "go down there" in the South End "and get those niggers and burn their shacks"; and had told the crowd at the Labor Temple to go home and get weapons and come back ready to do battle. But the prosecution could not find anyone willing to testify under oath that Brockway had murdered anyone. Brockway was convicted of conspiracy to cause rioting and was sentenced to five years in the state penitentiary.[7]

By December, tragedy had turned into sad farce. Former night chief of police Cornelius Hickey and five other policemen were set to go on trial for failing to perform their duties during the riot. Then, someone lost the original indictment. Judge Crow, a political hack who had been known to fall asleep on the bench after drinking lunch, discovered that the indictment was missing and quickly dismissed the charges before someone found it. Crow and fellow circuit judges also dismissed the charges against Mollman.[8]

The farce continued into the next year.

Six policemen, including Hickey, had also been charged with murder or conspiracy to riot by the grand jury. Three of them, including Hickey, were charged in the July 3 shootings in which one black man was shot to death, another was seriously wounded, and part of a black woman's arm was blasted off. Dan McGlynn, a city hall and courthouse regular and a member of the chamber of commerce's reform group, the Committee of One Hundred, was one of the defense attorneys for the policemen. By the time Mc-Glynn was through working deals, seven months had passed since the riot and an extraordinary arrangement had been worked out with the prosecution, which seems to have been dubious that it could find twelve white men who would convict any white policemen of crimes against blacks during the July riot. The murder charges would be dropped on the condition that any three policemen among the six charged with various felonies would plead guilty to the single charge of rioting. On February 5, 1918, the six policemen drew numbers from a hat to choose which three would plead guilty. Judge Crow fined them a total of $150. All six men pitched in and paid the fine. The *St. Louis Argus* was outraged, suggesting that the "lottery" had effectively set the price for a license to kill or maim blacks in East St. Louis at $50.[9]

By then, a number of other cases, including ones in which whites allegedly had murdered blacks, had ended in plea bargains and minor sentences. In the end, as the cases against whites dragged on for months, with many of them being dismissed for lack of evidence, only nine whites were actually sent to prison, most of them on lesser sentences than those received by the twelve convicted and imprisoned blacks. Whites who pleaded guilty to misdemeanors, no matter how serious the original felony charges, usually got off with $50 fines or short terms in the county jail.[10]

The prosecution in the riot trials had been severely handicapped by the fact that very few white East St. Louisans would admit under oath to having seen anyone of the Caucasian race do much of anything illegal involving blacks on July 2 in downtown East St. Louis, even though the main intersections were packed with thousands of white people. A visitor asked the Reverend George W. Allison how it was possible on the night of July 2, when the town was lit by fires as if "by a blazing sun," everybody in town was "as blind as a bat to the destruction of human life?" Allison replied, "They are afraid to come to the front . . . afraid of their lives and property . . . I think that men here in town are cowards."[11]

The House Select Committee to Investigate Conditions in Illinois and Missouri Interfering with Interstate Commerce Between These States, also known as the Special Committee Authorized by Congress to Investigate the East St. Louis Race Riots, opened hearings on the morning of October 18 in the federal courtroom of the Metropolitan Building in downtown East St. Louis, about three blocks east of the epicenter of the riot. The committee had five members. Two were from Illinois: George Foss, fifty-four years old, a Republican; and Martin Foster, fifty-six, a Democrat. John Raker, fifty-four, was a California Democrat who had grown up in Illinois. Henry Cooper, a sixty-seven-year-old, eleven-term Republican, was from neighboring Wisconsin and was old enough—and fiercely moralistic enough—to have been an abolitionist as a boy. The fifth member was Ben Johnson, a crusty fifty-nine-year-old Kentuckian who, it later became apparent, chose to think the riot was mainly the fault of black ne'er-do-wells who would have been better off staying in the paternalistic South.[12]

The first witnesses represented business and industry, and they said, yes, interstate commerce definitely had been interfered with by the July 2 riot, getting that constitutional formality out of the way on the first day. On the second day, witnesses began answering questions about the real reason the hearings were being held.

Business blamed labor for the riots, and labor responded by blaming business. Robert Conway, general manager of the Armour meatpacking plant, charged the riots were inspired by "agitation on the part of the disturbing element among the Aluminum Ore Company strikers." He said, "There was common talk around town here that they were going to drive the niggers out." Labor leaders begged to differ; they placed the blame on Conway and the other meatpackers and industrialists who kept hiring untrained blacks to replace experienced whites and flooding the city with African Americans.[13] As the hearings proceeded in the federal courtroom, outside, in the fading October sun, men in white robes and hoods paraded slowly up and down the street or stood silently, arms folded in front of them, their expressions hidden by gathered cloth. Congressman Henry Cooper decided the costumes looked very much like the ones worn by the hooded nightriders in the movie *The Birth of a Nation*, and took the occasion to decry the "curse" that movie had put on the nation, the "terrible passions" it had aroused.[14]

In fact, the resurgent Ku Klux Klan was on the rampage across the South and lower Midwest, and racial hatred was not its only cause. On October 28, men in white robes and hoods kidnapped a pacifist minister in Cincinnati, took him across the Ohio River into Kentucky and, in a dense wood, horse-whipped him nearly to death. They acted, they said, "in the name of Belgian women and children." A couple of weeks later, seventeen members of the International Workers of the World who had been accused of plotting terrorism in the oil fields were kidnapped from police custody in Tulsa, Oklahoma, stripped, tied to whipping posts, flogged with a cat of nine tails, and tarred and feathered by a gang of sixty men in black robes and hoods. They called themselves the Knights of Liberty. The leader shouted, "In the name of the outraged women and children of Belgium," as he spread hot pitch on the bleeding backs of the pacifistic Wobblies. The city attorney of Tulsa refused to file any charges. The assaults were among many across the country as American troops began dying in Europe and self-proclaimed patriots who had stayed home assaulted and in some cases lynched their fellow citizens who opposed the war or made statements judged unpatriotic.[15]

At the congressional hearings, witness after witness testified that East St. Louis had become, as one man put it, "a rendezvous for thugs, yeggmen, pickpockets and thieves" over the past decade. The Reverend George Allison and labor leader Harry Kerr accused slum landlords like Thomas Canavan and his partner, Locke Tarlton, of helping to cause the riot by charging blacks such exorbitant rents that as many as three dozen men were crowded into one small house. There were no jobs for these men once the meat and industrial plants had a sufficient supply of strikebreakers, Kerr said, and they crowded downtown and lingered on the streetcars for hours—some of them eating and sleeping there—and they turned to panhandling and some to crime. When Congressman Raker heard descriptions of the sordid, crowded conditions in the black sections of downtown, with prostitutes selling their bodies to a dozen or more men a day and lying with them on filthy mattresses in shacks without indoor plumbing, he exclaimed, "Why it would keep a frog busy trying to stay healthy down in that hole!"[16]

G. E. Popkess, Paul Anderson, and other reporters blamed the riots on a complex array of factors, from simple racial prejudice to rampant crime among both blacks and whites, manipulation of blacks and whites by both labor and management, and corruption and ineptness that began with Mayor Mollman. James Kirk, owner and editor of the *East St. Louis Daily Journal,* said "The graft, rottenness and corruption which we have endured here is beyond the power of words to describe."[17]

On November 8, in the midst of the hearings, the committee was given a dramatic demonstration of one reason there were so many unemployed young men in East St. Louis. Eleven black men who had arrived in East St. Louis earlier in the week were brought in to testify that they had been brought up from Mississippi on a pass by a railroad straw boss. They had been promised $2 a day and board, plus a trip home every two weeks, to lay and raise track for the Alton and Southern Railroad, a belt line that ran to the Aluminum Ore Company plant and was owned by it.

When they arrived, they discovered the pay was actually $1.40 a day, less than some of them had been making in Jackson; the meals were bread and molasses with a small piece of pork fatback; and the sleeping quarters were a bare railroad car where they had to pay $4.50 for a set of comforters for a bed. The foreman threatened to throw them in jail if they tried to leave. Some of the men walked away in anger anyway and were scrambling for jobs to make enough money to buy a ticket home. One of the workers, Lee Cox, said he discovered in the railroad yards that the straw boss brought gangs up every week, and many men walked off the job when they found out they had been cheated.

The straw boss was located. He told the congressmen that there had been some misunderstandings about pay and board. But, he said, labor agents had been bringing trainloads of blacks to East St. Louis for more than a year, and he had learned, "The more you pay one of them, the better you feed him, the less work you will get out of him."[18]

As the congressional committee was hearing about the weekly importation of blacks to East St. Louis by the railroads, importation that continued despite the worst race riot in decades, word came to the United States from the Russian capital of Petrograd that armed Bolsheviks had stormed the Winter Palace of the tsars, deposed the provisional government that had held shakily to power since the overthrow of Tsar Nicholas in March, and taken over the government of Russia. To follow were a bloody civil war and a dictatorship that would last three quarters of a century, murder millions, and imprison millions more.

On November 16, after lengthy testimony by Paul Anderson on the suspicious links between levee board funds in the Illinois State Bank and a personal slush fund maintained by Locke Tarlton, president of the levee board, the committee adjourned the hearings. In its final report, the committee asserted that, long before the riot, "Sodom and Gomorrah were model Christian communities in comparison" to East St. Louis and judged that "No terms of condemnation applied to the men who were responsible for these appalling conditions . . . can be too severe. No punishment that outraged citizens can wish upon them will be adequate. In many cases they deserve the extreme penalty; in every case they merit the execration of a despoiled and disgraced community."

The committee decided that "the men who were responsible" for the riot, in great part, were "the politicians of both political parties who found East St. Louis respected and prosperous, and in a few years robbed its treasury, gave away valuable franchises, sank it into the mire of pollution and brought upon it national censure and disgrace." The committee also castigated the chamber of commerce and "the owners of great corporations . . . who live in other cities [and] pocket their dividends without concern for the dishonesty and neglect that wasted the taxes, and without a thought for the thousands of their own workmen, black and white, who lived in hovels, the victims of poverty and disease."

Industrialists, including the railroads and the Aluminum Ore Company, the committee charged, "pitted white labor against black" and "stirred the fires of racial hatred until it finally culminated in bloody, pitiless riot, murder and wanton arson."

The report ran for twenty-four pages, detailing the horrors of July 2 and 3, the carloads of whites speeding through black neighborhoods firing guns, the fatal shooting of the two policemen, the bullet-riddled car sitting in front of police headquarters as a call to arms, the broad-daylight attacks on innocent men, women, and children in the streets of downtown East St. Louis. The committee reported that 312 buildings had been destroyed by fire. "It is not possible to give accurately the number of dead," the committee decided. "At least 39 Negroes and 8 white people were killed outright, and hundreds of Negroes were wounded and maimed."[19] (The St. Clair County coroner fixed the number of dead whites at nine, and it is generally accepted that at least thirty-nine blacks and nine whites were killed in the riot.)[20]

The committee specifically rebuked:

Mayor Fred Mollman, "personally honest, maybe, but so weak, so feeble and so easily influenced that the conspirators were able to dictate his policies, and in the shadow of his stupidity loot the municipality."

Political boss–slum landlord Locke Tarlton, who controlled the mayor and whose "cunning mind . . . helped develop the schemes by which he and his associates were enriched" through a crooked partnership with the State Bank of Illinois, which helped him skim thousands of dollars a year from the levee board.

Tom Canavan, superintendent of public improvements, Tarlton's partner: "Their minds met in countless devious plans for personal gain and political advantage."

Alexander Flannigen, "an attorney of some ability and no character [whose] speech to an excited crowd of workingmen . . . the night of May 28 practically advised them to kill and burn the houses of the Negroes . . . Flannigen has long been a menace to decency and order in East St. Louis."

State's Attorney Hubert Schaumleffel, who "held in his hand the moral destiny of this city" but was "devoid of character . . . the boon companion of the low and the dissolute; the ready servant of scheming politicians; at heart, a sympathizer with criminals whom he should have prosecuted relentlessly . . . His love for liquor seems to have stripped him of all moral courage and manhood, and left him naked and unashamed."

Colonel S. O. Tripp, a "hopeless incompetent": "Responsibility for much that was done and left undone must rest on him . . . He was a hindrance instead of a help to the troops . . . He was ignorant of his duties, blind to his responsibilities, and deaf to every intelligent appeal that was made to him."

The "great majority" of the police, who turned hundreds of rioters loose without bond and did nothing to stop savage attacks on blacks. "The police," the committee charged, "shot into a crowd of Negroes who were huddled together [in a] particularly cowardly exhibition of savagery" and destroyed the cameras and film of newspaper photographers, threatening them with arrest "if any attempt was made to photograph the rioters who were making the streets run red with innocent blood."

A few came in for praise, including Lieutenant Colonel E. P. Clayton, for "his promptness and determination" in stopping the mob from committing "many more atrocities"; Paul Anderson, for reporting "what he saw without fear of consequences" and rendering "an invaluable public service by his exposures," despite running "a daily risk of assassination," and the Reverend George W. Allison "for "fighting with all his splendid power the organized forces of evil" despite "conspiracies against his character and threats against his life."

But in the main the report was a shattering condemnation of greedy capitalists, crooked politicians and judges, dishonest and uncaring policemen, and the vicious criminals, black and white, they turned loose on the citizens of East St. Louis.[21]

In mid-October, Dr. Leroy N. Bundy was extradited from Ohio, brought to the St. Clair County jail in Belleville, and charged with inciting to riot. Dr. Bundy was in his mid-thirties, a handsome, charismatic, ambitious man who had grown up in Cleveland, where his father was a prominent minister and a trustee of Wilberforce University. A 1903 graduate of Case Western Reserve dental school, Bundy had lived in Detroit and Chicago before coming to East St. Louis about 1909. He and his wife, Vella, had no biological children but had adopted a small boy from Africa. In addition to practicing dentistry, he was an entrepreneur, setting up a service station, a garage, and a small car agency. He was also a skilled politician, serving a term on the St. Clair County Board of Supervisors. White politicians considered him to be the key to the black vote in East St. Louis, although many whites found Bundy to be too aggressive and outspoken. The *Post-Dispatch* remarked, "He was known as a vigorous advocate of 'equal rights' and this had brought him into conflict with white people more than once."[22]

After six weeks in jail, Bundy gave a sworn statement to Illinois attorney general Edward Brundage alleging massive fraud in the East St. Louis mayoralty elections of 1915 and 1917, won by Fred Mollman, and a levee district election in 1916 in which Locke Tarlton was reelected district president. Bundy implicated himself in the fraud, along with Mollman, Tarlton, Canavan, and numerous other political figures, including a few Republicans among the many Democrats, telling the attorney general that he and other "pay off men" had been given thousands of dollars to buy black votes at between $1 and $5 a head. In response to the charges, both federal and state authorities announced they would launch major investigations into vote fraud in East St. Louis, but the investigations never materialized—perhaps because Bundy had cast such a wide net, naming prominent members of both major political parties, including St. Clair County's Republican state's attorney Hubert Schaumleffel.[23]

Mayor Mollman, whom Bundy had said was not "the real mayor" but a figurehead for Tarlton and Canavan, called Bundy's charges "a malicious lie." Mollman also said, probably accurately, that the Republican Bundy was trying to influence the Republican attorney general to drop or lessen the murder charge against him. If so, Bundy failed, and at the same time he alienated his most powerful supporters.

In the aftermath of the conviction in early October of ten black men for the murder of Coppedge, men whose defense had been supported in part by the St. Louis branch of the NAACP, the association's national office arranged for prominent lawyers, white and black, to work in Bundy's defense, including Charles Nagel, former secretary of commerce and labor in the Taft administration. Bundy quickly became a cause célèbre among blacks and white liberals. One black newspaper called his case "not just the trial of an individual" but "the trial of the Race." W. E. B. Du Bois wrote, "Here we understood was a successful professional man, a leader of his local group in East St. Louis, who, when riot was threatened, advised the colored people to arm themselves and . . . because of this he was arrested, thrown into jail and accused of murder and inciting to riot. This seemed to us an ideal case. We were determined to leave no stone unturned to secure vindication for Dr. Bundy and, with this, the great and sacred right of self-defense for American Negroes in the face of the mob."[24]

But after Bundy confessed that he had been the spigot through which thousands of dollars in election bribes had flowed to black voters, the "ideal case" seemed less so to the NAACP. Du Bois wrote:

> It was an outrageous action and it put his attorneys and especially the National Association for the Advancement of Colored People

in a most difficult position . . . We were making a hero of Bundy.
We were holding him up as a brave and persecuted man, who in
the midst of crime and lawlessness, had told the people to arm
in self defense. In the midst of all this Mr. Bundy comes out and
confesses that he is hand and glove with the men and is part of the
system which made East St. Louis a city of corruption and made
it possible for such a horrible riot to go on without interference by
the authorities.

In April of 1918, with the matter still up in the air, the St. Louis branch
of the NAACP reported that Bundy was out on bond and wanted to go on
a lecture tour and raise $50,000 for himself in addition to the money the
NAACP was supplying. Bundy, the branch reported, was "intolerant of the financial plan of this branch, which was devised to forestall money scandals."
Bundy also refused to go back to work and, the St. Louis branch charged,
wanted the NAACP to support him and his wife and pay $2,000 in back bills.
The branch recommended dropping support of Bundy. Three months later, in
an angry meeting in New York with the directors of the NAACP, Bundy refused to agree to any financial accounting of the money he was receiving from
the NAACP, or from any other source. Afterward, the NAACP announced it
was "no longer connected in any way with the further defense of Dr. Leroy N.
Bundy." The *Chicago Defender* and other black papers were sharply critical of
the NAACP for deserting Bundy, and the *Cleveland Gazette* advised its readers
to resign from the "white-man controlled" organization.[25]

Bundy, who had continued to raise money on his own and was represented by three white lawyers and four black ones, finally went on trial for the
murder of Coppedge and inciting to riot in March of 1919. The venue had
been shifted to the rural town of Waterloo, Illinois, twenty miles from East St.
Louis, on arguments by the defense that the jury pool in East St. Louis had
been irrevocably polluted by numerous front-page stories that had described
Bundy as the leader of the men who shot detectives Coppedge and Wodley.[26]

At the trial, which attracted national attention, a number of white witnesses testified that they had seen a crowd of blacks, some of them armed,
gathering near Bundy's house and the garage and gasoline station that adjoined it on the evening of July 1. And several white men said that, in the
months before the July riot, guns had been stored in Bundy's house and

garage, and Bundy's yard, porch, and living room became the place for blacks to hang out and argue about race and politics. Most of the witnesses admitted on cross-examination that they had not seen Bundy himself in the crowd near his house, at Seventeenth and Bond, nor anywhere else in East St. Louis on the night the policemen were shot. They had seen a red touring car driving around with armed black men in it, and Bundy owned a red touring car, a Hupmobile.

One witness who said he *had* seen Bundy near the scene of the shooting that night was Gus Masserang, the hoodlum and jitney driver who, according to a witness, drove a car that ended up parked in front of the Commercial Hotel riddled with holes on July 2. Masserang, it was established, had been treated at a hospital for superficial shotgun wounds early the morning of July 2. The defense fought its way through strenuous prosecution objections to suggest for the record that Masserang had been wounded while driving men firing guns through black neighborhoods and that he had made a deal to avoid prosecution and was finally holding up his end of it. It was even suggested that the men firing from Masserang's car were policemen, which would certainly help to explain why blacks would shoot at the police car holding Wodley and Coppedge.[27]

Bundy's legal septet shredded Masserang's testimony and put on a detailed defense that attacked alleged sightings of Bundy and of his expensive red car in East St. Louis on the night of the shootings. Witnesses testified that neither Bundy's red Hupmobile nor Bundy himself was anywhere near Tenth and Bond when the shootings occurred.[28] But Edward Wilson, the black iceman whose testimony had been crucial to the ten convictions in the first trial for the murder of Coppedge, appeared again and said Bundy had been in the mob that had shot the policemen. In rebuttal, two defense witnesses testified that Wilson had told them that he had been beaten by police while in jail until he agreed to testify against Bundy and the other defendants. They said Wilson had confided to them that Bundy had not been in the mob. Still, the all-white jury found Bundy guilty, and sentenced him to life in prison. His lawyers appealed to the Illinois Supreme Court, which eventually overturned the conviction on the grounds that the prosecution had not proven its case. Wilson's key testimony was completely discredited by the court. Bundy was freed after having served about a year in the state prison at Menard, where he worked as the prison dentist.[29]

Bundy moved back to Cleveland and got a law degree from Western Reserve. For a time, he headed up the large Cleveland chapter of Marcus Garvey's United Negro Improvement Association. The flamboyant black nationalist had gone to Bundy's support after the NAACP dropped him and, in a so-called court ceremony held in Harlem, Garvey anointed him "Sir Leroy Bundy." The two headstrong men split in an argument over finances and Bundy entered local politics. He served as a city councilman from 1929 to 1937. In the pivotal year of 1936, with black allegiance shifting from the Republican to the Democratic Party in national politics, he helped lead the partly successful fight at the Republican National Convention in Cleveland to block the seating of delegations from Southern states that excluded blacks.[30]

In 1918, as the Great War ground into its final grueling year—with tens of thousands of American doughboys shipping out for Europe every week—the Great Migration of African Americans from South to North continued, although few came to East St. Louis. Indeed, thousands of blacks who fled the city in July of 1917 never returned, and by the census of 1920 the black population of East St. Louis was just under seventy-five hundred—roughly the same as it had been in 1914, before the migration had begun. An uneasy racial peace, if not harmony, prevailed in the slowly rebuilding river city, perhaps in some part because violence-prone residents of the area had a new outlet for their prejudices—jingoism.[31]

In early April of 1918, in Collinsville, Illinois, a small town about ten miles east of East St. Louis, a German-born Socialist miner named Robert Prager made a speech critical of Woodrow Wilson and American participation in the Great War. He was accused of "disloyalty," assaulted, rescued by police, dragged from police protection by a mob of three hundred men, paraded through town wrapped in an American flag, and hanged from a tree. According to the *St. Louis Globe-Democrat*, the lynching was "the first killing for disloyalty to the United States." Several weeks earlier, four men, including a Catholic priest of Polish descent, had been tarred and feathered in a nearby mining town as part of a widespread campaign, as the *Globe-Democrat* put it, "to drive disloyal persons from southern Illinois." Similar attacks were becoming increasingly common in towns and cities across the country.[32]

On July 26, not long after a jury had acquitted the men who had lynched Robert Prager, President Woodrow Wilson finally issued a statement condemning lynching and "the mob spirit which [has] frequently shown its head among us, not in any single region, but in many and widely separated parts of the country."

Although the carefully worded statement contained no specific references to lynching of blacks, the *New York Times* seemed to read Wilson's mind in reporting that the president was moved to condemn lynching not only by "mob action against those suspected of being enemy aliens or enemy sympathizers" but by "lynchings of negroes in the South." The paper explained, "It is known that the lynchings of negroes, as well as attacks upon those suspected of being enemies or enemy sympathizers, have been used by the German propaganda throughout Central and South America as well as in Europe, to contend that the stand of the United States as a champion of democracy is a sham. Deeply concerned by the situation, the president decided to address his fellow countrymen, and to declare that 'every mob contributes to German lies about the United States.'" The NAACP printed and distributed fifty thousand copies of the president's address, although W. E. B. Du Bois wondered rhetorically why it had taken the death of a white man to inspire the president finally to speak up when so many hundreds of blacks had been lynched over the years.[33]

Ironically, on the very day that the president condemned lynching and mob violence, a race riot broke out in Philadelphia, which had seen its share of them over the decades. Indeed, the previous year, a brutal race riot with several deaths had struck Chester, Pennsylvania, just southeast of the city. In the war years, thousands of blacks had crowded into the southern part of Philadelphia, lured by jobs in a new shipbuilding complex. The immigrants pushed the boundaries of established black neighborhoods. Beginning in late June, blacks were attacked in the streets by their white neighbors. On the last Friday in July, after a black woman—a city probation officer—had moved into a house she had recently bought in a white neighborhood, a white mob gathered on the street, chanting and cursing and throwing stones through the windows. The terrified woman fired a warning shot from a second-story window, bringing police, who were finally able to break up the crowd.

Further attacks on African Americans on Saturday, in the main ignored by police, led to pitched battles in the streets between blacks and whites armed with guns, clubs, razors, and bricks. The riot lasted four days. A white policeman was shot and killed trying to take a pistol away from a black man who was defending himself from a white mob, and another white man was killed when a black man fired into a crowd of whites that was chasing him. The third person killed in the riot, a black man, was shot by a policeman while in custody. In the riot's immediate aftermath, black leaders formed a Colored Protective Association and protested the prisoner's killing and other police actions—and inactions—charging the "incompetent police force" with "hobnobbing with the mob" during and "for a long time" before the riot, ignoring "the beating up of Negroes, the stoning of their homes and the attacking of their churches." The black leaders' persistent complaints in the wake of the riot eventually led to a major shakeup of the Philadelphia police department.[34]

There were small, comparatively brief racial clashes that year in several other cities, including New York, where blacks battled whites in both Brooklyn and Harlem, but relatively few fatalities and no large-scale arson resulted, nothing approaching the horror of East St. Louis. In part, perhaps, that relatively low level of violence came because so many young men had left home for the military. By the time of the armistice in November of 1918, four million Americans were in uniform. Also, the United States was increasingly preoccupied with "disloyalty" at home. And, in the second half of 1918, the nation was stunned by the influenza epidemic, which killed half a million Americans in less than a year.

But by the spring of 1919, the influenza epidemic had run its course and millions of former soldiers, including 350,000 African Americans, were home, having been trained in warfare and the use of weapons. The blacks had served their country in wartime and were impatient for the so-called democracy their president had promised the world. As for the whites, according to James Weldon Johnson of the NAACP, "Reports from overseas had come back warning that the returned Negro soldiers would be a dangerous element and a menace [who] had been engaged in killing white men, that . . . they had frequently been given the treatment accorded only to white men in America and, above all, that many of them had been favorably regarded by white women. One of the chief recruiting slogans of the Klan was the necessity of united action to keep these men in line."[35]

There were eighty-three cases of lynching in America in 1919, nineteen more than the year before. And there were many race riots. The generally accepted figure is roughly two dozen, and the *New York Times* reported in October of 1919 that there had been "38 race riots and clashes in cities and other communities in various parts of the country" so far that year. The summer of 1919 was so racially violent that James Weldon Johnson named it "the Red Summer." The reference was to the color of blood, although America was also at the peak of a "red scare," as right-wing congressmen and federal officials found Bolsheviks under the beds and inside the skin of every militant labor leader, pacifist, and advocate of black civil rights.[36]

The two most notorious riots of the Red Summer were in Chicago and Washington, although the deadliest may have been in Phillips County in Arkansas's cotton belt, where black tenant farmers who were essentially slaves to their debt tried to organize to get a fairer deal from landowners. After a rumor spread that the county's blacks were planning a massacre of whites, a sheriff's posse fired on a meeting of tenant farmers and in the resulting melee a white deputy sheriff was killed. White mobs went on a rampage reminiscent of the worst days of Redemption. Officially, fourteen blacks were killed, but James Weldon Johnson contended that "between two hundred and three hundred Negroes were hunted down in the fields and swamps to which they fled, and shot down like animals." Blacks were blamed for the riot, and in subsequent trials in Arkansas seventy-nine blacks were speedily convicted of murder. Twelve of them were sentenced to death. The NAACP fought the case all the way to the Supreme Court, which ruled that the seventy-nine men had been denied the right to a fair trial, and freed them.[37]

The 1919 riot in Washington, D.C., once a rare refuge of hope for blacks but now, with Woodrow Wilson in the White House, an increasingly segregated Southern city with very high black unemployment, began on a hot, muggy night in mid-July. The story is a tragically familiar one. The four daily newspapers, including the *Washington Post*, had been stirring up the city's white population with repeated lurid stories about a "Negro Fiend" who was attacking white women. A few days before the riot, the NAACP sent warnings to the four papers that they were "sowing the seeds of a race riot by their inflammatory headlines."

The city was crowded with soldiers and sailors home from the Great War, and the mood of drunken celebration turned ugly when the rumor circulated that a man suspected of being the Negro Fiend had been arrested and then released by Washington police. The morning of the riot, the *Washington*

Post published a front-page article headlined MOBILIZATION FOR TONIGHT. The story reported, erroneously, that all service personnel in the city were to report to Seventh Street and Pennsylvania Avenue at nine P.M.. for "clean-up" duty. That evening, a white mob that included many servicemen formed in a seedy saloon district off Pennsylvania Avenue and began chasing and beating black men and women. Whites dragged hundreds of blacks off of streetcars and beat and shot them. More than five hundred guns were sold to whites at pawnshops, and black veterans, many of whom had brought weapons back from France, fought back. What ensued was not so much a riot as a small-scale race war. Officially, at least thirty-nine blacks and whites were killed.[38]

Two weeks later, Chicago exploded in riot. The black population of Chicago had virtually doubled in the war years, inevitably pushing the boundaries of the so-called Black Belt on the South Side. Racial antagonism had been intensified by the hiring of black strikebreakers to replace white stockyard and slaughterhouse workers. That summer, there were frequent attacks on blacks with little response from police. Black homes were torched, along with the offices of real estate agents who sold to blacks. Chicago black leader Ida B. Wells-Barnett cried out to city officials and the public, "I implore Chicago to set the wheels of justice in motion before it is too late, and Chicago be disgraced by some of the bloody outrages that have disgraced East St. Louis."

The riot began on Sunday, July 27, after a white man threw a rock at a black boy who was swimming close to what whites considered to be a white-only beach on Lake Michigan. The rock struck the boy on the head and he drowned. Fights between blacks and whites broke out on the beach and spread into the city. Roving white mobs attacked badly outnumbered blacks. Whites in automobiles sped through black neighborhoods, firing at people on the street and into homes. Black snipers fired back. The riot, which ranged into the Loop and across much of the city, lasted five days. A thousand black families were left homeless by the burning and destruction, and thirty-eight people—twenty-three of them black—were killed, at least officially. Black leaders charged that many more than that had died and that black bodies had been thrown into the Chicago River and its tributaries and burnt up in the hundreds of buildings that were reduced to cinders and rubble.[39]

It is worth noting that, with the addition of Chicago to East St. Louis and Springfield, three of the worst race riots of the first two decades of the twentieth century took place in Illinois, the home of Abraham Lincoln and the first martyr of abolition, Elijah Lovejoy.

After the Chicago riot, W. E. B. Du Bois, continuing on the course he had set after visiting a devastated city at the other end of Illinois two years before, wrote a declaration that made him a hero to generations of black radicals: "For three centuries we have suffered and cowered. No race ever gave Passive Resistance and Submission to Evil longer, more piteous trial. Today we raise the terrible weapon of Self-Defense. When the murderer comes, he shall no longer strike us in the back. When the armed lynchers gather, we too must gather armed. When the mob moves, we propose to meet it with bricks and clubs and guns."[40]

Once again, as in 1917, the attacks on blacks in the Red Summer of 1919 led thousands of blacks and white liberals to strengthen their commitment to civil rights for African Americans. Membership in the NAACP more than doubled to ninety-one thousand between the end of 1918 and the end of 1919, boosted in part by the publication of the NAACP study *Thirty Years of Lynching in the United States, 1889–1918,* which stated that 2,522 blacks and 702 whites had been lynched in thirty years, many more than had been legally executed in the same period.[41]

With the lynching study as added ammunition, in 1919 James Weldon Johnson and the NAACP began intense lobbying in support of the Dyer Bill, which designated lynching as a federal crime. The bill had evolved from discussions between black leaders and Republican congressman L. C. Dyer of St. Louis in the aftermath of the East St. Louis race riot. After years of stalling, in January of 1922, the U.S. House of Representatives finally passed the bill by a vote of 230 to 119. The bill was subsequently reported favorably out of committee in the Senate, but it was killed by a filibuster of Southern Democrats.[42]

Numerous similar bills went down to defeat in years and decades to come. Those few that passed the House died in the Senate. Finally, in 2005, the U.S. Senate approved a resolution that, in effect, apologized for never passing an antilynching law, expressing "the deepest sympathies and most solemn regrets of the Senate to the descendants of the victims of lynchings, the ancestors of whom were deprived of life, human dignity, and the constitutional protections accorded all citizens of the United States." The resolution, which was passed by a voice vote, was cosponsored by eighty of the one hundred members of the Senate. Among the twenty nonsponsors—nineteen Republicans and one Democrat—was former Senate majority leader Trent Lott. The Mississippi Republican, who had lost his leadership position because of remarks seen as racially divisive, said of the resolution, "Where do we end all this? Are we going to apologize for not doing the right thing on Social Security?"[43]

In the spring of 1921, the final major race riot of the World War I era hit Tulsa, Oklahoma. The city's black population had grown from just under two thousand in 1910 to almost nine thousand in 1920, and blacks, who made up about 12 percent of the populace, were blamed for much of the crime in the vice-ridden oil-patch city. On May 31, riot fever was stirred up in the white population by an inflammatory, misleadingly lurid news story about a young black man's "assault" on a white woman on a downtown elevator. Apparently, the elevator lurched, they were thrown together, and she screamed and accused him of attacking her. Police arrested the young black man. That evening, a rumor swept through the city's black community that a lynch mob was gathering downtown near the city jail and courthouse, and some blacks headed that way to defend the prisoner. A counter-rumor spread like an oil-field fire among the city's whites—that a gang of armed blacks was on the way downtown to break the black prisoner out of jail before the whites could lynch him. Whites broke into sporting goods and hardware stores, grabbing hundreds of rifles and guns and cases of ammunition, and began shooting and beating blacks. They invaded Tulsa's black section, Greenwood, setting fire to homes.

By the next morning, thirty-five blocks of the city were in flames. A small group of armed blacks fought back. By then, National Guard troops had reached Tulsa, and the guardsmen fired on the blacks with mounted machine guns. The official death toll was thirty-six, including twenty-six blacks. Once again, historians and civil rights leaders have estimated that one hundred or more blacks were actually killed, their bodies hauled by the truckload to the outskirts of town and secretly buried in mass graves, or incinerated in their homes beyond human recognition, or dumped in the Arkansas River, whose treacherous waters, according to the enduring oral tradition of Tulsa's African Americans, "ran red" with the blood of blacks on the first day of June in the year of 1921.[44]

CHAPTER 13

The Deal with the Devil

East St. Louis, with its mile upon mile of utterly meaningless streets and mean houses, with something extraordinarily brutal and even threatening in the air, is the most perfect example, at least in America, of what happens under absentee ownership.

—Sherwood Anderson

During and immediately after the First World War, as hundreds of thousands of Southern blacks moved to the North in search of decent jobs and better lives, more than two dozen American cities and towns exploded in riot. The first and officially the deadliest of these race riots took place in East St. Louis. Why?

One way that East St. Louis differed from many Northern cities, it could be argued, was that it and the rest of southern Illinois were distinctly Southern in racial attitudes, more akin to the former slave states of Kentucky and Missouri on its riverine borders than to northern Illinois. The blacks who came to East St. Louis from the South by the thousands in 1915, 1916, and the first half of 1917 had been led to expect better treatment in the North. As the congressional committee that investigated the East St. Louis riot observed, "They swarmed into the railroad station on every train, to be met by their friends who formed reception committees and welcomed them to the financial, political and social liberty which they thought Illinois guaranteed." But East St. Louisans were not ready to grant those liberties, and resented the black newcomers for acting as if men and women with black skin were entitled to be treated as equals.

According to one East St. Louis business executive, "Being as close to the Mason Dixon line as we are, we naturally resent it when a Negro assumes the attitude of being able to do anything that he chooses . . . for instance getting on a streetcar and crowding up as close to a white woman as he can, and assuming that attitude." Another executive said that East St. Louis whites "didn't represent the Northern sentiment," which seems an understatement. The Ku Klux Klan was active in southern Illinois in 1917, even marching in robes through the streets of East St. Louis as hearings and trials were being held in the aftermath of the riot.

The relatively small size of the city may also have been a factor. The first major race riots of the twentieth century took place in towns and small cities in Missouri, Ohio, and Indiana, not in major metropolises like Chicago or Washington, D.C. In smaller cities and towns, blacks tended to live in the oldest sections, which almost always meant near downtown. The black ghetto inevitably would not be all that far from city hall and the central business district. In Chicago, most whites had little daily contact with the Black Belt on the city's South Side. In a small city like East St. Louis, much of the commercial, financial, governmental, and even social life of the city was conducted in the stores, theaters, meeting halls, and private and public office buildings of downtown. A large percentage of the population went downtown on a regular basis, where they inevitably saw large numbers of blacks and, in many cases, reacted negatively. In the congressional hearings, one white witness who worked downtown testified that on main downtown streets like Collinsville Avenue and Broadway, blacks often outnumbered whites, and another man said of blacks, "The streets were full of them."[1]

Also, the notion that there was a relatively large black population in East St. Louis was more than an illusion, at least in comparison to larger Northern cities. The black population of Chicago, the Promised Land to so many Southern blacks in the period, had reached 110,000 by 1920, the year after that city's riot, but blacks still made up only about 4 percent of the total population. At the time of the East St. Louis riot, blacks represented about 15 percent of the total population of the city. That may not seem like such a large percentage to contemporary readers, but the Great Migration had just begun in 1917 and at least one East St. Louis business executive, Raymond Rucker of the Aluminum Ore Company, said that the black population was "sufficient here to impress upon us that we have a native colored population, one which is a problem to deal with." The impression that downtown was swarming with blacks also may have been reinforced by the fact that East St. Louis was the northern and/or western terminus for several large railroads— a major regional transfer point—so at least some of the blacks downtown were waiting for trains to carry them to other cities to the north and west.[2]

Over the long term, probably the most important factor in laying groundwork for the riot was pervasive corruption. Few if any other American industrial cities, no matter how corrupt they may have been—and Chicago, Houston, and Tulsa, among others, were indisputably corrupt—had been so thoroughly turned over to its criminals and thugs as East St. Louis. The city's relatively small size and absentee ownership made it easier for it to be dominated by malign elements. The great majority of the residents were poor—in 1918, the U.S. Census Bureau named East St. Louis the second-poorest city in the country—with little political clout except in the weeks before municipal elections. Criminals and their hirelings ruled, with the help of corrupt police and politicians and judges.[3]

By the time of the riot, East St. Louis for several decades had been a city where street crime and sudden violence had become such an expected part of daily life that many ordinary citizens carried guns to town. "We had such corruption," newspaper publisher James Kirk remarked to the congressional investigating committee, "such maladministration, such robbery of the city treasury, such wholesale plundering, such crimes and vice and theft and utter disregard of the public interest that you would think the community would rise up in rebellion and go down to City Hall . . . and demand a change." In a sense, of course, much of the community did rise up on July 2, 1917, but the main targets were not in city hall.[4]

Numerous witnesses at the congressional riot hearings blamed black crime for inflaming whites in 1917. "One thing that helped lead up to the riot," said W. A. Miller, director of the downtown YMCA, "was a lawless element of colored fellows—may not be more than two or three—who were practicing robbing down in this Valley section. Every night there would be two or three robberies down there, and occasionally some fellow who refused to be robbed would be injured, maybe shot in the arm or leg, and . . . the police were never getting them." Even when these black holdup men were arrested, he said, they were soon out on bail and the case was "done away with" in the corrupt police courts.

"It is my opinion," Miller said, "that the race riot came as a result of the people who indulged in it coming to feel that there was no law in East St. Louis."[5]

The contribution of blacks to that lawless atmosphere was exaggerated, as even Miller suggested by observing that perhaps "no more than two or three" black robbers were operating in the Valley. A military board of inquiry looking into the performance of the National Guard during the July riot noted after several days of hearings that there was "no evidence tending to show that the lawless element among negroes is large or abnormal." Instead, the board said, "evidence tends to show that the negro citizens of the community and those who have come into East St. Louis within the last six to eight months are law abiding working people." As for assaults on white women—part of the festival of rumors that stoked the small city's racial fires in the first half of 1917—the military board of inquiry specifically asked East St. Louis mayor Fred Mollman if blacks, in the months leading up to the riot, were guilty of "any sex outrages."

"No," he replied.

"No complaints or prosecutions that white women were outraged by colored men?" he was asked.

"No, sir."[6]

What is almost certainly true is that crime was on the rise in the war-boom years of 1916 and 1917 among both blacks and whites. Blacks were blamed, in part because of the play given to blacks attacking whites in the *East St. Louis Daily Journal* and some other area newspapers. But in East St. Louis much of the crime in the streets was committed by whites. One particularly noxious plague zone surrounded the Commercial Hotel—a haunt of hoodlums and holdup men, pimps and whores, pickpockets and gamblers—less than two blocks from the main police station. The hotel's saloon and another one adjacent to it at Third and Missouri had been closed for several months by Mayor Fred Mollman in the winter and early spring. But Mollman had allowed the saloons to reopen after his landslide electoral victory in April, "adding to the already terrible lawless conditions of this section," said W. A. Miller, whose YMCA sat right across the street. At least one carload of gunmen who shot up black neighborhoods on July 1 seems to have come from the Commercial Hotel, so in that sense it had a direct causative connection to the riot.

In a letter to Mayor Mollman on May 25, three days before the first riot, Miller complained about the "daily practice of robbing and killing" around the hotel, and warned that because of "the lawless element harbored by saloons licensed by the city to operate in a section of vice and crime not equaled in any city in the West, I predict that more blood of good citizens will be spilled as a price of these saloon licenses."[7]

The reference to saloon licenses was not just a casual one. Because of cozy deals between businessmen and politicians, East St. Louis was starving for funds and as a result, ironically, crime, vice, and drunkenness had become integral to the city's fiscal survival. The single largest source of income to the city were saloon licenses.

That seems an astonishing statement, but in 1916 saloon licenses brought $175,000 into the coffers of East St. Louis, 43 percent of the city's $400,000 income for the year. By comparison, in roughly the same period, saloon licenses provided about 4.5 percent of the annual budget of St. Louis. In 1917, East St. Louis desperately tried to balance the city's books, which were soaked in red ink, by raising the price of a saloon license from $500 to $750 a year. Closing down all the city's noxious saloons simply did not make fiscal sense to the political machine that ran East St. Louis.[8]

In addition, fines for illegal and unlicensed saloons (and brothels and gambling joints) were crucial to the city. The money went into the public coffers after the unsalaried justices of the peace took their cuts. Unlicensed "blind tigers" in the Valley—black and white—were fined repeatedly, even after they had paid the routine bribes that police counted on to supplement their low salaries of $70 to $80 a month. The dives were never shut down for very long. The city needed them to reopen so it could fine them again. And East St. Louis also needed the fines and bribes paid by the hundreds of prostitutes, black and white, who worked the streets in twelve-hour shifts. One prostitute who worked for several decades and became known as the "Mother of the Valley" was arrested more than one hundred times, and she alone paid out several thousand dollars in fines and court costs.[9]

With the hundreds of prostitutes came dozens if not hundreds of pimps, men with strong arms and bad tempers, adding to the potential for violence. And the saloons and gambling joints and whorehouses lining the streets, particularly in the Valley and along the so-called Whiskey Chute across St. Clair Avenue from the stockyards, depended upon cadres of hoodlums and street toughs to maintain a semblance of order. In the years leading up to the riot, an untold number of criminals, white and black, arrived in East St. Louis—some of them from as far away as Chicago and New York—drawn by the small midwestern industrial and transportation center's reputation as a wide-open town with corrupt police and a notably forgiving judiciary. Most of these petty criminals were armed—guns could be bought for as little as fifty cents in downtown pawnshops—and the laws against carrying pistols were generally ignored. Some of the men were prone to acts of great brutality, like the notorious 1916 beheading of a three-year-old boy whose father would not stop complaining to police about criminal activity in his neighborhood.

East St. Louis's deal with the devil meant that when July of 1917 rolled around, the city was full of thugs and saloon brawlers, many of them armed, all of them prone to violence, with little regard for the social compact. Witness after witness at trials and hearings after the riot testified that many of the rioters came from the dozens of low dives jammed together side by side throughout the main part of the city, barrelhouses where the back bar might be a plank laid out over empty whiskey barrels, where whiskey was sold for a nickel a shot, with gambling in the back room and prostitutes upstairs.

East St. Louis had been prepared for the murderous onslaught of July 2, 1917, by decades of lawlessness, brutality, greed, selfish ambition, and racial animosity, much of it aroused by the cynical men who owned and controlled the city, although they did not necessarily live in it—or pay taxes to it. Some corporate executives tried to shift the blame to the unions, particularly members of the marginalized aluminum workers union. But Paul Anderson, among others, said he hadn't seen any men he associated with organized labor in the riot. Instead, "The men who seemed to take the most active part," Anderson said, "were the type that you would call saloon loungers; the kind of men who inhabit wine rooms and places of that character." Congressman John E. Raker, after hearing two weeks of searingly detailed testimony, described the men who led the rioting as "barrelhouse loafers."[10]

But what is surprising is the number of ordinary working people, not all of them poor, some of them middle-aged, who joined the riot and even helped lead it: a chauffeur, a railroad switchman, a messenger boy, an ice-wagon driver, a salesman of photo supplies, a security guard. Why did these seemingly ordinary people decide to join in the murder of black men, women, and children and the burning of more than a dozen square blocks of their hometown? And why did thousands of their fellow citizens let them do it, and in many cases cheer them on as they committed acts of shocking brutality against men, women, and children?

Race riots, including the one in East St. Louis, have been studied in great detail by sociologists, psychologists, and historians. It seems clear that what happened that hot July day in 1917 on the east bank of the Mississippi is what usually happens in a riot once it gets started. Mob psychology takes control and people do or acquiesce to horrible things most of them ordinarily would find repellent.

In an "emergent norm" event like the East St. Louis riot, leaders rise from a crowd riding a wave of rumor, fear, prejudice, hatred, and anger, and establish a new and more radical norm of behavior. The crowd becomes a mob and a mob has its own standards. The rioters become possessed by what lawyer-scholar Donald L. Horowitz has called a "lucid madness," not so much going out of control as shifting into a new mode of rationality in which killing members of another race becomes the logical and even moral thing to do. Dissenters are cowed into silence by assertive leaders as the mass moves toward a unanimity of rageful action.[11]

According to Horowitz, professor of political science and law at Duke University, racial, ethnic, and religious riots are often particularly brutal. Horowitz has studied ethnic and religious violence all over the world, genocidal tribal warfare in Africa and religious slaughter in Asia as well as American race riots like the one in East St. Louis. He observes, "Although atrocities and mutilations are occasionally present in other forms of violence, they are pervasive in the deadly ethnic riot."[12]

In most riots, the violence rises in an escalating rhythm, with leaders periodically giving the mob a jolt of energy by taking the action to a new and momentarily shocking level—killing the first person, hanging the first person, attacking women or children for the first time. Each step upward creates a new and even more murderous norm. The rules of civilized behavior no longer apply as the mob is caught up in the fury of the increasingly sadistic rising action.

British historian Malcolm McLaughlin, who has studied and written about the East St. Louis riot extensively, argues that the leaders who emerged from the crowd in East St. Louis were often people with a particular axe to grind—for example, white pimps and prostitutes and other petty criminals trying to exact revenge on the black competition and drive it out of town. These people, McLaughlin says, "physically orchestrated the violence, shaping and reshaping norms of behaviour in the riot, driving it forward . . . With a bold leading figure or subgroup acting consistently and with vigour, the crowd on July 2 came to accept greater and greater acts of violence . . . Simply put, whites in East St. Louis got 'caught up in the mood' of the riot."[13]

Significantly, he notes, reporter Roy Albertson remarked that, in the early stages of the riot, the rioters "were just running around . . . promiscuously from one end of the street to the other." After a while, Albertson said, "they would get tired of beating up negroes there and they would look for some other new game . . . As the day wore on, the rioting grew more serious."[14]

McLaughlin writes:

> Over the day, attacks became increasingly focused on killing—not simply beating—and involved increasingly systematic searches for African Americans . . . stopping streetcars, searching them for black passengers, dragging out those they found, and beating them with brickbats . . . Then, soon after 1 o'clock, two wagon drivers, Charles Hanna and John Dow, who were leading the assaults, dragged Edward Cook and his foster son from a streetcar and shot and killed them. From that point a new murderous intent became established . . . [A]n almost casual attitude developed towards murder once the behavioural boundary had been crossed; in the early afternoon, rioters "calmly" shot and killed prone victims. And while these core rioters broke increasingly brutal ground, the crowd followed behind them, not participating but cheering and "hissing" at dissenters to maintain unanimity.[15]

Later in the afternoon, white police officers reportedly suggested the rioters loot a pawnshop for weapons, and word spread that the police were on the side of the rioters, which helped make them feel their actions were more legitimate. After that, rioters with guns torched buildings in the black neighborhood along Third Street and shot blacks as they ran from them. Rioters were not just attacking passing blacks, as they had in the morning. They were looking for blacks to kill.

About three forty-five, a national guardsman asked a rioter to stop beating a black man, saying he had "done enough." The rioter immediately shot the black man through the head.

"Murder was now the established norm," observes McLaughlin. He goes on:

> By early evening, the brutal element was holding sway, controlling the riot at the "storm center" of Fourth and Broadway. It was after six o'clock, at the height of the violence, that the news reporter Paul Anderson, for example, saw a rioter sit on a black man and shoot not one but "several shots" into that man's head; one victim was shot in the face and then hanged; another was hanged and then shot twice in the head. There seems also to have been a degree of sadistic delight, which shocked watching reporters; a man being hanged was teased with "good natured jabs in the ribs" as a noose was placed around his neck . . .
>
> [T]he worst of the violence was carried out by a leadership core. Even when certain crowd members participated in a limited way, they still looked to the mob leadership to approve and orchestrate killings. When some crowd members beat two fleeing black men they did not kill them, but passed them on to more active rioters, shouting "hang them" and "swing 'em up." On another occasion, the crowd set two black men against a wall for three armed whites to shoot and kill . . .
>
> Undoubtedly, that assembled crowd bears responsibility for eventually supporting indiscriminate murder. However, without prodigiously violent individuals at the core of the mob, willing to break new violent ground, it seems far from certain that the riot would have ended in bloody tumult at Fourth and Broadway.[16]

Studies of riots and laboratory experiments suggest that being part of a mob, paradoxically, gives a rioter both anonymity and an identity. He embraces a collective vision—establishing that he is a right-thinking member of the group committing the violent acts—and at the same time he avoids personal responsibility by being a faceless member of the crowd. In general, the larger the lynch mob, the more terrible the atrocities it commits. And "deindividualization" in a mob attack does not apply only to the rioters. The victims are deprived of their individuality, their humanness, and thus become more easily attacked.[17]

For a rioter, being a member of a racist mob also makes it clear, to others as well as to himself, that he is not a member of the despised group. Jeremy Krikler, a British historian from South Africa, compares the East St. Louis riot to a racial massacre in 1922 in the streets of the Rand, Johannesburg's gold-mining district, during a long and bitter strike by miners. Mine owners had crushed the white miners' union by refusing to negotiate and by bringing in black strikebreakers. The government sided with the owners. Union leaders were arrested. Police and troops were mobilized to protect the strikebreakers and keep the mines open. Strikers were killed in street battles. And after two months of painful losses, amid false rumors of black uprisings, the defeated miners and other whites rose up and attacked black neighborhoods, killing as many as forty people, few of them having any direct involvement with the strike. The government had to call in the air force to quell the violence.

One reason for the degree of brutality in South Africa, Krikler speculates, is that the white miners were desperate to prove their own whiteness in a circumstance in which all of the powerful forces in their community were insisting that they were no better than the blacks—indeed, perhaps not as good. He sees a similar dynamic motivating the rioters in East St. Louis, a fear among poor whites of plunging lower than the lowest stratum of society and a need to identify with those higher up. He calls the massacre in East St. Louis "a collusion" of white assailants with police and National Guard:

> Given that not long before this, white para-military or military personnel had been used to suppress white workers' militancy in East St. Louis, is it not possible that the carnival of slaughter in 1917 was linked subconsciously to an attempt to restore that community of whites which had earlier been shattered by class conflict? What could do this better than working with the forces of law and order earlier used against strikers? Rumours of this time in East St. Louis—that formations (even "armies") of blacks were about to slaughter whites—are not very different from the kinds of rumour that plagued white working-class communities in 1922 on

the Rand and, significantly, they were the kinds of rumours that effaced all distinctions among whites since they gestured at a common threat to all classes.[18]

The Rand riot was fed by what was known as the "Black Peril," the enduring and periodically intensified fear that the black majority would swoop down upon the white invaders, killing, raping, and pillaging. White fear, racial paranoia, guilt, and rage coalesced to deadly effect. Similarly, the East St. Louis riot could be seen as resulting from the fear of a black uprising, spurred on by reports that the blacks were preparing to massacre whites on July 4 and that Dr. Leroy Bundy was training an armed cadre of blacks.

Those may have been false rumors, but there is no question that blacks in East St. Louis took a radical step on the first day of July in 1917. They armed themselves and gathered in the streets for self-defense, responding to months of attacks that culminated on July 1 in whites driving through black neighborhoods firing guns. To many whites, the armed blacks must have personified an American version of the Black Peril.

In other riots before East St. Louis, notably in Atlanta, blacks had used guns to defend their neighborhoods, but only after a riot was well under way, after homes had been burned down and blacks had been killed. What happened in East St. Louis was new, and that may well go a long way toward explaining why East St. Louis was the first city of the World War I period to erupt into race riot. For the first time, dozens if not hundreds of armed blacks assembled before the riot started. They were prepared to fight, to shoot and kill if necessary, in defense of their neighborhoods and their lives.

The fear of blacks organizing to repel white attacks with guns explains why whites were so alarmed at reports of the black Odd Fellows marching with weapons near Bundy's house earlier in the year; reports of a church bell ringing to signal blacks to arm themselves and get ready to fight; reports of blacks firing back at white gunmen riding through their neighborhoods late on the night of July 1. Those acts implied planning, preparations for a battle, for what de Tocqueville almost a century earlier had described as "the nightmare constantly haunting the American imagination"—that blacks would make war on the race that had enslaved them. The Black Peril in America.[19]

The attack on the police, which seems to have been a tragic mistake, gave whites a further reason for racial fear and anger. Not only were the blacks armed and organized, not only had they fired back at men who had driven through their neighborhoods shooting guns, but they had attacked the guardians of the white power structure. Two of the first race riots of the twentieth century were triggered by the killing of black policemen in small midwestern cities: in 1903 in Evansville, Indiana, and in 1904 in Springfield, Ohio. In East St. Louis, when a police car was attacked and two white policemen were fatally shot, it was as if all the worst rumors and racial fears were confirmed. The blacks were finally rising up and killing whites, and they needed to be stopped.

As far as many black leaders were concerned, the central issue in the trials of Leroy Bundy and the other black men for killing the two policemen was not murder or inciting to riot but black self-defense. In their eyes, the killing of the two policemen was, at worst, an understandable if regrettable accident whose root cause was the months-long reign of terror against African Americans. In both trials for the murder of the policemen, lawyers for the defense tried repeatedly—if futilely—to introduce evidence that the armed black men had assembled on the night of July 1 to defend themselves from nightriders firing into their homes. As W. E. B. Du Bois said in explaining the NAACP's initial decision to defend Bundy, "We were determined to leave no stone unturned to secure vindication for Dr. Bundy and, with this, the great and sacred right of self-defense for American Negroes in the face of the mob." The questions of self-defense and of responding with violence to white attacks and white oppression would continue to haunt the civil rights movement for decades to come.[20]

Finally, it cannot be forgotten that the riot in East St. Louis came at one of the most violent periods in history, as the United States and the world were struggling to absorb all the staggering changes—political, social, cultural, scientific, and technological—that came with the twentieth century. Empires were shattering, class structures were warping, traditional belief systems were evaporating, social compacts were being ripped up, and alliances were being torn apart. Europe was in the midst of a great war in which millions died in Sisyphean trench warfare, blown to bits by long-range shells from unseen artillery guns or choked to death from poison gas, a weapon so cruel it was banned in the war's aftermath.

The riot came at the midpoint of a notably bloody year in a notably bloody decade, a year whose pivotal events would haunt the world for the rest of the century and beyond. As blacks were being slaughtered in East St. Louis, American soldiers began dying in France. In Russia, the violent period that came to be known as the July Days commenced in the embattled streets of the capital, days of slaughter that led four months later to the Bolshevik Revolution. To the south of Russia, Turks continued the ethnic cleansing that, by the end of the year, would leave 1.5 million Armenians dead. And Germany introduced mustard gas to the battlefield—a weapon of appalling cynicism and cruelty, designed not to kill but to maim and thus add to the cruel burden of the enemy. Meanwhile, the British army marched into Jerusalem to fight the Turks in the name of establishing a Jewish state in Palestine. Thousands died, as many thousands more would die in years to come.

In America in 1917, labor disputes turned violent across the nation, from the shipyards of Brooklyn to the coal mines of southern Illinois, the lead mines of southeastern Missouri, and the steelyards of San Francisco, where marines were sent in to protect plants from twenty thousand striking ironworkers. By the end of the year, there had been forty-two hundred strikes nationwide, far more than in any previous year. Nightriders lynched blacks across the South, and throughout America dissenters from the war fever that seized the nation were brutally beaten, hanged, shot, and burned with hot tar. In the spring of 1917, as he prepared to bring the nation into what he would describe to Congress quite accurately as "the most terrible and disastrous of all wars," President Woodrow Wilson said despairingly, "Once lead this people into war, and they'll forget there ever was such a thing as tolerance."[21]

The World War I years were a time of great intolerance brutally expressed, of war and revolution and global chaos, the first movement of a dissonant century of unparalleled freedom and democracy and unparalleled tyranny and mass murder. As Hannah Arendt so eloquently has written, the "magnitude of the violence let loose in the First World War might have been enough to cause revolution in its aftermath even without any revolutionary tradition and even if no revolution had ever occurred before." It was a period whose defining notions came from nineteenth-century thinkers like Marx, Freud, Darwin, and Nietzsche, their theories and musings often perverted by vengeful demagogues. It was a period dominated by the new religions of class struggle, historical inevitability, survival of the fittest, racial purity, and the deep desires of the subconscious, a world many saw as purged of moral absolutes, where nothing was forbidden and everything was permitted. "The blood-dimmed tide is loosed, and everywhere the ceremony of innocence is drowned," a great poet wrote despairingly in 1919. The East St. Louis race riot and those that followed it were, in one sense, yet another bloody episode in the continuing American tragedy whose precipitating event was slavery. In another sense, they were manifestations of the agony of the emerging twentieth century, the most violent century of them all.[22]

The East St. Louis Blues

Bluesman Henry Townsend, who worked juke joints with Robert Johnson during the Depression and was still performing in his nineties, ran away from home as a boy in 1919 and rode an Illinois Central freight train 125 miles north from the river town of Cairo, Illinois. When he climbed down in the freight yards of East St. Louis, he discovered the riot was still "a fresh thing, it hadn't cooled off."

"Being a nine-year-old kid, I still knew what was happening," he recalled eighty years later. "I had to know because I'm still here . . . East St. Louis was a major migration area for people from the South. And everybody out of the South had a .45 or a .38 or something. And that was underestimated among the whites that got this thing kicked off."[1]

In the years following the riot, the black migration to East St. Louis slowly resumed. Even though the black population of East St. Louis remained a minority until the 1960s, the small city on the east bank of the Mississippi—in spite of the riot, or perhaps in part because of it—became known as a regional center of black life, epitomized by the impassioned music the migrants brought up from the fields and crossroads and whitewashed country churches of the South. "The East St. Louis Blues," essentially the lament W. C. Handy had heard on the St. Louis levee decades earlier, was recorded by Blind Willie McTell, Mississippi Fred McDowell, and Furry Lewis, among other historically important blues musicians. And in 1927, Duke Ellington celebrated East St. Louis's reputation as a tough, bluesy old town with one of his greatest compositions, "East St. Louis Toodle-Oo," for many years his theme song.

The riot was not forgotten, at least not among blacks. In 1932, in "East Chicago Blues," the Sparks Brothers sang, "East St. Louis is burning down." In the early 1940s, Harlem artist Jacob Lawrence made the East St. Louis riot integral to his "The Migration of the Negro" series with a highly stylized tempera view of a prone black man being attacked by whites with clubs and knives, now in the Museum of Modern Art. And in February of 1952, Josephine Baker spoke of the East St. Louis riot at length and with great passion when she came back to her hometown for the first time since the early 1920s. She talked and sang and danced and modeled the latest Paris fashions for a crowd of about six thousand at Kiel Auditorium in downtown St. Louis. The crowd was racially mixed—a rarity in the St. Louis area in those days.

Baker, who had lived for many years in France, where she was revered as an artist, a humanitarian, and a hero of the resistance, was on a rare tour of the United States. She had tears in her eyes as she looked out into the vast auditorium.[2] "Ladies and gentlemen," she said, "believe me when I say that it makes me profoundly happy, it makes my heart swell with pride to see in this beautiful audience tonight, salt and pepper. I mean by that colored and white brothers mingling."

She recalled that she had left St. Louis many years before in great part because of the East St. Louis riot:

> I can still see myself standing on the west bank of the Mississippi looking over into East St. Louis and watching the glow of the burning of Negro homes lighting the sky. We children stood huddled together in bewilderment . . . frightened to death with the screams of the Negro families running across this bridge with nothing but what they had on their backs as their worldly belongings . . .
>
> So with this vision I ran and ran and ran . . . but that glow in the sky of burning houses, the screams, the terror, the tears of the unfortunate children that had lost their parents—this kept coming before me on the stage, in the streets, in my sleep . . . I was haunted until I finally understood that I was marked by God to try to fight for the freedom of those that were being tortured.

She said she had finally decided to return to America and use her position of prominence to speak out about the tragedy of racial prejudice. She said, "Americans, the eyes of the world are upon you. How can you expect the world to believe in you and respect your preaching of democracy when you yourself treat your colored brothers as you do?"[3]

In the early and mid-1950s, another wave of blues musicians came up to East St. Louis from the South, including bandleader Ike Turner, singer Little Milton Campbell, and guitarist Albert King. Chuck Berry would drive over from St. Louis to play guitar and sing with pianist Johnnie Johnson at the Cosmopolitan Club at Seventeenth and Bond. In 1958, a teenage girl from St. Louis named Annie Bullock with an exhilarating gospel-drenched voice began singing in East St. Louis with Ike Turner. Soon, she married him and became Tina Turner. Many years later, after she had become an international singing star, she recalled that St. Louis was "a fairly sedate place" in the mid-fifties. But across the river, particularly after hours, East St. Louis was something else entirely. "East St. Louis had *action*, and it never seemed to stop."[4]

East St. Louis black poet Eugene Redmond calls his hometown "East Boogie." "This was the hotbed, Paradise and Mississippi," said Redmond, gesturing at a now-vacant intersection of unpaved streets in Rush City, a section of East St. Louis between the South End and Monsanto chemical plants, whose stacks tower over the landscape from the adjoining company town of Sauget. "You could hear Ike and Tina Turner, B. B. King, Lightning Hopkins, Jimmy Reed. When I was a kid, the population of Rush City was around fifteen hundred people. Now it's down to perhaps two hundred."

"Paradise Street," he said, laughing. "From time to time, Monsanto would emit a colorless, odorless gas that would send the people of Paradise Street choking to the emergency room." There were a few remaining shotgun houses and trailers scattered among the weeds along Paradise Street. In the distance, on the opposite shore, we could see the gleaming Gateway Arch, a monument to westward migration.

Redmond, a poet and professor of English at Southern Illinois University in suburban Edwardsville, grew up in East St. Louis in the 1940s and 1950s, spending the early years of his life on Paradise Street. Like Miles Davis two decades earlier, and like thousands of other black kids growing up in these parts over the years, Redmond heard about the massacre of 1917 long before he started grade school. "There has never been a time when the riot was not alive in the oral tradition," he said.

He was conducting a personal and historical tour of his hometown, something he frequently does for visitors, who come in increasing numbers from as far away as Europe and Japan to see the town that produced Miles Davis and Ike and Tina Turner.

Redmond has been a professor and poet-in-residence at colleges across the country, from Oberlin in Ohio to California State University at Sacramento, but he came back to East St. Louis in 1986 because of "a chronic case of homesickness." Redmond then became poet-in-residence for the schools of East St. Louis, going into some of the toughest classrooms in the country and encouraging kids to learn about the rich history and culture of African Americans, getting them to write poems and essays and short stories. Redmond has been the mentor of several generations of writers from the area and he is the editor of a literary magazine, *Drumvoices Revue*, which publishes local poets and fiction writers alongside the work of nationally prominent black writers like Amiri Baraka and Maya Angelou. Eugene Redmond is the official poet laureate of East St. Louis, a title he takes seriously, always working on the next gala poetry reading or jazz concert or cultural celebration in his hometown. His latest project was what he called "a mini-World's Fair" in 2008 to celebrate black culture and the large role East St. Louis has played in it. "East St. Louis ain't dead yet," Eugene Redmond says. "I got the scars and tattoos to prove it."

Redmond, wearing an African black-leather hat, circular with a slanted top like a beret, and an old sweatshirt promoting the Miles Davis Arts Festival, put his battered old compact car in gear and we left Rush City and headed north, past acres of rubble-strewn vacant lots struggling to become prairie once again.

We crossed into the South End, bouncing across rails—not an old streetcar track, a freight rail line that runs right down the middle of a wide street with houses on either side. There were many vacant lots in this part of the city, south and east of the shabby downtown business district, but the houses that remained were larger than the tiny ones in Rush City.

He slowed down as he said, "This neighborhood was prosperity for the blacks in the early part of the twentieth century, and the rioters sacked it. A lot of it was never built back up."

We drove past houses where well-known East St. Louisans had grown up: Olympic champion Jackie Joyner-Kersee; film-director brothers Warrington and Reginald Hudlin; Barbara Ann Teer, who founded the National Black Theater in Harlem; Miles Davis. Redmond pointed out the red shotgun house where Ike and Tina Turner lived. In the African tradition, poets are part magician, and Redmond has an almost mystical belief in the ability of East St. Louis to turn out exceptional people. He has a point. There is something remarkable about the number of prominent men and women who have come from its financially gutted schools, its dilapidated housing, its polluted environment, and its mean streets. East St. Louis not only turns out athletes and musicians and other people in the arts, but also people like Senate Democratic leader Richard Durbin, Donald McHenry, ambassador to the United Nations under Jimmy Carter, and Ellen Soeteber, editor of the *St. Louis Post-Dispatch* from 2001 to 2005.

We crossed Bond Avenue, a main thoroughfare for aspiring blacks in the first half of the twentieth century, and, in July of 1917, the street where two white policemen were fatally shot to trigger the deadliest race riot of an era. We continued through the city to the North End and the old stockyards. The cows and pigs and sheep were all gone, and what remained had an ominous post-apocalyptic feel—bare pillars and weather-eaten smokestacks and multilevel structures that look like ruined parking garages three and four and five stories high, where pigs by the thousands once walked up ramps to slaughter. We stopped for a moment. "Listen," says Redmond. The wind rustled through the weeds and thistles and moaned around the bare superstructures of the abandoned slaughterhouses. Redmond smiled sadly, and gently shook his head.

"I come here and meditate on East St. Louis and sometimes I can hear the squeals of the pigs that died here when I was a child."

We headed east past the abandoned stockyards and turned onto an interstate highway. "They built the first freeway in 1964, and it ruined East St. Louis," Redmond said. "Now the rich people could just drive right past it, right over it." We were still well within the limits of East St. Louis, driving east through land that was mostly vacant, land that Redmond envisioned just waiting for the bulldozer or the plow. "The city is twelve square miles. See all this land?" he asked. "There is enough land to feed everybody."[5]

The population of East St. Louis hit its peak of eighty-two thousand in 1950, when the city was still predominantly white. The tipping point—when blacks began to outnumber whites—came in the very early 1960s, and the departure of whites became a panicked exodus. By 1970, the total population had fallen to seventy thousand, about 70 percent black.[6]

The dancer and choreographer Katherine Dunham, who, like Josephine Baker, was at least as well known in Paris and Rome as she was in the United States, came to East St. Louis in 1964 as part of an extended visit to Southern Illinois University's Edwardsville (SIUE) campus. Dunham, who brought African tradition into modern dance, had grown up in the Chicago suburb of Joliet. She was seven years old when the riot ripped the heart out of East St. Louis, and, like Baker, she never forgot it.

When she saw the poverty and desolation of so much of East St. Louis almost five decades later, she typically became inspired to start a new project—to help save East St. Louis. She became artist in residence at SIUE. Periodically, she would leave—to choreograph a show in Rome for Marcello

Katherine Dunham

Mastroianni, to direct dance troupes and to perform herself in Paris and New York, Senegal and Haiti. Haiti became her second home. But she kept coming back to southern Illinois. She bought a house in East St. Louis and established a performing arts center nearby to teach dance and martial arts to young people of the city.[7]

In the summer of 1964, a white policeman shot an unarmed black fifteen-year-old in Harlem, and in response a black mob looted and burned white-owned stores in Harlem and in the Brooklyn neighborhood of Bedford-Stuyvesant. Race riots hit other American cities that year, and in 1965, when the six-day Watts riot in Los Angeles resulted in the death of thirty-four people, twenty-five of them black. The riots continued in the late 1960s, an era of great social change, like the 1910s. But these riots — some blacks called them "uprisings" — were different in several significant ways from those of the World War I period. Perhaps most important, although whites were often attacked and sometimes killed in the course of the riots, and hundreds of millions of dollars' worth of white-owned property was destroyed, there was very little of the relentless racial stalking and slaughter that marked the riots in East St. Louis, Tulsa, and elsewhere earlier in the century. These were not racial massacres.[8]

In September of 1967, a race riot broke out in East St. Louis. It grew out of protest marches inspired by a visit from militant H. Rap Brown. A young black protester was shot to death when he ran from police, who were questioning him in a stockyards parking lot, and about thirty blacks marched on the East St. Louis police station. Shortly afterward, gangs began looting and burning white-owned businesses in the South End and attacking the cars of white motorists. After two days and about thirty-five arrests, the riot died down. The only fatality was the young black man shot by police.[9]

After the riot, Katherine Dunham intensified her work with young people in the city and in 1970 she took forty-three students from East St. Louis to Washington, where they performed African dance and karate at the White House. Over the years since then, students from the Katherine Dunham center in East St. Louis have performed across the country, and the center has worked with thousands of young people, bringing in teachers from around the world.[10]

In the 1970s, a black political machine took over the government of East St. Louis from the white political machine that had run the city for one hundred years. The stockyards closed in the 1960s and early 1970s and some of the major industries left the area as well, leaving nationally prominent hazardous waste sites in their wake. By the 1980s, when author Jonathan Kozol visited East St. Louis for *Savage Inequalities*, his excoriating and anguished examination of the raw deal poor kids were getting in America's public schools, East St. Louis was 98 percent black, and poorer than it had ever been. In fact 75 percent of the city's population was on some form of welfare. The Department of Housing and Urban Development described East St. Louis as "the most distressed small city in America." Chemical plants in nearby company towns so polluted the air that East St. Louis had one of the highest rates of child asthma in the United States. At the pitiful public housing projects in the city, raw sewage backed up into sinks and bathtubs, into shower rooms at a public school, and into a children's playground, forming what Kozol described as "an oozing lake . . . a lagoon" filled with billions of bacteria where more than one hundred children played every day. And the city could not afford the $5,000 needed to fix the old vacuum truck used to unclog sewers. Dozens of children were discovered to have frightening amounts of lead in their blood and brains. Dangerously high levels of arsenic, mercury, and lead, as well as steroids used by the stockyards to plump up cattle, were detected in the soil. The mayor of East St. Louis announced he might have to sell city hall and six fire stations to meet the budget, which didn't even have funds to heat city buildings or supply them with toilet paper.[11]

And yet the story of East St. Louis was not entirely a negative one.

Jacqueline Joyner and her older brother Al grew up poor in the 1960s in the South End of East St. Louis, in a tiny, badly heated house on Piggott Avenue between Fifteenth and Sixteenth streets. She later described her neighborhood as a "rough and tumble precinct"—and when children refer to their neighborhood as a "precinct," you can be pretty sure it is known for crime.[12]

Jackie was an exceptionally athletic child. In 1969, when she turned seven, the city-supported Mary E. Brown Community Center opened near her house, and the gymnasium and basketball court became her second home. Eight years later, at Lincoln High School, she was beating all comers in track and field, her specialties being dashes, hurdles, and the long jump. In 1981, in her freshman year at UCLA, her mother collapsed from a bacterial infection back home in East St. Louis. Mary Joyner was only thirty-seven years old. Jackie rushed home and found her mother on a respirator with irreversible brain damage. Jackie was the one who finally had to make the decision to discontinue life support.

Devastated by grief, she quietly left her childhood home, which was filled with mourners, and walked in the gray January cold to the Mary E. Brown Community Center, where she hoped to spend a few minutes shooting baskets to try and take her mind off the tragedy. She was stunned to discover that it was closed.

"I didn't realize the center was boarded up," she recalled. "I thought, 'Where do the kids go?' . . . At the place that I had grown up and gotten used to, the doors were no longer open and I thought about the other kids in the neighborhood."

At UCLA, Joyner married another young track star, Bob Kersee, who became her coach. By the time she graduated with a degree in history in 1986, she had become the greatest female athlete in the world. She tried several times to get the Mary E. Brown center reopened, but there was no money, and she was far from rich. Frustrated, she raised enough money to fly a group of children from East St. Louis to New York for the Macy's Thanksgiving Day Parade.

In 1988, Jackie Joyner-Kersee set new records in the heptathlon and the long jump, and she would continue her dominance in international competition for much of the next decade. The same year, she and her husband established the Jackie Joyner-Kersee Youth Center Foundation to raise funds for a recreational center for young East St. Louisans. The foundation raised twelve million dollars, and in 1999 and 2000, on a thirty-seven-acre site in East St. Louis, built the forty-one-thousand-square-foot Jackie Joyner-Kersee Youth Center, affiliated with the national Boys and Girls Club. The Joyner-Kersee Center has its own stop on St. Louis's MetroLink light rail system.[13]

In early July of 1997, St. Louisan Gary Kennedy, whose grandmother Katherine and father Samuel had escaped from the 1917 riot on a raft, led a ceremony in downtown East St. Louis to commemorate the eightieth anniversary of the tragedy. Several hundred people from St. Louis and East St. Louis, including survivors of the riot and their descendants, joined the commemoration. Gary Kennedy said he wanted "to honor the people of both races who perished in the riot and to encourage unity and healing." He also spoke of his father, who, after a long struggle with poverty—at one point, he made his living boxing on the streets of St. Louis—became the president of a local textile workers union and, in 1962, a St. Louis alderman. He served until his death in 1988. The following year, his son Terry, Gary's twin brother, was elected to succeed him.[14]

By the 2000 census, eight out of ten East St. Louis families were headed by single mothers. And eight out of ten children at a representative middle school in the city received government assistance. The population of East St. Louis had shrunk to 31,450, and one fifth of those people lived in public housing. East St. Louis was one of the most segregated cities in America, and one of the poorest.[15] Poverty, mismanagement, and corruption in the city had by then resulted in the establishment of the East St. Louis Financial Advisory Authority, a state board with wide-ranging powers over the city, including control over its budget and finances.[16]

In 2004, the young black cartoonist Aaron McGruder (*The Boondocks*) collaborated with East St. Louis–raised filmmaker Reginald Hudlin to create a satirical graphic novel called *Birth of a Nation*. In the book, the mayor of East St. Louis—"the inner city without an outer city"—secedes from a racist nation after a radical right-wing junta headed by a dim-witted Texas governor steals the presidency by denying 1,023 perfectly honest black citizens of East St. Louis their legal right to vote on the grounds that they are felons. The Supreme Court, by a 5 to 4 vote, refuses to overturn the election.

So East St. Louis becomes Blackland, with a national anthem sung to the tune of the theme from *Good Times* and Ike Turner's face slated to adorn the $5 bill. Back in Washington, the bellicose new president and his eager-to-please African American secretary of state decide to send in the troops to effect a regime change. East St. Louis stands its ground in the face of attack. Finally, the president backs down, and East St. Louis—Blackland—is on its own, an independent nation.

On July 2, 2004, Anne Walker, a Dunham dancer and teacher who founded a black history organization called Freedom Trails, Legacies of Hope, organized a downtown commemoration of the eighty-seventh anniversary of the 1917 riot that had so horrified Katherine Dunham as a young girl. The commemoration has become an annual event, with a procession from downtown to the Eads Bridge to drop a wreath on the Mississippi. The procession is silent save for the beat of drums in conscious emulation of the original Silent Parade.

In 2005, in part inspired by recent intensive investigations into riots in Tulsa, Wilmington, N.C., and the demolished black town of Rosewood, Florida, investigations that led to calls for compensation to the descendants of riot victims, the Illinois General Assembly approved a joint resolution to create the Illinois Riot and Reparations Commission. It was charged with reexamining race riots in the state, including the one in East St. Louis in 1917, and making a report by January 7, 2009.[17]

In May of 2006, one month shy of her ninety-seventh birthday, which she had hoped to celebrate in East St. Louis, Katherine Dunham died at her home in New York. Her birthday and her passing were celebrated in East St. Louis by four generations of her students with dance and music and poetry and African drums.[18] About the same time, the chief of police of East St. Louis was sent to prison for taking a gun out of evidence and selling it back to the criminal suspect it had been confiscated from.[19]

The following spring, Alvin L. Parks, a former councilman and city manager who had the backing of the city's Democratic central committee, was elected mayor of East St. Louis. Like many mayors-elect before him, Park vowed to clean up the city's streets and riverfront, get rid of drug dealers, promote economic development, and strengthen the police department. The citizens of East St. Louis, he said, wanted and deserved "a life more abundant."

"I know you've heard a thousand people say this," he told a visitor. "I truly believe in the future of East St. Louis."[20]

Acknowledgments

First of all, I would like to express my deep gratitude to Andrew Theising for teaching me about East St. Louis and to Eugene Redmond for showing me its soul. Writing *Never Been a Time* would have been much more difficult, and much less enjoyable, without their help. Andy, author of *Made in USA: East St. Louis*, was also kind enough to read my manuscript and share with me and my publisher the extensive file of photos and illustrations from his book. Eugene, poet and educator, was always eager to help and his wisdom and enthusiasm were an inspiration.

I would like to thank my agent, Matthew Carnicelli, and my publisher, George Gibson, for agreeing with me that this was a story that needed to be told and one that would be read. I am also grateful to George and editor Jacqueline Johnson for insisting that the story needed its roots firmly planted in the tragic history of race relations in America. At Walker and Company, I would also like to thank Laura Keefe, Peter Miller, Michele Lee Amundsen, Michael O'Connor, and Paula Cooper.

For help in research, I am indebted to Adele Heagney, Joseph Winkler, and Keith Zimmer of the main branch of the St. Louis Public Library, as well as the staff of the Julia Davis branch, with its extensive and invaluable collection of thousands of books and other documents of African American history, much of it assembled by the teacher whose name the branch bears. I am also grateful to Duane Sneddeker of the Missouri Historical Society Library, Deborah Cribbs of the St. Louis Mercantile Library, Walter Hill and Rodney Ross of the National Archives, Janet Cameron Levkowicz of the libraries of the University of New Orleans, Elaine Pichaske Sokolowski of the Peoria

(Illinois) Public Library, and the staffs of the Omer Poos Law Library at St. Louis University, the Olin Library at Washington University, the Lovejoy Library at Southern Illinois University Edwardsville, the Ellis Library at the University of Missouri–Columbia, and the public libraries of the cities of East St. Louis and Belleville, Illinois.

For help along the way, I would like to thank Paul Solman, Joe Klein, Jill-Ellyn Riley, Diane McWhorter, Durb Curlee, Dan McGuire, Anne Walker, Gary and Terry Kennedy, Dan Martin, Susan Luberda, Matthew Fernandes, Hillary Levin, Ernest Stadler, June and Larry Rouse, and Charles Lumpkins. Finally, I was helped and inspired by the work of three writers now deceased who preceded me in recounting the tragedy of the East St. Louis riot of 1917: Paul Y. Anderson and Carlos Hurd of the *St. Louis Post-Dispatch* and Elliott Rudwick, author of the superb 1964 study *Race Riot at East St. Louis*.

Notes

INTRODUCTION: A HISTORY OF VIOLENCE

1. H. Rap. Brown, head of the Student Non-Violent Co-Ordinating Committee, said in 1967 of the black race riots of the era, "I say violence is necessary. It is as American as cherry pie." See *NYT*, July 28, 1967. Woodson, *A Century of Negro Migration*, 3.

2. Numerous scholarly sources, such as Henderson H. Donald in *Negro Migration*, 18–19, and George W. Groh in *The Black Migration*, 48, postulate a total northward migration of five hundred thousand or more in the decade from 1910 to 1920, as do standard references such as the *Encyclopedia Britannica* and *Africana: The Encyclopedia of the African and African American Experience*. With its release of the 1920 census, the United States Census Bureau reported, "While it is impossible to calculate exactly the extent of this [black] migration during the recent decade, the available data indicate that approximately 400,000 [blacks] left the South subsequent to April 15, 1910." Censuses and other surveys traditionally have undercounted blacks, poor people, and immigrants, all categories that apply to statistics on African Americans moving to the northern United States. (See Donald, *Negro Migration*, preface, 15.)

3. Myrdal, *An American Dilemma*, 566.

4. The exact number of blacks in East St. Louis at the time of the riots in 1917 is difficult to determine, in part because the black population peaked in the spring, just before the May riot, and plunged immediately after the July riot. For his meticulous and authoritative book on the 1917 riot, *Race Riot at East St. Louis, July 2, 1917*, Southern Illinois University sociologist Elliott Rudwick examined the records of the strictly segregated East St. Louis school system and selective service records. He estimated that the black population of East St. Louis went from about 8,200 in 1916 to between 10,600 and 13,000 in the spring of 1917, suggesting roughly 2,500 to 5,000 blacks arrived in a year or so. At that point, the total population of East St. Louis was roughly 75,000, up from 72,000 in 1915. See *Statistical Abstract of the*

United States, 1915, no. 38, published in 1916 by the Department of Commerce; Rudwick, *Race Riot 1917*, 160–70; McLaughlin, *Power, Community, and Racial Killing*, 11; and Rudwick, "Colonization," 42.

CHAPTER 1: BROTHERLY LOVE

1. Historical Census Statistics.
2. Runcie, "Hunting," 189.
3. Du Bois, *The Philadelphia Negro*, chap. 4, sec. 10.
4. Woodson, *A Century of Black Migration*, 43; Runcie, "Hunting," 187.
5. Runcie, "Hunting," 210.
6. Gilbert, *Westering Man*, 13–25.
7. Schecter, *The Devil's Own Work*, 36; Runcie, "Hunting," 199.
8. Runcie, "Hunting," 206–13.
9. Du Bois, *Philadelphia Negro*, chap. 13, sec. 37.
10. Ibid., chap. 18, sec. 58.
11. Ibid., chap. 4, sec. 10.
12. Jefferson, *Notes on the State of Virginia*, 291; Baldwin, *The Fire Next Time*, 4.
13. Schecter, *Devil's Own Work*, 40–45.
14. Woodson, *A Century of Black Migration*, 57–58.
15. Primm, *Lion of the Valley*, 182–85.
16. Schechter, *Devil's Own Work*, 47.
17. Lincoln, *Collected Works of Abraham Lincoln*, vol. 1, 109–10.
18. Schecter, *Devil's Own Work*, 51; Franklin, *From Slavery to Freedom*, 228.
19. Schecter, *Devil's Own Work*, 33.
20. Ibid., 4–8, 148–52.

CHAPTER 2: RECONSTRUCTION AND REDEMPTION: FROM HOPE TO DESPAIR

1. Historical Census Statistics. Note: High black death rates and low black birth rates in Northern cities in the nineteenth and early twentieth centuries meant that virtually all population growth came from migration. In some Northern cities, and in New York State as a whole, deaths among blacks significantly exceeded births from 1895 to 1915, so the population of blacks in those areas actually would have shrunk if it were not for migration. In that period, more than one fourth of black infants in the North died before the age of one, which was twice the death rate for white infants. Black adults also died at a much higher rate than whites in the cities of the North. Also, many of the migrants to the North were single men and women, others were married men who left their wives and families at home, at least for the time being, as job-seeking immigrants often do, so there was a relatively low birth rate among blacks in the North. See Henri, *Black Migration*, 112–13, and Scroggs, "Interstate Migration of Negro Population," 1039.
2. Eric Foner, *Reconstruction*, 261–63.

3. Du Bois, *Black Reconstruction*, 678.
4. Eric Foner, *Reconstruction*, 140–42.
5. Du Bois, *Black Reconstruction*, 671–78.
6. Ibid., 678.
7. Ibid., 676.
8. Lemann, *Redemption*, 3–22.
9. Foner, *Reconstruction*, 558; Williams, "Long Hot Summers," 13.
10. Foner, *Reconstruction*, 558–63.
11. Du Bois, *Black Reconstruction*, 30.
12. Matison, *Labor Movement and the Negro*, 430–31.
13. Spero and Harris, *Black Worker*, 23–24.
14. Foner, *Reconstruction*, 512–13.
15. Franklin, *From Slavery to Freedom*, 310–11.
16. Historical Census Statistics.
17. Scott, *Negro Migration*, 4–6.
18. Bontemps and Conroy, *Anyplace But Here*, 57–71; Scott, *Black Migration*, 6; Historical Census Statistics: Between 1870 and 1880, according to the U.S. Census Bureau, the black population of Kansas increased from 17,000 to 43,000.
19. Woodson, *A Century of Negro Migration*, 142.
20. Bontemps and Conroy, *Anyplace But Here*, 65.
21. Douglass, *Life and Times*, 433–35.
22. Bontemps and Conroy, *Anyplace But Here*, 61.
23. Historical Census Statistics.
24. Logan, *Negro in American Life and Thought*.
25. Henri, *Black Migration*, 10.
26. Tuskegee Institute.
27. Tolnay and Beck, *Festival of Violence*, 119–37.
28. Benedict, *Race*, 151.
29. Wells-Barnett, *Crusade for Justice*, 18–20, 52.
30. Wells-Barnett, *On Lynchings*, 14–29; Wells-Barnett, *Crusade for Justice*, chap. 5.
31. Harlan, *The Making of a Black Leader*, 163.
32. Ibid., 210–17.
33. Ibid., 219–20.
34. Ibid., 222–28.
35. Lewis, *Biography of a Race*, 175, 206.
36. Harlan, *Making of a Black Leader*, 225–26; Wells-Barnett, *Crusade for Justice*, 265; Myrick-Harris, "Ida B. Wells."
37. Henri, *Black Migration*, 14–15.
38. Much of the information on the riot comes from the official *Wilmington Race Riot Report*. See also Tyson, "The Ghosts of 1898."
39. Tyson, "The Ghosts of 1898."
40. "Alex Manly—Wilmington Race Riots," *Encyclopedia of the State Library of North Carolina*.

41. *Wilmington Race Riot Report*, chap. 8.
42. Historical Census Statistics.

CHAPTER 3: A HARVEST OF DISASTER

1. Franklin, *From Slavery to Freedom*, 341; Harlan, *Wizard of Tuskegee*, 3–6.
2. Tolnay and Beck, *Festival of Violence*, 119–37; Historical Census Statistics.
3. Franklin, *From Slavery to Freedom*, 340–46; Henri, *Black Migration*, 52, 112–13.
4. Lewis, *Biography of a Race*, 222; Foner and Lewis, *Black Workers*, 286.
5. Williams, "Long Hot Summers," 14; *Monett (Mo.) Times,* Aug. 10, 2001; *NYT, PD,* June 8, 1903.
6. Godshalk, *Veiled Visions*, 59.
7. Lewis, *Biography of a Race*, 226.
8. Du Bois, *Souls of Black Folk*, 48.
9. Ibid., 14, 45–49.
10. Lewis, *Biography of a Race*, 320–25.
11. Godshalk, *Veiled Visions*, 13–25.
12. Lewis, *Biography of a Race*, 332–35.
13. Godshalk, *Veiled Visions*, 39–47.
14. Baker, *Following the Color Line*, 4–8.
15. Lewis, *Biography of a Race*, 330; Godshalk, *Veiled Visions*, 74–76.
16. Baker, *Following the Color Line*, 9–10.
17. Godshalk, *Veiled Visions,* 86–115.
18. Lewis, *Biography of a Race*, 333–40.
19. Godshalk, *Veiled Visions*, 123, 191–92.
20. Ibid., 143–50; *NYT*, Sept. 24, 2006.
21. Godshalk, *Veiled Visions,* 182–83.
22. Lewis, *Biography of a Race*, 376–87.
23. Senechal, "The Springfield Race Riot," 22–32.
24. Ibid., 25.
25. Lewis, *Biography of a Race*, 386–407; Wells-Barnett, *Crusade for Justice*, 324–26.

CHAPTER 4: EAST ST. LOUIS AND THE GREAT EXODUS

1. Information on the early development of East St. Louis and St. Louis comes from Theising, *Made in USA*, chaps. 2–4, and Primm, *Lion of the Valley*, chaps. 1–3.
2. *Journal*, Sept. 24, 1916.
3. Southern, "In Retrospect," 85–86.
4. Handy, *Father of the Blues*, 26–27, 120–21.
5. Theising, *Made in USA*, 105–13.
6. Congressional Hearings, 1912–13; McLaughlin, *Power, Community, and Racial Killing*, 12–15.
7. Tuttle, *Red Summer*, 120–22.
8. Wells-Barnett, *Crusade for Justice*, 310.

9. Rudwick, *Race Riot*, 165; McLaughlin, *Power, Community, and Racial Killing*, 10–11.

10. Scott, *Negro Migration*, 41.

11. Ottley, *The Lonely Warrior*, 121–37.

12. Ibid., 105–15.

13. Ibid., 138–40, 126.

14. Ibid., 133–34, 159–70.

15. Ibid., 144–46.

16. *Defender*, Feb. 24, 1917.

17. Lemann, *The Promised Land*, 15–17.

18. Historical Census Statistics; Scott, *Negro Migration*, 3.

19. Spero, *The Black Worker*, 151.

20. Arnesen, *Brotherhoods of Color*, 8, 44.

21. Foner and Lewis, *Black Workers*, 306–7.

22. Donald, *Negro Migration*, 20.

23. Epstein, *The Negro Migrant in Pittsburgh*, 31–32.

24. Foner and Lewis, *Black Workers*, 318.

25. Donald, *Negro Migration*, 29.

26. Primm, *Lion of the Valley*, 434–39.

27. Lewis, *Biography of a Race*, 506. See also "D. W. Griffith's *The Birth of a Nation*" on the PBS Web site http://www.pbs.org/wnet/jimcrow/stories_events_birth.html.

CHAPTER 5: A NEST OF CRIME AND CORRUPTION

1. Congressional Hearings, 1755–84.

2. Ibid., 1190.

3. Rudwick, *Race Riot*, 5–6.

4. Davis, *Miles*, 15–16, 38.

5. *PD*, July–Aug. 1916.

6. Rudwick, *Race Riot*, 91; *Journal*, Sept. 30, 1917.

7. Rudwick, *Race Riot*, 20–21.

8. Congressional Hearings, 2055–56; Rudwick, *Race Riot*, 20.

9. Congressional Hearings, 1525, 2150–53; *Journal*, Oct. 9–10, 1916.

10. Congressional Hearings, 1828–30.

11. Rudwick, *Race Riot*, 17.

12. *Journal*, Oct. 8, 9, 1916.

13. Rudwick, *Race Riot*, 13–14; *Argus*, Oct 6, 20, 1916.

14. Henri, *Black Migration*, 252–55; Lewis, *Biography of a Race*, 423; Wolgemuth, "Woodrow Wilson and Federal Segregation," 158–73.

15. *Argus*, Nov. 3, 1916; Lewis, *Biography of a Race*, 522.

16. Henri, *Black Migration*, 256–58; Rudwick, "Colonization," 40; *GD*, Oct. 17, 1916.

17. *Journal*, Oct. 10, 1916.

18. *Journal* (reprint of *News-Democrat* article), Nov. 1, 1916.

19. Lumpkins, "East St. Louis Pogrom," 7.
20. Rudwick, *Race Riot*, 119–20; *Defender*, Oct. 20, 1917.
21. *Journal*, Oct. 6, 18–19, 1916. See also Rudwick, "Colonization Conspiracy."
22. *GD*, Oct. 26, 30, 1916.
23. Rudwick, *Race Riot*, 136; *Journal*, Nov. 9, 1916.
24. Congressional Hearings, 579; Rudwick, "Colonization Conspiracy," 39.
25. Military Board of Inquiry, 20–23.

CHAPTER 6: THE MAY RIOT

1. Congressional Hearings, 616, 1173.
2. Ibid., 3787–90.
3. Ibid., 3638; *Journal*, Feb. 15–25, 1917.
4. Ottley, *The Lonely Warrior*, 162–72.
5. Tuttle, *Red Summer*, 90.
6. Congressional Hearings, 1025–26.
7. Ibid., 1531.
8. Rudwick, *Race Riot*, 18–23; Foner and Lewis, *Black Worker*, vol. 5, 284. McLaughlin, *Power, Community, and Racial Killing*, 16.
9. Sinclair, *The Jungle*, 123–24.
10. Ibid.
11. *Journal*, March 27, 1917; Congressional Hearings, 1792–98.
12. Brecher, *Strike!*, 115–19; Bing, *War-Time Strikes*, 7–9, 293.
13. Foner and Lewis, *Black Workers*, 288; Lewis, *Biography of a Race*, 419–20.
14. *Journal*, March 30, 1917.
15. Congressional Hearings, 3511.
16. Theising, *Made in USA*, 142–44; *Report of Special Committee Authorized by Congress*, 10–11.
17. Rudwick, *Race Riot*, 187–88.
18. *PD*, Nov. 19, 1917; Congressional Hearings, 3508–27.
19. *Journal*, April 4, 1917; Congressional Hearings, 3564–65, 3723.
20. *Journal*, April 14, 1917.
21. Congressional Hearings, 4073, 4102.
22. *Journal*, April 19, 1917.
23. Rudwick, *Race Riot*, 18–23; *Journal*, April 26, 1917.
24. *Journal*, May 11, 1917.
25. Ibid., May 14–16; Congressional Hearings, 3125.
26. *New Orleans Times-Picayune*, April 27–29, 1917.
27. Congressional Hearings, 1999, 2055, 4185.
28. Ottley, *The Lonely Warrior*, 161.
29. Rudwick, *Race Riot*, 160–70; Congressional Hearings, 1026–42, 1710. See also introduction, note 7.
30. Analysis by author. Also see Rudwick, *Race Riot*, 8–9, 213–15.
31. *Journal*, May 24–25, 1917; Congressional Hearings, 3525.

32. *Journal*, May 25–28, 1917; Rudwick, *Race Riot*, 27–28; Congressional Hearings, 3121, 3141, 2569, 2401.

33. *Journal*, May 28, 1917.

34. Rudwick, *Race Riot*, 27–35.

35. Congressional Hearings, 2875.

36. Ibid., 3126–93.

37. Ibid., 3824; Flannigen obituary, *Journal*, May 12, 1926.

38. Congressional Hearings, 1916, 4310–18.

39. Rudwick, *Race Riot*, 28–30.

40. Congressional Hearings, 3882, 2028–32.

41. Ibid., 3125–27, 3155.

42. See Horowitz, *The Deadly Ethnic Riot*, chap. 3.

43. *PD, Journal, Republic*, May 29–30, 1917; Rudwick, *Race Riot*, 27–32.

44. Congressional Hearings, 3375–80.

45. Ibid., 2240–45.

46. Rudwick, *Race Riot*, 28–33.

47. Congressional Hearings, 1418–20.

48. Ibid., 1346–50.

49. *Journal, PD*, May 29–31, 1917; Rudwick, *Race Riot*, 30–33.

50. *Journal*, May 29, 1917; *Argus*, June 1, 1917.

51. *PD*, May 29–30, 1917.

CHAPTER 7: SHOTS IN THE DARK

1. *Journal*, June 4, 1917.

2. Ibid., June 8–10, 1917.

3. *Report to the Illinois State Council of Defense*, 1–6.

4. *Journal*, June 18, 22, 1917; Rudwick, *Race Riot*, 36–39.

5. *The Trial of Leroy Bundy*, 765, 796–99, 824–25; Congressional Hearings, 686.

6. Congressional Hearings, 1078–80.

7. Ibid., 2060–61, 1355–57.

8. *Journal*, June 11, 1917.

9. Congressional Hearings, 2369.

10. Ibid., 686, 1350; Rudwick, *Race Riot*, 37.

11. Congressional Hearings, 3527–30.

12. *The Trial of Leroy Bundy*, 732–35; Congressional Hearings, 1107; Rudwick, *Race Riot*, 38–39.

13. Congressional Hearings, 1138–40.

14. Ibid., 1105–19.

15. Ibid., 674, 1064–70; Rudwick, *Race Riot*, 38.

16. *The Trial of Leroy Bundy*, 752, 770–72; Congressional Hearings, 1106–9.

17. Congressional Hearings, 1106–9.

18. Ibid., 1065–76, 673.

19. Ibid., 477–82.

20. Roy Albertson obituary, *Journal*, July 28, 1960. Note on Frank Wodley's name: In his 1964 book on the riots, *Race Riot at East St. Louis, July 2, 1917*, sociologist El- liott Rudwick spells Wodley's name "Wadley" throughout. But the name is spelled "Wodley" in the 1916 East St. Louis city directory, and the *St. Louis Post-Dispatch* and *Globe-Democrat* spelled the name with an "o" consistently, from the riot in July of 1917 through the trials that stretched from the fall of 1917 to the spring of 1922. The *East St. Louis Journal*, in its initial coverage of the riot, spelled the name "Wadley," but by the time of its coverage of indictments and trials growing out of the riot in the fall of 1917 it had changed the spelling to "Wodley." See, for exam- ple, *Journal* riot indictment stories on Sept. 26 and 30 and Oct. 1, 1917.

21. Congressional Hearings, 477–78.

22. *The Trial of Leroy Bundy*, 353–56; Rudwick, *Race Riot*, 39.

23. Congressional Hearings, 479–82. See also *The Trial of Leroy Bundy*, 354–55, 364–65, 385–86.

24. Congressional Hearings, 546–65, 1233.

25. Congressional Hearings, 480–81. See also *Republic*, July 2, 1917.

26. Congressional Hearings, 589–92, 3390.

27. Ibid., 3546–47, 4089.

28. Ibid., 589–92.

29. Ibid., 484.

30. Ibid., 485.

31. Ibid., 1140–42.

32. Ibid., 505.

33. Ibid., 756.

34. Ibid., 2039–41.

35. *Republic*, July 2, 1917.

36. *Argus*, July 6, 1917.

CHAPTER 8: THE JULY RIOT BEGINS

1. Congressional Hearings, 250–51.

2. Anderson obituaries, *NYT*, *PD*, Dec. 7, 8, 1938; *PD*, Dec. 14, 2003; Military Board of Inquiry, Anderson testimony, 319.

3. Congressional Hearings, 403–5.

4. *Republic, Journal*, July 3, 1917.

5. Congressional Hearings, 757, 809, 823; Tripp obituary, *Peoria Star*, Nov. 2, 1938.

6. Congressional Hearings, 591; Rudwick, *Race Riot*, 81–86.

7. Congressional Hearings, 753–57; Rudwick, *Race Riot*, 41.

8. *Report of the Special Committee*, 20–22; *Journal*, Aug. 15, 1917.

9. Military Board of Inquiry, Clayton testimony, 1–15; Klauser testimony, 2–3. Con- gressional Hearings, 486, 494–95, 509; *Report of the Special Committee*, 20–22; Rudwick, *Race Riot*, 82–83.

10. For troop arrivals, see Military Board of Inquiry, *Report to Adjutant General*, 10, and Exhibit D.

11. Congressional Hearings, 486.
12. Ibid., 407–10.
13. Ibid., 683–85. Much of the information on Richard Brockway comes from coverage of his trial, *PD, Journal*, Nov. 13–25, 1917.
14. *PD*, Nov. 14, 1917; Rudwick, *Race Riot*, 41, 106–8.
15. Congressional Hearings, 1110.
16. Ibid., 2039–41.
17. Ibid., 3653.
18. Ibid., 388.
19. *Journal, PD*, Nov. 14, 1917.
20. Except as noted, descriptions of the riot come from *Journal* and *PD*, July 2–4, 1917, and *GD* and *Republic*, July 2–5, 1917.
21. Military Board of Inquiry, *Report to Adjutant General*, 16–17. Congressional Hearings, 109–10.
22. Congressional Hearings, 253.
23. Ibid., 1359–62.
24. Ibid., 250–60, 591.
25. Military Board of Inquiry, Mollman testimony, 40–45.
26. Congressional Hearings, 576.
27. Ibid., 1071–80.
28. Ibid., 269.
29. Ibid., 862–78.
30. Ibid., 924–25.
31. Ibid., 623–25.
32. Ibid., 3099.
33. Ibid., 260–67.
34. Ibid., 3385.
35. For a detailed discussion of the "emergent norm" situation in the East St. Louis riot, see McLaughlin, "Reconsidering the East St. Louis Race Riot of 1917," 203–9.

CHAPTER 9: "THIS WAS THE APOCALYPSE"

1. Congressional Hearings, 118–23; Roger obituary, *Journal*, June 2, 1953.
2. Congressional Hearings, 112–23, 999–1003; Military Board of Inquiry, Roger testimony, 204–11.
3. Congressional Hearings, 766.
4. *Argus*, July 6, 1917.
5. Congressional Hearings, 488–92, 210–12, 232–38.
6. Ibid., 412.
7. Ibid., 250–60.
8. Letters from Carlos Hurd to Katherine Cordell Hurd, July 1917, courtesy of Ernest Stadler, in possession of author. Carlos Hurd obituaries, *PD, NYT*, June 9, 1950. See also Carlos Hurd and Frances Hurd Stadler files at the Missouri Historical

Society and Gillespie, *The Titanic Man*. For troop arrivals, see Military Board of
Inquiry, *Report to Adjutant General*, 10, and Exhibit D.

9. Congressional Hearings, 490–92.
10. Baker, *Josephine*, chap. 1, especially 1–3.
11. Congressional Hearings, 1072–80.
12. Ibid., 3100.
13. Ibid., 775–80.
14. Ibid., 1150–60.
15. Ibid., 1056–58, 2041, 2462.
16. Ibid., 3707–79.
17. Ibid., 106–16.

CHAPTER 10: A DRAMA OF DEATH

1. *PD*, July 3, 1917.
2. Congressional Hearings, 1389–99.
3. Ibid., 109–10.
4. Ibid., 576.
5. *PD*, July 3, 1917.
6. Congressional Hearings, 263–70.
7. Ibid., 3658.
8. *PD*, July 3, 1917.
9. Congressional Hearings, 578.
10. Ibid., 402, 413–14.
11. Ibid., 492–95.
12. *GD*, July 3, 1917.
13. Congressional Hearings, 2868.
14. Ibid., 778–81.
15. Military Board of Inquiry, *Report to Adjutant General*, 10, and Exhibit D; Congressional Hearings, 778–83.
16. Congressional Hearings, 1309–16; *PD*, Oct. 27, 1917.
17. Interviews with Terry and Gary Kennedy in St. Louis, Nov. 16, 20, 2007.
18. Congressional Hearings, 1420–31.
19. Ibid., 1695–98.
20. *Republic*, July 3, 1917; *Argus*, July 6, 1917.
21. *PD*, July 3, 1917.
22. Ibid.
23. Congressional Hearings, 267, 597.
24. Military Board of Inquiry, Fekete testimony, 23–24; Congressional Hearings, 592–97.
25. Congressional Hearings, 780–84.
26. *PD*, July 3, 1917.
27. Congressional Hearings, 384–87, 395–99.
28. Ibid., 1360–62.

29. Ibid., 857.
30. Markham, *Bovard of the Post-Dispatch*, 70, 135–36.
31. Letters from Carlos Hurd to Katherine Cordell Hurd, July 1917, courtesy of Ernest Stadler, in possession of author.

CHAPTER II: LEGACY OF A MASSACRE

1. Congressional Hearings, 933–65.
2. Military Board of Inquiry, *Report to Adjutant General*, 10, and Exhibit D.
3. Rudwick, *Race Riot*, 52–53; Congressional Hearings, 1305–13; *PD*, Oct. 27, 1917.
4. Congressional Hearings, 285–91, 1259–65, 1373–80.
5. Ibid., 1144–45, 1190–97.
6. Ibid., 1211–25.
7. *Journal*, July 5–6, 1917; Schmidt, *Red Scare*, 67–68.
8. Rudwick, *Race Riot*, 4, 49–50; "Mississippi rarely returns what currents snatch away," *PD*, March 29, 2002.
9. Rudwick, *Race Riot*, 49–50; Congressional Hearings, 271; *Report of the Special Committee Authorized by Congress*, 4; *Argus*, July 6, 1917; *Crisis*, Sept. 1917; *PD*, Aug. 15, 1917.
10. Congressional Hearings, 3636.
11. Ibid., 3710–15.
12. Ibid., 1947–61, 2616.
13. Ibid., 499–500, 539.
14. Wells-Barnett, *Crusade for Justice*, 383–85.
15. Foner and Lewis, *The Black Worker*, vol. 5, 307.
16. *GD*, July 5, 1917.
17. Wells-Barnett, *A Black Holocaust*, 1–6; Wells-Barnett, *Crusade for Justice*, 383–95.
18. *PD*, *NYT*, July 7, 1917; Rudwick, *Race Riot*, 134.
19. *NYT*, July 5, 1917.
20. *Chicago Tribune*, *GD*, July 4, 1917.
21. Rudwick, *Race Riot*, 58–62.
22. *Atlanta Constitution*, reprinted *GD*, July 5, 1917.
23. *NYT*, July 17, 1917.
24. *Survey*, Aug. 18, 1917, 447–48.
25. Ridge, *The Ghetto and Other Poems*, 80–81.
26. *Journal*, July 5, 1917.
27. *Survey*, July 14, 1917, 331–33.
28. Congressional Hearings, 2039.
29. Rudwick, *Race Riot*, 95–106.
30. Lewis, *Biography of a Race*, 536–40; *Argus*, July 13, 1917.
31. Du Bois, *Oxford W. E. B. Du Bois Reader*, 525–26.
32. "The Massacre of East St. Louis," *Crisis*, Sept. 1917.
33. *Crisis*, March, 1918.

34. *NYT*, July 29, 1917; Lewis, *Biography of a Race*, 539; Bundles, *On Her Own Ground*, 206–7; Rudwick, *Race Riot*, 134–35.

35. Morrison, *Jazz*, 53–54.

36. Bundles, *On Her Own Ground*, 205–12, 270–72.

37. Schmidt, *Red Scare*, 67–68.

38. Bundles, *On Her Own Ground*, 208–9; *Argus*, July 13 and Aug. 10, 1917; Rudwick, *Race Riot*, 138; Kellogg, *NAACP*, 221–32.

39. Rudwick, *Race Riot*, 96–98; *PD*, Aug. 15–19 and Sept. 9, 1917; *Journal*, Aug. 13–19 and Sept. 9–13, 1917.

40. *PD*, *Journal*, Aug. 15, 1917; *Report of the Grand Jury*, 3.

41. *Report of the Grand Jury*, 1–7.

42. Congressional Hearings, 3636.

43. *PD*, *Journal*, July 3, 1917; McLaugllin, *Power. Community, and Racial Killing*, 187; *Journal*, July 12, 13, 1921.

44. *Journal*, Aug. 17, 1917.

45. *PD*, Aug. 15, 1917. "Brockway, Richard," Biographical Sketch Index, Belleville Public Library, Belleville, Ill. *People v. Richard Brockway, et al.* Note: The transcript of the Brockway trial along with many other transcripts from the period of the riot were shredded when the St. Clair County Circuit Court moved to a new building in 1971. Some pre- and post-trial motions and similar records remain.

46. *Journal*, July 20, 1911; *PD*, Nov. 2, 1917; Congressional Hearings, 280–81.

47. *PD*, *GD*, *Journal*, Aug. 19, 1917; Rudwick, *Race Riot*, 96–97.

48. *Journal*, Aug. 23, 1917.

49. Haynes, *A Night of Violence*, 57–60.

50. Ibid., 83.

51. Ibid., 86.

52. Ibid., 296–304.

53. Lewis, *Biography of a Race*, 539–44; Berg, *The Ticket to Freedom*, 23; Kellogg, *NAACP*, 225; Garvey, "The Conspiracy of the East St. Louis Riots," 300–301.

54. Bundles, *On Her Own Ground*, 212, 270–72.

CHAPTER 12: JUDGMENT DAYS

1. *Argus*, Oct. 5, 1917.

2. *PD*, Oct. 1–8, 1917; Rudwick, *Race Riot*, 112–15.

3. *PD*, Oct. 8–13; *GD*, Oct. 9–14; Rudwick, *Race Riot*, 102–32.

4. *PD*, Oct. 18–19, 1917; *Journal*, Oct. 16–18, 1917.

5. *PD*, Oct. 18, 1917.

6. *PD*, Oct. 23, 1917.

7. *PD*, *Journal*, Nov. 13–27, 1917.

8. *Journal*, Dec. 9, 1917.

9. Ibid., Feb. 6, 1918; *Argus*, Feb. 8, 1918; Rudwick, *Race Riot*, 98–99.

10. Rudwick, *Race Riot*, 95–106.

11. Congressional Hearings, 3649.

12. *PD*, Oct. 18, 1917.
13. Congressional Hearings, 125–40, 4185–90.
14. Ibid., 1855.
15. *PD*, Oct. 29, Nov. 10, 1917.
16. Congressional Hearings, 1866–70, 1902–6, 3532–34; *PD*, Nov. 6, 1917.
17. *PD*, Nov. 8, 9, 1917.
18. Congressional Hearings, 3248–78, 3300, 3344, 3390; *PD*, Nov. 8, 1917.
19. *Report of the Special Committee*, 1–10.
20. Congressional Hearings, 1229; Rudwick, *Race Riot*, 50.
21. *Report of the Special Committee*, 11–24.
22. *GD, Journal*, Oct. 12–14, 1917; *PD*, March 20, 1919; Rudwick, *Race Riot*, 119–23.
23. *Journal*, Nov. 26, 1917; Rudwick, *Race Riot*, 188–90.
24. Du Bois, "Leroy Bundy," 16–21; Rudwick, *Race Riot*, 122–23.
25. Du Bois, "Leroy Bundy," 19–21; Rudwick, *Race Riot*, 123; *Defender*, Sept. 14, 1918.
26. *PD*, March 20–28, 1919.
27. *The Trial of Leroy Bundy*, 251–303; *PD*, March 21, 1919.
28. *The Trial of Leroy Bundy*, 861–83, 994–1062, 1106–32.
29. *PD*, March 28, 1919; Rudwick, *Race Riot*, 122–31; Bundy obituary, *Journal*, June 8, 1943.
30. Du Bois, "Leroy Bundy," 16; *NYT*, June 9, 1936.
31. Rudwick, *Race Riot*, 165.
32. *GD*, April 5, 1918.
33. *NYT*, July 27, 1918; Kellogg, *NAACP*, 228.
34. Franklin, "The Philadelphia Race Riot of 1918," 316–28; *NYT*, July 29, 1918.
35. Johnson, *Writings*, 511–12.
36. Tuskegee Lynching Statistics, Tuttle, *Red Summer*, 14; *NYT*, Oct. 5, 1919.
37. Johnson, *Writings*, 512–13; Tuttle, *Red Summer*, 14; Henri, *Black Migration*, 321.
38. "Race Riot of 1919 Gave Glimpse of Future Struggles," *Washington Post*, March 1, 1999.
39. Tuttle, *Red Summer*, 3–10, 75–76, 238–40.
40. *Crisis*, Sept. 1919.
41. Berg, *The Ticket to Freedom*, 23; NAACP, *Thirty Years of Lynching*, 5–8.
42. Johnson, *Writings*, 530–50.
43. *NYT*, June 14, 19, 2005.
44. Hirsch, *Riot and Remembrance*, 38, 77–113, 117–19.

CHAPTER 13: THE DEAL WITH THE DEVIL

1. Congressional Hearings, 3202; Rudwick, *Race Riot*, 161.
2. McLaughlin, *Power, Community, and Racial Killing*, 10–11; Tuttle, *Red Summer*, 76; Rudwick, *Race Riot*, 165–66, 217–18; Congressional Hearings, 1850–51.
3. Theising, *Made in USA*, 144.

4. Congressional Hearings, 3222–23.
5. Congressional Hearings, 4075–82.
6. Military Board of Inquiry, *Report to Adjutant General*, 5; Mollman testimony, 21. Rudwick, *Race Riot*, 213–15.
7. Congressional Hearings, 4075–82.
8. Rudwick, *Race Riot*, 190–96; St. Louis license statistics courtesy of Adele Heagney, reference librarian, St. Louis Public Library.
9. *Journal*, Sept. 19, 1921.
10. Ibid., 280–307; *PD*, Nov. 1, 1917.
11. Horowitz, *The Deadly Ethnic Riot*, 124 and chap. 3.
12. Ibid., 117.
13. McLaughlin, "Reconsidering the East St. Louis Race Riot of 1917," 205–7.
14. Congressional Hearings, 489.
15. McLaughlin, "Reconsidering the East St. Louis Race Riot," 206–7.
16. Ibid., 207–9.
17. Horowitz, *The Deadly Ethnic Riot*, 116–17.
18. Krikler, "Inner Mechanics," 1051–75.
19. De Tocqueville, *Democracy in America*, 357.
20. Du Bois, "Leroy Bundy," 170.
21. Bing, *War-time Strikes*, 7–9, 293; Morison, *Oxford History*, 858–59.
22. Arendt, *On Revolution*, 9.

EPILOGUE: THE EAST ST. LOUIS BLUES

1. Townsend, *A Blues Life*, 14–15.
2. *PD*, Feb. 4, 1952.
3. Baker, Speech at Kiel Opera House.
4. Turner, *I, Tina*, 44–46.
5. Interview by the author with Eugene Redmond, East St. Louis, Jan. 18, 2006.
6. Theising, *Made in USA*, 13, 196. Some information on population and racial trends in East St. Louis comes from the East St. Louis Action Research Project of the University of Illinois at Urbana–Champaign, http://www.eslarp.uiuc.edu.
7. Donloe, *Katherine Dunham*, particularly 165–86.
8. *Los Angeles Times*, Aug. 11, 2005.
9. *PD*, Sept. 11–15, 1967.
10. Interview by the author with Anne Walker, East St. Louis, Nov. 7, 2007.
11. Kozol, *Savage Inequalities*, 7–39.
12. Joyner-Kersee, *A Kind of Grace*, 14–15.
13. Kramer, "An Olympic Champion Comes Home," 40–47. Some information on the center comes from the Jackie Joyner-Kersee Foundation.
14. Interviews by the author with Terry and Gary Kennedy, St. Louis, Nov. 16, 20, 2007.
15. *PD*, June 20, 2001.
16. Theising, *Made in USA*, 223.

17. Interview by the author with Anne Walker, East St. Louis, Nov. 7, 2007. For Illinois Riot and Reparations Commission legislation, see Senate Joint Resolution 0044, Ninety-fifth General Assembly, at http://www.ilga.gov/legislation/.
18. *PD*, May 22, June 23, 2006.
19. *PD*, March 21, 2006.
20. *PD*, May 11, July 8, 2007.

Bibliography

PRINCIPAL NEWSPAPER SOURCES

Chicago Defender (Defender)
East St. Louis Daily Journal (Journal)
New York Times (NYT)
St. Louis Argus (Argus)
St. Louis Globe-Democrat (GD)
St. Louis Post-Dispatch (PD)
St. Louis Republic (Republic)

BOOKS AND LARGE COLLECTIONS OF FILES

Acquaviva, Mike. *Guide to "The East St. Louis Race Riot of 1917."* Printed guide accompanies eight reels of microfilm. Frederick, Md.: University Publications of America, 1985. See *The East St. Louis Race Riot of 1917.*

Arendt, Hannah. *On Revolution.* A Compass Book. New York: Viking Press, 1965.

Arnesen, Eric. *Brotherhoods of Color: Black Rail Workers and the Struggle for Equality.* Cambridge, Mass.: Harvard University Press, 2001.

Baker, Josephine, and Jo Bouillon. *Josephine.* New York: Marlowe and Company, 1998.

Baker, Ray Stannard. *Following the Color Line: American Negro Citizenship in the Progressive Era.* New York: Harper & Row, 1964.

Baldwin, James. *The Fire Next Time.* New York: Vintage, 1993.

Benedict, Ruth. *Race: Science and Politics.* New York: Viking Press, 1950.

Berg, Manfred. *The Ticket to Freedom: The NAACP and the Struggle for Black Political Integration.* Gainesville: University of Florida Press, 2005.

Berry, Chuck. *Chuck Berry: The Autobiography.* New York: Harmony Books, 1987.

Bing, Alexander M. *War-Time Strikes and Their Adjustment.* New York: Dutton, 1921.

Bontemps, Arna, and Jack Conroy. *Anyplace But Here.* (Originally called *They Seek a City,* 1966, 1945.) Columbia, Mo.: University of Missouri Press, 1997.

Bracey, John H., with August Meier and Elliott Rudwick, eds. *Black Workers and Organized Labor.* Belmont, Calif.: Wadsworth Publishing, 1971.

Brecher, Jeremy. *Strike!* Boston: South End Press, 1997.

Bundles, A'Lelia. *On Her Own Ground: The Life and Times of Madam C. J. Walker.* New York: Scribner, 2001.

Cha-Jua, Sundiata Keita. *America's First Black Town: Brooklyn, Illinois 1830–1915.* Urbana and Chicago: University of Illinois Press, 2000.

Congressional Hearings. Reels 1–5 of *The East St. Louis Race Riot of 1917.* Edited by Elliott M. Rudwick. Frederick, Md.: University Publications of America, 1985.

Cottrell, Robert C. *Roger Nash Baldwin and the American Civil Liberties Union.* New York: Columbia University Press, 2000.

Davis, Miles, with Quincy Troupe. *Miles: The Autobiography.* New York: Simon & Schuster, 1989.

Daniels, Josephus. *The Life of Woodrow Wilson.* Philadelphia: Winston, 1924.

Department of Justice (Bureau of Investigation) files on the East St. Louis riot of 1917: Glasser File: *Records Relating to a Study of the Use of Force in Internal Disturbances by the Federal Government, 1915–1949.* Central Files, 1904–1967: File number 186835, *Correspondence on the East St. Louis Riot of 1917.* National Archives, College Park, Md.

De Tocqueville, Alexis. *Democracy in America.* Translated by George Lawrence. Edited by J. P. Mayer. New York: HarperCollins Perennial Classics, 1988.

Directory of East St. Louis. East St. Louis: Carroll, 1893, 1916, 1918, and 1921.

Directory of St. Louis. St. Louis: Polk, 1917.

Donald, Henderson H. *The Negro Migration of 1916–1918.* Washington, D.C.: Association for the Study of Negro Life and History, 1921.

Donloe, Darlene. *Katherine Dunham.* Los Angeles: Melrose Square Publishing, 1993.

Douglass, Frederick. *Life and Times of Frederick Douglass, Written by Himself.* New York: Collier Books, 1962.

Du Bois, W. E. B. *Black Reconstruction in America, 1860–1880.* New York: Free Press, 1998.

———. *The Oxford W. E. B. Du Bois Reader.* Edited by Erica J. Sundquist. New York: Oxford University Press, 1996.

———. *The Seventh Son: The Thought and Writings of W. E. B. Du Bois.* Edited by Julius Lester. New York: Random House, 1971.

———. *The Souls of Black Folk.* Mattituck, N.Y.: Amereon House, 1994.

———. *The Philadelphia Negro.* New York: Lippincott, 1899. Available at the Pfeiffer University Web site at http://www2.pfeiffer.edu/~lridener/DSS/DuBois/pntoc.html.

———. *Writings.* New York: Library of America, 1986.

Early, Gerald, ed. *Ain't but a Place: An Anthology of African American Writings About St. Louis.* St. Louis: Missouri Historical Society Press, 1998.

The East St. Louis Race Riot of 1917. Frederick, Md.: University Publications of America, 1985. Edited by Elliott M. Rudwick. Eight microfilm reels include five reels of testimony before the U.S. House of Representatives Select Committee to Investigate

Conditions in Missouri and Illinois Interfering with Interstate Commerce Between These States, which investigated the 1917 race riot in East St. Louis. The hearings were held in East St. Louis in October and November of 1917. Also included are a draft of the final report of the committee, the report of the military board of inquiry investigating conduct of soldiers during the riot, the full transcript of the trial of N. Leroy Bundy, and many other documents relating to the riot.

Epstein, Abraham, *The Negro Migrant in Pittsburgh.* New York: Arno Press, 1969.

Foner, Eric. *Reconstruction: America's Unfinished Revolution, 1863–1877.* New York: Harper & Row, 1988.

Foner, Philip S., and Ronald L. Lewis. *The Black Worker: A Documentary History from Colonial Times to the Present.* Vol. 5. From 1900 to 1919. Philadelphia: Temple University Press, 1978.

Foner, Philip S., and Ronald L. Lewis. *Black Workers: A Documentary History from Colonial Times to the Present.* (Abridged version of multivolume edition above.) Philadelphia: Temple University Press, 1989.

Franklin, John Hope. *From Slavery to Freedom: A History of African Americans.* New York: Alfred A. Knopf, 2000.

Gillespie, Vera and John. *The Titanic Man: Carlos F. Hurd.* Mattituck, N.Y.: Amereon House, 1995.

Godshalk, David Fort. *Veiled Visions: The 1906 Atlanta Race Riot and the Remaking of American Race Relations.* Chapel Hill: University of North Carolina Press, 2005.

Goggin, Jacqueline. *Carter G. Woodson: A Life in Black History.* Baton Rouge: Louisiana State University Press, 1993.

Groh, George W. *The Black Migration: The Journey to Urban America.* New York: Weybright and Talley, 1972.

Hagedorn, Ann. *Beyond the River: The Untold Story of the Heroes of the Black Underground.* New York: Simon & Schuster, 2002.

Handy, W. C. *Father of the Blues.* New York: Macmillan, 1943.

Harlan, Louis R. *Booker T. Washington: The Making of a Black Leader, 1856–1901.* New York: Oxford University Press, 1975.

Harlan, Louis R. *Booker T. Washington: The Wizard of Tuskegee, 1901–1915.* New York: Oxford University Press, 1983.

Harlan, Louis R., ed. *The Booker T. Washington Papers.* Vol. 3. Urbana: University of Illinois Press, 1974.

Hasse, John Edward. *Beyond Category: The Life and Genius of Duke Ellington.* New York: Simon & Schuster, 1993

Haynes, Robert V. *A Night of Violence: The Houston Riot of 1917.* Baton Rouge: Louisiana State University Press, 1976.

Henri, Florette. *Black Migration: Movement North, 1900–1920.* Garden City, N.Y.: Anchor Press/Doubleday, 1975.

Hirsch, James S. *Riot and Remembrance: The Tulsa Race War and Its Legacy.* Boston: Houghton Mifflin, 2002.

Horrigan, Kevin. *The Right Kind of Heroes: Coach Bob Shannon and the East St. Louis Flyers.* Chapel Hill, N.C.: Algonquin Books, 1992.

Horowitz, Donald L. *The Deadly Ethnic Riot.* Berkeley: University of California Press, 2001.

Jaspin, Elliot. *Buried in the Bitter Waters: The Hidden History of Racial Cleansing in America.* New York: Basic Books, 2007.

Jefferson, Thomas. *Notes on the State of Virginia.* New York: Library of America, 1984.

Johnson, James Weldon. *Writings.* New York: Library of America, 2004.

Joyner-Kersee, Jackie. *A Kind of Grace: The Autobiography of the World's Greatest Female Athlete.* New York: Warner Books, 1997.

Kellogg, Charles Flint. *NAACP: A History of the National Association for the Advancement of Colored People.* Baltimore: Johns Hopkins Press, 1967.

Kelly, Frank K. *The Fight for the White House: The Story of 1912.* New York: Crowell, 1961.

Kozol, Jonathan. *Savage Inequalities.* New York: Crown, 1991.

Lahs-Gonzalez, Olivia, ed. *Josephine Baker: Image and Icon.* St. Louis: Reedy Press, 2006.

Lemann, Nicholas. *The Promised Land: The Great Migration and How It Changed America.* New York: Vintage Books, 1992.

Lemann, Nicholas. *Redemption: The Last Battle of the Civil War.* New York: Farrar, Straus and Giroux, 2006.

Lewis, David Levering. *W. E. B. Du Bois: Biography of a Race, 1868–1919.* New York: Henry Holt, 1993.

Lincoln, Abraham. *The Collected Works of Abraham Lincoln.* Edited by Roy P. Basler. Vol. 1. New Brunswick, N.J.: Rutgers University Press, 1953.

Logan, Rayford W. *The Negro in American Life and Thought: The Nadir, 1877–1901.* New York: Dial Press, 1954.

Markham, James W. *Bovard of the Post-Dispatch.* Baton Rouge: Louisiana State University Press, 1954.

Marx, Karl. *The Eighteenth Brumaire of Louis Bonaparte.* Based on the third edition, prepared by Friedrich Engels. Moscow: Progress Publishers, 1937. Available at www.marxists.org/Archive.

McCombs, William Frank. *Making Woodrow Wilson President.* New York: Fairview, 1921.

McGruder, Aaron, and Reginald Hudlin. *Birth of a Nation.* Illustrated by Kyle Baker. New York: Crown Publishers, 2004.

McLaughlin, Malcolm. *Power, Community, and Racial Killing in East St. Louis.* New York: Palgrave Macmillan, 2005.

McMurry, Linda O. *To Keep the Waters Troubled: The Life of Ida B. Wells.* New York, Oxford University Press, 1998.

Military Board of Inquiry, *Reports and Testimony.* Reel 6 of *The East St. Louis Race Riot of 1917.* Edited by Elliott M. Rudwick. Frederick, Md.: University Publications of America, 1985.

Morison, Samuel Eliot. *The Oxford History of the American People.* New York: Oxford University Press, 1965.

Morrison, Toni. *Jazz.* New York: Alfred A. Knopf, 1992.

Myrdal, Gunnar. *An American Dilemma: The Negro Problem and Modern Democracy.* New York: Harper & Brothers, 1944.

National Association for the Advancement of Colored People. *Thirty Years of Lynching in the United States, 1889–1918,* New York: NAACP, 1919.

Ottley, Roi. *The Lonely Warrior: The Life and Times of Robert S. Abbott.* Chicago: H. Regnery Co., 1955.

Primm, James Neal. *Lion of the Valley: St. Louis, Missouri.* St. Louis: Western Urban History Series. 1990, paperback, second ed.

Report of the Grand Jury of St. Clair County, Illinois, August 14, 1917. Reel 7 of *The East St. Louis Race Riot of 1917.* Edited by Elliott M. Rudwick. Frederick, Md.: University Publications of America, 1985.

Report of the Special Committee Authorized by Congress to Investigate the East St. Louis Race Riot. "The East St. Louis Riots," House of Representatives Document No. 1231. Sixty-fifth Congress, Second Session, July 15, 1918, 1–24.

Report to the Illinois State Council of Defense on the Race Riots at East St. Louis by the Committee on Labor. Reel 7 of *The East St. Louis Race Riot of 1917.* Edited by Elliott M. Rudwick. Frederick, Md.: University Publications of America, 1985.

Ridge, Lola. *The Ghetto and Other Poems.* New York: Huebsch, 1918.

Roediger, David. *Working Toward Whiteness: How America's Immigrants Became White.* New York: Basic Books, 2005.

Rudwick, Elliott M. *Race Riot at East St. Louis, July 2, 1917.* Cleveland and New York: World Publishing, 1966.

Sandweiss, Lee Ann, ed. *Seeking St. Louis: Voices from a River City, 1670–2000.* St. Louis: Missouri Historical Society Press, 2000.

Schecter, Barnet. *The Devil's Own Work: The Civil War Draft Riots and the Fight to Reconstruct America.* New York: Walker & Company, 2005.

Schmidt, Regin. *Red Scare: The FBI and the Origins of Anti-Communism in the United States.* Copenhagen: Museum Tusculanum, 2000.

Scott, Emmett J. *Negro Migration During the War.* New York: Arno Press and the New York Times, 1920, 1969.

Senechal, Roberta. *The Sociogenesis of a Race Riot: Springfield, Illinois in 1908.* Chicago: University of Illinois Press, 1990.

Sinclair, Upton. *The Jungle.* New York: Penguin Books, 1985.

Smith, Gene. *When the Cheering Stopped: The Last Years of Woodrow Wilson.* New York: Morrow, 1964.

Smith McKoy, Sheila. *When Whites Riot: Writing Race and Violence in American and South African Cultures.* Madison: University of Wisconsin Press, 2001.

Spero Sterling D., and Abram L. Harris. *The Black Worker.* New York: Atheneum, 1968.

Theising, Andrew J. *Made in USA: East St. Louis: The Rise and Fall of an Industrial River Town.* St. Louis: Virginia Publishing Co., 2003.

Thompson, Mildred I. *Ida B. Wells-Barnett: An Exploratory Study of an American Black Woman, 1893–1930.* Brooklyn: Carlson Publishing, 1990.

Tolnay, Stewart E., and Em. M. Beck. *A Festival of Violence: An Analysis of Southern Lynchings, 1882–1930.* Urbana: University of Illinois Press, 1995.

Townsend, Henry, as told to Bill Greensmith. *A Blues Life.* Urbana and Chicago: University of Illinois Press, 1999.

The Trial of Leroy Bundy. Reels 7–8 of *The East St. Louis Race Riot of 1917.* Edited by Elliott M. Rudwick. Frederick, Md.: University Publications of America, 1985.

Trotter, Joe William Jr., and Eric Ledell Smith, eds. *African Americans in Pennsylvania: Shifting Historical Perspective.* University Park, Pa.: Pennsylvania State University Press, 1997.

Tucker, Mark. *Ellington: The Early Years.* Urbana and Chicago: University of Illinois, 1991.

Turner, Ralph H., and Lewis M. Killian. *Collective Behavior.* Englewood Cliffs, N.J., Prentice-Hall, 1957.

Turner, Tina, with Kurt Loder: *I, Tina: My Life Story.* New York: William Morrow and Co., 1986.

Tuttle, William M. *Race Riot: Chicago in the Red Summer of 1919.* Urbana and Chicago: University of Illinois Press, 1996.

The WPA Guide to Illinois. New York: Pantheon, 1983.

Wells-Barnett, Ida B. *A Black Holocaust in America: The East St. Louis Massacre of 1917.* Milwaukee: Black Holocaust Society, 2002.

———. *Crusade for Justice: The Autobiography of Ida B. Wells.* Chicago: University of Chicago Press, 1970.

———. *On Lynchings.* New York: Humanity Books, 2002.

Wood, Ean. *The Josephine Baker Story.* New York: Sanctuary, 2000.

Woodson, Carter. *A Century of Negro Migration.* New York: Russell and Russell, 1969.

ARTICLES, INTERNET SITES, AND MISCELLANEOUS

"Alex Manly—Wilmington Race Riots." *Encyclopedia of the State Library of North Carolina.* http://statelibrary.dcr.state.nc.us/nc/bio/afro/riot.htm.

Anderson, Sherwood. "Nobody's Home." *Today*, March 30, 1935, 6–10.

Baker, Josephine. Speech at Kiel Opera House on February 3, 1952. University of Missouri–St. Louis Black History Project, Western Historical Manuscripts Collection, University of Missouri–St. Louis.

Du Bois, W. E. B. "Leroy Bundy." *Crisis*, Nov. 1922, 16–21.

———. "The Massacre of East St. Louis." Originally in *Crisis*, September 1917. Reprinted in *The Seventh Son*, 80–106.

East St. Louis Action Research Project. University of Illinois at Urbana-Champaign. http://www.eslarp.uiuc.edu.

Franklin, V. P. "The Philadelphia Race Riot of 1918." Reprinted in Trotter and Smith, *African Americans in Pennsylvania*, 316–29.

Freund, Charles Paul. "The Secret History of Woodrow Wilson." *Reason*, March 2003 Print Edition. http://www.reason.com.

Garvey, Marcus. "The Conspiracy of the East St. Louis Riots." Speech in New York on July 8, 1917. Reprinted in Early (ed.), *Ain't But a Place*, 300–306.

"The Great Migration." *Africana: The Encyclopedia of the African and African American Experience.* Appiah, Kwame Anthony, and Henry Louis Gates Jr., eds. New York: Basic Civitas Books, 2004, 869–72.

Gibson, Thomas. "Bloody Island: Race Riots of East St. Louis." Documentary on videocassette. Produced and directed by Thomas Gibson. New York: Filmmakers Library, 1998.

Bibliography

Historical Census Statistics on Population Totals by Race, 1790 to 1990, and by Hispanic Origin, 1970 to 1990, for the United States, Regions, Divisions and States. Compiled for the U.S. Census Bureau by Campbell Gibson and Kay Jung. Working Paper Series No. 56. Sept. 2002. The paper, which is referred to throughout the book, reinterprets data from the census. http://www.census.gov/population/www/documentation/twps0056.html.

Kramer, Staci D. "Jackie: An Olympic Champion Comes Home." *St. Louis*, July 1998, 40–47.

Krikler, Jeremy. "The Inner Mechanics of a South African Racial Massacre." *Historical Journal* 42, no. 4 (Dec. 1999): 1051–75.

Lapsansky, Emma Jones. " 'Since They Got Those Separate Churches: Afro-Americans and Racism in Jacksonian Philadelphia." Reprinted in Trotter and Smith, *African Americans in Pennsylvania*, 93–120.

Leonard, Oscar. "The East St. Louis Pogrom." *Survey*, July 14, 1917, 331–33.

Linzee, David. "Bob Shannon." *St. Louis*, Dec. 1998, 28–33.

Lumpkins, Charles L. "To Smash Decades of Black Political Activism: The East St. Louis Pogrom of July 1917." Paper presented at the Southern Historical Association Conference, Nov. 18, 2006. Courtesy of the author.

Matison, Sumer Eliot. "The Labor Movement and the Negro During Reconstruction." *Journal of Negro History* (Oct. 1948): 426–68.

McLaughlin, Malcolm. "Reconsidering the East St. Louis Race Riot of 1917." *International Review of Social History* (Aug. 2002) Cambridge, England: 187–212.

Menees, Charles. "Audience of 6000 for Josephine Baker." *St. Louis Post-Dispatch*, February 4, 1952.

Myrick-Harris, Clarissa. "Ida B. Wells and Her Brave Fight Against Lynching." *Smithsonian*, July 2002.

People v. Richard Brockway, et al., September 1917, St. Clair County Circuit Court, County Courthouse, Belleville, Ill. Transcript destroyed in 1971. Remaining miscellaneous files include pre- and post-trial motions.

"The Race Riot of 1919." *Washington Post*, March 1, 1999.

Rudwick, Elliott M. "East St. Louis and the 'Colonization Conspiracy' of 1916." *Journal of Negro Education* (Winter 1964): 35–42.

Runcie, John. " 'Hunting the Nigs' in Philadelphia: The Race Riot of August 1834." *Pennsylvania History* (April 1972): 187–218.

Scroggs, William O. "Interstate Migration of Negro Population." *Journal of Political Economy* 25, no. 10 (Dec. 1917): 1034–43.

Senechal, Roberta. "The Springfield [Ill.] Race Riot of 1908." *Illinois History Teacher* 3, no. 2 (1996): 22–32. The essay is a summary of the findings of her book, *The Sociogenesis of a Race Riot*.

Southern, Eileen. "In Retrospect: Letters from W. C. Handy to William Grant Still, Part 2." *Black Perspective in Music* 8.1 (Spring 1980): 65–119.

Tuskegee Institute. "Lynchings: By Year and Race." Available on the Web site of the law school of the University of Missouri at Kansas City. http://www.law.umkc.edu/faculty/projects/ftrials/shipp/lynchstats.html.

Tyson, Timothy B. "The Ghosts of 1898: Wilmington Race Riot and the Rise of White Supremacy." *Raleigh News & Observer*, Nov. 17, 2006.

Welding, Pete. Notes to *The Blues in St. Louis 1929–1937*. Original Jazz Library CD reissue. OJL-20.

Williams, John A. "The Long Hot Summers of Yesteryear." *History Teacher* (March 1968): 9–23.

Wilmington Race Riot Report. North Carolina Department of Cultural Resources, 2006. http://www.ah.dcr.state.nc.us/1898-wrrc/.

Wolgemuth, Kathleen L. "Woodrow Wilson and Federal Segregation," *Journal of Negro History* (April 1959): 158–173.

Photo Credits

Index

A Note on the Author

Harper Barnes is a longtime editor and cultural critic for the *St. Louis Post-Dispatch*. He edited the Boston *Phoenix* and also has written for the *Atlantic Monthly*, *Rolling Stone*, and the *Washington Post*. Barnes is author of *Blue Monday*, a historical novel, and *Standing on a Volcano: The Life and Times of David Rowland Francis*, a biography. He lives in St. Louis with his wife, Roseann Weiss, and enjoys bicycling, canoeing, and fishing in the nearby Ozarks.